praise for

FAST FENG SHUI

9 Simple Principles for Transforming Your Life by Energizing Your Home

"*Fast Feng Shui* is a delightful book and filled with great tips and lots of positive affirmations. It is good for beginners and for advanced students. You can open it at any page and find useful information. I love this book!"

— LOUISE L. HAY
author, *You Can Heal Your Life*
and *Empowering Women*

"In the often complex world of feng shui, *Fast Feng Shui* is a breath of fresh air. Stephanie Roberts takes ancient concepts and makes them applicable to modern life in a way that is fun, valuable, and fast."

— DENISE LINN
author, *Feng Shui for the Soul*,
Sacred Space, and *Space Clearing*

"Creatively integrates your personality type and the power of intention with the basics of Western Feng Shui."

— JAMI LIN
internationally renowned Feng Shui expert,
instructor, and author

"Finally, a fun and easy-to-understand feng shui book that is logical, coherent, and user friendly.... I highly recommend this book to beginners as well as seasoned practitioners."

a

"*Fast Feng Shui* is a fabulous, f
empower yourself and your e
attract and create the life you
mystical easy and accessible. Stephanie Roberts is brilliant!"

— SONIA CHOQUETTE, PhD
author, *Your Heart's Desire, True Balance*,
and *The Pyschic Pathway*

Also by Stephanie Roberts:

Clutter-Free Forever! Home Coaching Program
Fast Feng Shui
Fast Feng Shui for Singles
The Pocket Idiot's Guide to Feng Shui (Alpha Books)

coming soon:

Fast Feng Shui for the Home Office

FAST FENG SHUI for Prosperity

8 Steps on the Path to Abundance

STEPHANIE ROBERTS

Lotus Pond Press
Kahului, HI

Published by Lotus Pond Press, LLC, 415 Dairy Rd. #E-144, Kahului, HI 96732
www.lotuspondpress.com

"Fast Feng Shui" is a trademark of Lotus Pond Press, LLC

cover concept by Kathi Dunn, executed by Yellowbird Graphics
author photo by Shasta Rose

Publisher's Cataloging-in-Publication Data
(provided by Quality Books, Inc.)

Roberts, Stephanie, 1958-
Fast feng shui for prosperity : 8 steps on the path to abundance / Stephanie Roberts.
-- 1st ed.
p. cm. (Fast feng shui series)
Includes index.
LCCN: 2005900575
ISBN: 1-931383-09-X

1. Feng shui. 2. Wealth—Psychological Aspects.
3. Finance, Personal—Psychological Aspects. I. Title.

BF1779. F4R63 2004 133.3'337
QBI33-1793

printed in the United States of America

this book is dedicated to

Lakshmi

Hindu Goddess of Abundance

Thank you, Lakshmi, for all of your blessings!
om shrim maha Lakshmiyei swaha

ॐ

Foreword

Coming to terms with our relationship to money and balancing the core issues we have about money allows our lives to be rich and money to flow. *Fast Feng Shui for Prosperity* delivers profound ways to increase wealth potential by exploring how feng shui can be used to enhance the inner as well as outer aspects of wealth.

In this groundbreaking new book, Stephanie Roberts shows how our innermost thought processes can either support or sabotage our best efforts to raise our level of financial wellbeing. In the safe and private honesty of our own minds, with this book as our guide, we can analyze how thought and behavioral patterns either help us to achieve an experience of abundance (even with little money in the bank) or banish us to the poor house.

Part I of *Fast Feng Shui for Prosperity* provides a thorough introduction to the nine Fast Feng Shui principles as they apply specifically to money issues—from defining your goals and identifying key "power spots" in your home, to correcting feng shui problems, adding specific wealth enhancements and more. Readers with a sense of urgency may skip directly to Part III, to choose from a variety of cash flow cures drawn from a range of feng shui traditions.

It is the central section of this book that will lift your understanding of the relationship between feng shui and prosperity to an entirely new level. In *Part II: The Inner Path*, Stephanie revisits the feng shui *ba gua*—the energy template of Chinese metaphysics and the map that defines the energy centers in your home—and translates its archetypal energies into thought-provoking and evolutionary interpretations that help us understand our relationship with money.

With great psychological depth, Stephanie reveals how and why our own attitudes and actions are so powerfully implicated in the success or failure of standard feng shui strategies. The concrete action steps and practices that she provides for each step in this transformational model can lift your consciousness and catapult you to a higher experience of wealth.

As you follow the steps presented in this powerful book, you will discover the secrets revealed by your outer actions and innermost beliefs about wealth. *Fast Feng Shui for Prosperity* will guide you gently into a deeper and truer consciousness of how your own thoughts and actions are at the root of happiness—and how feng shui can be applied from the inside out to align those thoughts and actions with your most heartfelt dreams and desires.

Along the way, you will discover key insights such as: whether you are truly open to receive what you desire; how letting go of attachment can impact what you receive; why jealousy, envy, and shame keep you from experiencing the wealth you desire; what your financial habits reveal about your ability to care for and nurture yourself; why the true meaning of the "wealth corner" encompasses every kind of blessing whether financial in nature or not; and why learning to let go of doubt, worry anxiety is the key to a happy and rewarding life.

One of the most essential benefits of reading this book is that it invites you to embrace what I believe is the most important secret to living richly: When you stop worrying about your bills, and think instead about the sheltering roof over your head, the nourishing food on your table, the gift of your health, the love of your family and friends, and that you are alive, you realize that in this moment you really do have all that you need. Sure, we'd all like to have a higher income and of course we can look forward to a vacation or a new car, but in knowing that we have all we need right now, we can live a happy and full life in the moment instead of in thoughts of future desires. That's the easy part.

The hard part is to create conscious moments throughout your day when you remember all the good things that are present for you right now. This is a challenge for all who continually aspire to evolve into better and more enlightened human beings. For most of us, including me, when confronted with the day-to-day "afflictions of an imperfect world," our unconscious mind automatically runs the tape that includes all our frustrations, insecurities, and disappointments. I say this to you, as I daily remind myself: Be mindful when less-than-perfect situations occur, be kind to yourself, and take a grounding and patient breath. Know that you are human and full of grace.

Living more prosperously can start right now. When you wake up, review your good fortune. When you go to sleep, say thank you for all your blessings. Freedom comes more easily from relaxing and being happy within than it does from the relentless pursuit of more money. Ebb and flow are the essential cycles of nature, and financial challenges are a natural part of the life experience. Even in times of adversity, the road is rich when your attitude is uplifting, and the journey smoother when you use feng shui and inner serenity to smooth out the rough edges of experience. When we encounter these financial bumps in the road, the practical steps for both feng shui enhancement and self-inquiry that you will find in this book will help you proceed with grace and equanimity.

It has been an honor and privilege to introduce Stephanie Roberts's *Fast Feng Shui for Prosperity*. I encourage you to relish and process every morsel of this excellent offering.

To you dear reader, I wish great success in developing your inner and outer riches.

Jami Lin

Author of the *Masterful Result Feng Shui Home Study Program, Feng Shui Today*, and *The Essence of Feng Shui*.

For more wisdom and insight from Jami,
please visit her website at: www.JamiLin.com

Author's Note

In the years before I discovered feng shui, I was an independent training consultant in New York City. I made good money when I was working, but often the weeks between projects would stretch on for longer than was comfortable, and the balance in my "incredible shrinking bank account"—as I jokingly called it then—would get a little scary before a new project came along to fill it up again. As you will learn in Part II of this book, using those words to describe my finances was not a good idea. I wish I'd known that at the time!

As I began to study feng shui in the mid-1990s, and applied the principles that I now write about to my own life, I experienced enough pleasant surprises to convince me that these methods were having a positive effect.

When I moved to Hawaii in 1999 with my husband-to-be, I gave up my city lifestyle to live in a place where the natural beauty is almost as mind-boggling as the extremely high cost of living. Throughout the sometimes challenging process of writing and launching the Fast Feng Shui books and becoming Internet entrepreneurs, we have continued to use the principles that you will learn in this book to create both an inner and an outer environment that support our financial success.

Many people are attracted to feng shui by the idea that they might solve their money problems by making a few simple changes to their home. I can't promise that you will enjoy miraculous effects from feng shui, although it can work that way for some lucky people. For the rest of us, feng shui can help smooth the way to a promotion at work, bring new opportunities to earn and prosper, and ease the stress and anxiety that so often accompany our financial affairs.

If you see those around you enjoying a level of prosperity that you can't seem to achieve, no matter how hard you try, I've written this book for you. It's also for anyone who would like to experience more ease and abundance in all the financial aspects of his or her life.

The contemporary style of feng shui that I practice and write about (which is based on, but does not strictly follow, the BTB methods popular here in America) places a great deal of emphasis on the power of intention as a key factor of success. Intention is also the power behind what is called "deliberate creation," "prosperity consciousness," or "the law of attraction." This is the level at which we either attract into our lives that which we desire, or we trip ourselves up, get in our own way, and hold ourselves back—often without being aware how our unconscious attitudes and beliefs are making it difficult, or even impossible, to experience the abundance that we see others around us enjoying.

This book will teach you, step-by-step, how to apply key principles of the contemporary western style of feng shui to your home so you can find your prosperity power spots and make important corrections and enhancements right away. It also explores how each area of the *ba gua* (feng shui energy map) can be used to support greater abundance and corresponds to a key attribute of inner prosperity. By combining outer feng shui with inner realignment, the sometimes rocky and winding path to abundance becomes smooth and straight.

Wishing you a delightful and rewarding journey,

Stephanie R.

Table of Contents

INTRODUCTION

Prosperity Consciousness and the Feng Shui of Money

At a session of the first professional-level feng shui* training seminar that I attended many years ago, a student raised the question of what to tell a client who complains, "I've done everything you suggested, and it's not working." The instructor's reply was simple: When a client says that feng shui is not working, assume that the problem is with the client, not with feng shui. In other words, the feng shui fundamentals are always sound. If the client is prepared for a change in circumstances, something—either subtle or profound—will shift as a result of making feng shui changes. If, on the other hand, no shifts in circumstances arise, this is a clear sign that the process is being blocked by the client's doubt, fear or resistance.

This reply did not sit well with the class, many of whom had come to feng shui from a healing or helping profession such as massage therapy and social work. It sounded as though we were being told to take the easy way out. We'd expected, as concerned professionals, to be advised to be more diligent and creative in devising solutions that would work for our clients. But our well-intentioned dismay simply proved how unformed our budding understanding of feng shui still was.

In our zeal to be of service, we were overlooking two fundamental assumptions of feng shui: first, that everything—our thoughts and our emotions as well as our physical environment—is connected; second, that we are the strongest factor in the feng shui of our homes. If our energy is not in alignment with what we say we want, the feng shui alterations we make to our spaces are placed in a hostile environment.

* Say "fung shway."

Having made it through just the first page of this book, perhaps you wonder if this means that feng shui will not work for you. Not to worry; *Fast Feng Shui for Prosperity* will show you how to coordinate outer feng shui with the internal awareness that helps ensure success. The easy, effective feng shui principles you'll learn here are supported by a step-by-step plan for embracing prosperity consciousness—the missing ingredient in most other books about the feng shui of money.

We often think of money as a purely material concern. The term "materialistic," used to describe someone who cares only about money, implies a lack of spiritual depth. But the truth is that money is one of the most emotionally complex and challenging aspects of life, equalled—if not surpassed—only by love.

When we approach money and prosperity from a purely material or rational perspective, we miss the essential lessons that it can teach us about what we truly value and appreciate. If you think about it, you will recognize that what inspired you to pick up this book is not really a desire to have more money, but a longing for what we believe money will bring us: greater serenity; a peaceful and secure home life; the simple comfort of being surrounded by objects of beauty; and the freedom to follow the voice of your heart. Prosperity, in its deepest sense, is not about having money but about experiencing contentment in all aspects of our lives.

One of the greatest lies of our time is the belief that money is inherently incompatible with personal integrity and spirituality. Sure, money can corrupt, but only in the hands of those who are corruptible. Money is also one of the most powerful forces of good in our world, as proven across the ages by the generosity and vision of great philanthropists and patrons of the arts.

I remember an incident some years ago when I was living in New York City and the state Lotto jackpot had grown to a very tempting amount of something like 72 million dollars. I was engaged in that very pleasant weekend activity (to which New York City is so perfectly suited) of walking and talking and shopping with a friend, when I said that I wished to stop at the corner newstand to purchase a lottery ticket.

My friend responded with dismay that I would succumb to such a misleading temptation. Didn't I realize that my odds of winning were a gazillion-trillion to one? I was throwing my money away. Besides,

$72 million was a ridiculous amount of money, far more than I could possibly need.

"It is," I agreed as I reached for my wallet (the chance to win $72 million being my idea of a dollar well-spent). "And just think how much fun I could have giving the rest of it away!"

This is what prosperity consciousness is about: holding the unshakeable belief—despite all evidence to the contrary—that good fortune can be yours, coupled with a present-moment experience of delight fueled by anticipation. Pair this with the power of feng shui, and you've got a winning combination.

I didn't win that $72 million jackpot, by the way, but I didn't know about feng shui back then, so now perhaps someday I will...

What to Expect From Feng Shui

While feng shui may not result in that winning lottery ticket you dream of, it brings many other benefits by creating a more harmonious and balanced flow of *chi* through your home. Just as fresh air, clean water and natural foods support the physical health of our bodies, so does fresh, clean *chi*—the life force present in all things—support an energetically healthy home or workplace.

If the flow of *chi* in your space is blocked or weak you may feel tired, discouraged, and unable to focus on what steps to take next in order to increase your income or pay off your debts. Where *chi* flows too strongly you may feel out of control, overly emotional, or anxious much of the time. Your work life and finances may feel unstable as you struggle to "keep your head above water" through what may seem like an endless string of bad luck.

The objective of feng shui is to analyze the layout and decor of your home, diagnose problems, and prescribe appropriate solutions. Shape, color, texture, sound, light, imagery, and the arrangement of your furniture can all be used to adjust the energy of your home. The result is an attractive, safe, and nurturing space where you can live in comfort and more effectively and successfully pursue your goals for financial prosperity.

A key assumption of feng shui is that certain areas of your home impact specific aspects of your life. When the areas of your home that affect your finances are cluttered, stagnant, or missing from your floor plan, it can be difficult to attract or hold on to money. Other feng shui problems that can affect your finances include *sha chi* (harmful energy) such as "secret arrows" aimed your desk. Poor feng shui can lead to increased arguments and miscommunication, affect your reputation at work, and hinder your personal growth—all of which may contribute to financial difficulties.

Another key assumption of feng shui is that everything is connected. Your thoughts and feelings, even your behavior, can be influenced by your surroundings, while the state of your home or work space is a reflection of your mood and attitude.

A dark, dingy and untidy office, for example, contributes to an atmosphere of apathy and fatigue, which makes it harder for you to find the energy to clean the place up. Feng shui gives you the insight and incentive to become a mindful caretaker of your space. As a result, you live in greater harmony with your surroundings, which can better support you in achieving what you desire—in your finances and in all other aspects of your life.

Traditionally, feng shui is seen as one of five factors that influence a person's life. The other factors are your karma, luck, education, and actions, each of which may also contribute to the past, present, and future state of your finances. The impact of feng shui is most immediate when the difficulties you are experiencing are caused by poor feng shui in the first place. When other life factors are involved, feng shui can help you gain the perspective and insight necessary for getting your finances back on track.

Those who turn to feng shui hoping for a quick fix often discover that it brings them many opportunities to repeat old behavior patterns. If you are a chronic overspender or compulsive shopper, for example, feng shui might help to increase your income. But if you don't address the emotional issues that are driving your spending habits, the more money you have the more you will spend. And there you will be, staring with dismay at a mountain of debt in spite of your higher income.

For those who are ready and willing to change, however, feng shui can be a powerful ally on the path to personal growth and fulfillment.

THE FAST FENG SHUI™ APPROACH

The Fast Feng Shui Series provides an approach to contemporary feng shui that is easy to learn and simple to follow. It helps you figure out what changes to make in your home in order to address the issues that most concern you right now.

Fast Feng Shui for Prosperity follows the Western practice of aligning the *ba gua** to the main entry to a space, but it accommodates the compass orientation as well. I believe that feng shui should empower you as well as your home, and I encourage you to be creative and playful as you use feng shui to transform your home and your finances.

The Power of Your Intention

The strength of your intention is an integral part of your success with feng shui. Think of the difference in your energy when you are excited about something, compared to times when you feel anxious, unhappy, or depressed. When you dwell on how dissatisfied you are with a life situation, your energy becomes stuck there. Approach feng shui with confidence, optimism, and a sense of adventure. This will keep you motivated, and will help to shift the energy of your home.

THE "IVAG" EMPOWERMENT PROCESS

What is "empowerment"? It is a specific method that you will use each time you place a feng shui cure or enhancement in your home or office, with the intention of improving the feng shui of your space. It reinforces external changes with the power of your thoughts and feelings about the results that you desire to experience in your life.

The empowerment method given here greatly enhances your efforts by focusing the power of your body, speech and mind on what you are doing. In the previous Fast Feng Shui books, I have focused on the Intention, Visualization, and Affirmation steps, addressing Gratitude later as part of Fast Feng Shui Principle Nine. Over the years, however, I have become more and more convinced that Gratitude is the most important factor of them all. With this in mind, I now include Gratitude as a fourth key step in the empowerment process.

* The feng shui energy map.

Traditionally, after making your feng shui adjustments, you use the "dispelling mudra"* nine times while repeating the mantra, *om mani padme hum*, nine times. The *mudra*, or hand gesture, represents the power of body; the *mantra* is the power of speech, and visualizing your desired outcome while you use the *mantra* and *mudra* uses the power of mind. You may use this instead of or combined with my "IVAG" method:

1. INTENTION: As you are making feng shui changes to your space, stay focused on your intention that these changes will have a positive effect on your circumstances.
2. VISUALIZATION: Visualize your desired outcome in your mind, as if it has already taken place. Be as specific and concrete as possible, using all of your senses, so you experience the feelings of joy, satisfaction, or relief that your desired results will bring.
3. AFFIRMATION: Make a verbal affirmation, in the present tense, that clearly states the intended shift in your energy and/or circumstances. If you don't wish to say this aloud, it's okay to whisper it or to say it subvocally.
4. GRATITUDE: End your empowerment with a few moments of heartfelt gratitude. Imagine that everything you desire has been achieved, and express your thanks for all of these blessings as though you have already received them.

Steps 1-3 may be done in any order, or simultaneously. You can also place your cures (with intention) at any convenient time, then do steps 2 through 4 at another time. During the hours of 11 AM to 1 PM, and 11 PM to 1 AM, the energy of the day is shifting; these are good times to empower feng shui changes. If you follow Chinese or western astrology, you may use either of these systems to choose an auspicious day and time for your empowerments.

---

* Hold your index and pinky fingers straight and curl your middle and ring finger toward the palm, holding them with your thumb. (Women, use your right hand; men use your left hand.) Now flick the middle and ring fingers out to dispell negative energy from whatever you have flicked at.

How to Use This Book

If you are new to feng shui, you should begin by learning how to use the basic tools of the practice. These are the *ba gua* (a map that identifies which areas of your home impact your finances and other life aspects) and the five feng shui elements (key influences that help you balance and correct the *chi* of your home).

Because readers familiar with these tools will be eager to get to the main text, I've addressed the *ba gua* and the element cycles in the "Toolkit" Appendices at the back of the book. If you do not yet know how to apply the *ba gua* to your floor plan, or are not familiar with the various cycles of the elements, please read Appendices A and B first, before turning to Part I.

Part I reviews the nine Fast Feng Shui Principles from the perspective of applying them to your finances. Here you will learn how to locate your prosperity power spots, identify feng shui problems, and choose the right feng shui cures and enhancements. Readers of my other books will find this section a useful guide to applying their existing knowledge of feng shui to the challenge of increasing their prosperity.

In Part II, we take a closer look at all the areas of the *ba gua* to discover the supporting roles they can play in improving your wealth. I'll also take you in an inner journey through the *ba gua*, revealing the secret clues it holds for manifesting an abundant life experience from the inside out.

Part III provides detailed instructions for a variety of feng shui cash flow rituals. If you feel impatient for a positive change in your finances, you may wish to turn to that section first, so you can start practicing one of these methods right away while you study the rest of the book. I will caution you, though, that these special cures may be less effective if you have not yet mastered the rest of the material.

Keeping a Prosperity Journal

I recommend that you use a notebook or journal to write down your feng shui goals, actions, and results. Use your Prosperity Journal to:

- Make a list of potential changes you could make to your home, so you can more easily prioritize your feng shui tasks and track your progress.
- Write down the affirmations and visualizations you will use to empower your feng shui changes.
- Record the specific changes you make to your home, including when and why you made them.
- Record your answers to the questions about your experiences and attitudes that you will find in Part II.
- Keep track of the changes you experience as a result of feng shui, big surprises and rewards as well as the little synchronicities that are likely to start cropping up as a result of shifts in energy.
- Explore any emotional issues that come up for you as a result of your feng shui work.

Your journal doesn't have to be fancy, but why not choose one that reflects prosperous energy in some way? Green and purple are wealth colors in feng shui, so a green or purple cover (or paper) would be a good choice. Red is the feng shui power color, so that's another option. Whatever notebook you decide to use should be new—so it will have clean energy—small enough so it is easy to carry around, yet large enough to write and sketch in easily.

Be prepared to really use your journal: stuff things in it, tear pages out, be creative. As soon as you start changing things around in your home, your own energy will start to shift as well. When you do feng shui, you are likely to find yourself more creative in all aspects of life, seeing things from new angles and having new ideas. Write them all down!

Part One
Guiding Principles

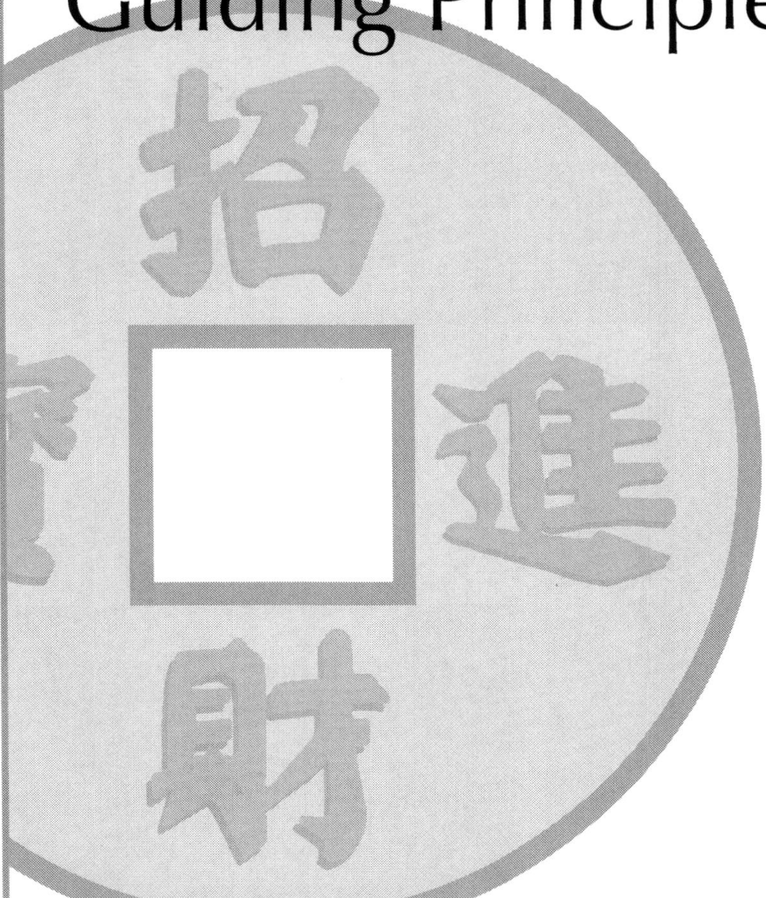

If you have read other books in the Fast Feng Shui series, you are familiar with the principles covered in this section. Here, we explore how these core principles apply to improving your prosperity. This section is essential reading for those who are new to feng shui or new to the contemporary style of practice. Experienced readers can use this section to deepen their understanding and practice.

Principle 1

Know What You Want

As you learned in the Introduction, feng shui is most effective when the changes that you make to your home are supported by deliberate, focused attention on a specific desired outcome. I assume, since you are reading this book, that you would like to increase your prosperity. Indeed, very few people would be disappointed to have more money. The important question is what what do you want it for?

Take a few minutes now to think beyond just wanting more money to the specific things that you would like to use it for once you have it. Here are some ideas to get you started:

- Get out of debt
- Buy a house or make home improvements
- Pay for education (your own or your children's)
- Buy a new car
- Lifestyle improvements: dining out, vacation, new clothes
- Peace of mind (my personal favorite!)
- Greater sense of self-worth*

As you apply feng shui to attracting a greater flow of prosperity into your life, it is important to define specific goals on which to focus the power of your intention. The more clearly you can define what you

* I don't mean to imply that you should be judged by yourself or by anyone else on how much money you make or have. However, if you've been struggling with the guilt and shame that often accompany being in debt—to mention just one possible money issue—getting out of debt is sure to help you feel better about yourself.

want to experience, the easier it will be to visualize receiving it, an important element of the empowerment practice that is fundamental to successful feng shui.

108 Desires

So, what do you want? Get out your Prosperity Journal (or create a new computer document) and make a list of 108 things you want to be, do, or have. Think in terms of:

- Material goods *(a new computer; remodeling the kitchen; a gold watch)*
- Activities and experiences (*a better job; a spa vacation; sky-diving lessons; getting your teeth whitened)*
- Taking care of business (*pay off your student loans; establish a "rainy day fund;" increase your insurance coverage*)

Most people discover that coming up with 108 desires is harder than it sounds, so don't expect to complete your list in one sitting. As you work on your prosperity issues, more and more ideas will come to you. Read through your list every morning, so you begin your day by focusing on what you intend to receive, feel, or experience.

Each time you receive something on your list, cross that item out and think of something new to add, so you always have an abundance of future delights to look forward to. If you find that an item you thought you wanted no longer appeals to you, delete it and come up with something new to take its place.

From your list of 108 desires, what three things do you most want? List them here or in your Prosperity Journal:

1. ______________________________

2. ______________________________

3. ______________________________

Principle 2

Locate Your Power Spots

When using feng shui to enhance prosperity, *hsun gua*—the section of the *ba gua** associated with wealth and abundance—is the key area to work with. Remember that there is a *ba gua* for your entire property, a *ba gua* for your house, and a *ba gua* for every room in your home. Some *hsun guas* will be good places for feng shui adjustments; others may have features that render them less useful. Follow these steps to find which *hsun gua* areas are your prosperity power spots:

1. Find *hsun gua* on your property. The lower edge of the *ba gua* is at the street, with *hsun gua* in the rear left corner of your plot. If part of your house overlaps this area, mark it on your floor plan:

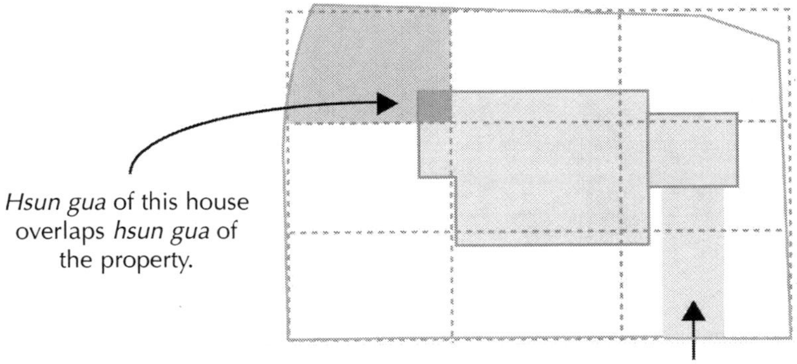
Hsun gua of this house overlaps *hsun gua* of the property.

* *Hsun* is pronounced "shun." If you are not yet familiar with the *ba gua* and how to use it, please read Appendix A to learn about this essential feng shui tool before continuing with this section.

2. Place the *ba gua* over your floor plan, aligning it with the front door. Where is *hsun gua* inside your home? Mark that area. (If your home is "missing" that corner, refer to pages 157-158 in Appendix A for recommended solutions.)

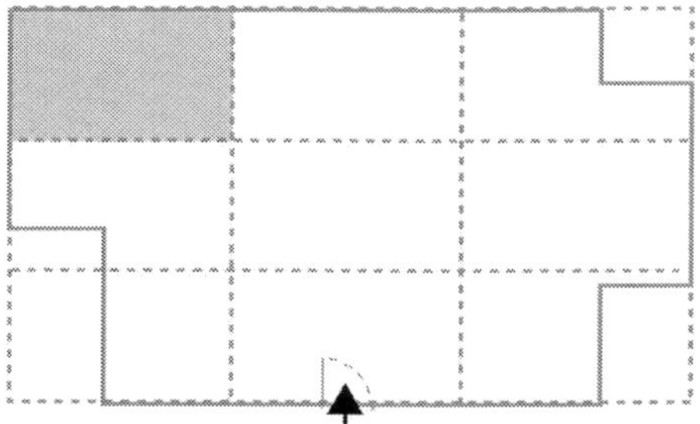

Hsun gua within the house

3. Now place the *ba gua* over any rooms you marked in Steps 1 & 2, one room at a time. Align the *ba gua* with the door to each space; it might be rotated one way or the other compared to the rest of the house. Where is *hsun gua* within each of those rooms?

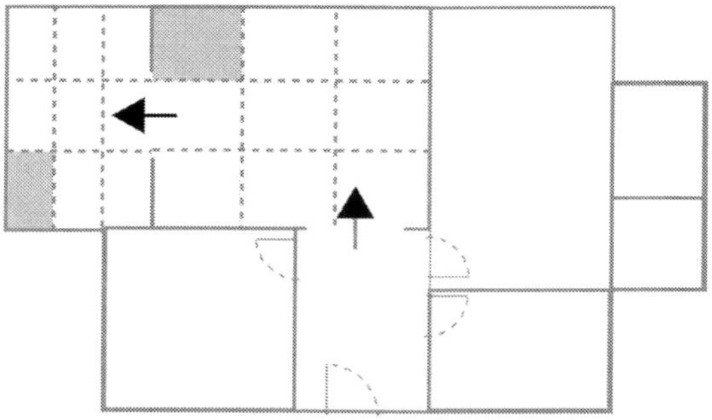

Hsun gua locations for two rooms in the house

4. Find *hsun gua* in your bedroom. This is a prosperity power spot regardless of its location within the larger *ba gua* of the home.

5. Find *hsun gua* in your living room and kitchen. These areas are often good power spots for prosperity.

6. When the *ba gua* is placed according to the compass directions, *hsun gua* is the southeast sector. Find the southeast area of your floor plan. Are any of the potential power spots you have already identified in that area? If so, they are likely to be important prosperity power spots for you.

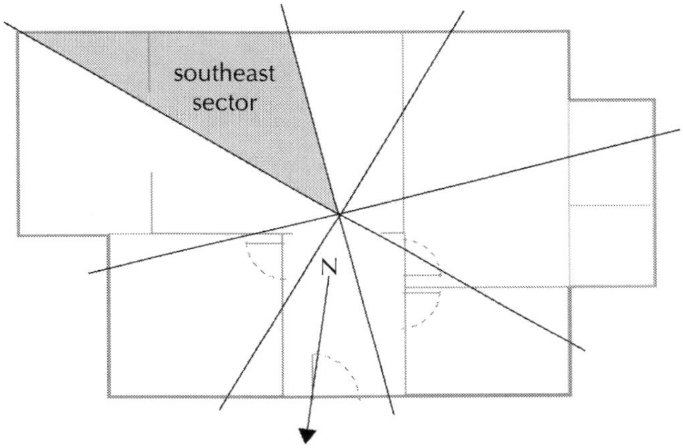

Hsun gua of the house, according to the compass

7. Review the potential power spots you identified in the previous steps and choose the best three to receive priority feng shui attention. Factors to consider are:

   - *Importance of the room*: Your bedroom, living room, kitchen, and home office (if you have one) are most important.
   - *Multiple influences*: Look for areas where *hsun gua* on one *ba gua* falls within *hsun gua* of another.
   - *Chi of the room*: any space that is cluttered, dark, cramped, dingy, neglected, or generally unappealing does not have strong *chi* and will not be a good power spot regardless of how well it meets the other criteria. You may be able to correct these problems with a good clutter clear-out, better lighting, and some basic home maintenance or a fresh coat of paint. Until you do, keep any space like this off your power spots list. Other spaces that are not good power spots include bathrooms, closets, narrow hallways, and stairways.

Principle 3

Create a Path for Chi

In order to increase prosperity, you want to ensure that *chi* flows from your front door to your prosperity power spots without being blocked or diverted along the way. Creating a path for *chi* involves getting rid of the stuff that piles up behind doors, arranging furniture to create a smooth traffic flow through the home, and using cures such as mirrors, wind chimes and faceted crystal balls to manage the flow of *chi*.*

Your Street

If you live on a busy street or on the outside of a curve, *chi* could be rushing right past your house. Without a good flow of *chi* onto your property, it will be difficult for your family to prosper. You can slow down passing *chi* with a large boulder or garden statue, and attract it into your yard with a flag, whirlygig or fountain.

Your Yard

A yard that slopes away in back of the house can be bad for prosperity. A fence or hedge at the back of the property will help keep *chi* in your yard, as will an uplight in *li gua* (fame) pointed up at the roof of the house, or a wind chime hung from a tree in *hsun gua*. A swimming pool in the backyard will also help to contain *chi*. If your house is much above street level, it's hard for *chi* to get uphill to your house. Flags, lights, or a wind chime will help to draw *chi* to the house, and a water feature in the front yard will help to hold *chi* on the property.

---

* See Appendix E for a quick reference guide to commonly used feng shui cures and accessories.

Your Front Path

Chi likes to meander, so a gently curving front path is good feng shui. A straight-as-a-ruler path from the street to the front door is considered less than ideal, because *chi* flows too quickly along it. This creates a subtle feeling of stress each time you leave the house, which can affect your mood and focus at work, which in turn could have an affect on whether or not you are offered a desired promotion or raise. It's a good idea to hang a wind chime near your front door to deflect this overly strong flow of *chi*. You can also soften the impact of a straight-line path by planting a curving border of flowers beside it.

The "Mouth of Chi"

Your front door is called the "mouth of *chi*" because it is the main way *chi* enters your home. If your mouth of *chi* has poor feng shui, you may find it difficult to recognize and respond to opportunities—which could mean missing out on chances to increase your income.

- Make sure your front door opens fully and that nothing is stored behind or around it in such a way that movement in and out of the house is restricted
- A bright light beside or over the front door attracts *chi* to the house
- Don't keep trash or recycling near the front door. If you must use this area for storage, make sure everything is as tidy and inconspicuous as possible.
- Keep the entire area around your front door clean, well-lit, and attractive. Pay attention to details like your house number and mailbox, and if that plant by the front door isn't looking very healthy these days, replace it with a bigger, prettier one.

If you never use your front door, you can't benefit from all the good *chi* that collects there. Make a point of using the front door at least once a week—preferably daily—instead of always going in and out through the back or side door. Each time you open the door, take a moment to mentally welcome prosperous *chi* into your home.

The Front Hall or Foyer

Narrow or shallow entry areas make it hard for *chi* to get into your home. If you want to have more money coming in, take a look at this space and see if it needs to be visually opened up. Mirrors are a good way to make a small space seem larger, and they can be used to good effect here.

BLOCKED ENTRY

A wall less than six feet in front of you when you enter your home may be blocking your ability to get ahead in life. The solution for this is to use a large mirror to visually open up the space:

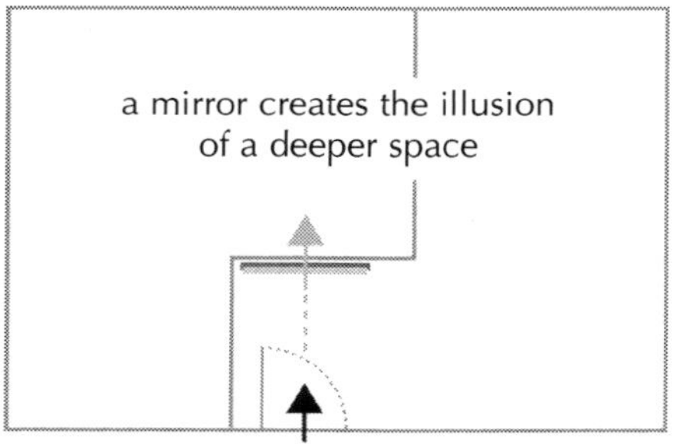
a mirror creates the illusion
of a deeper space

Some feng shui experts feel that a mirror directly opposite the door will bounce the *chi* right back out again, but a mirror brightens and expands the space, which is what this kind of entry needs. Another solution is to hang a landscape painting or poster opposite the door. The image should be large and have a distant horizon; this will visually open up the space and allow you to "see" into the distance.

"PINCHED NOSE" ENTRY

Another problem, the "pinched nose" entry, occurs when the front door opens onto a very narrow hallway. This is thought to restrict the flow of *chi* and opportunities into the home.

The best solution is to mirror the entire wall beside the open side of the door (not the hinge side). If you can't do that, a large mirror hung close to the door will also work.

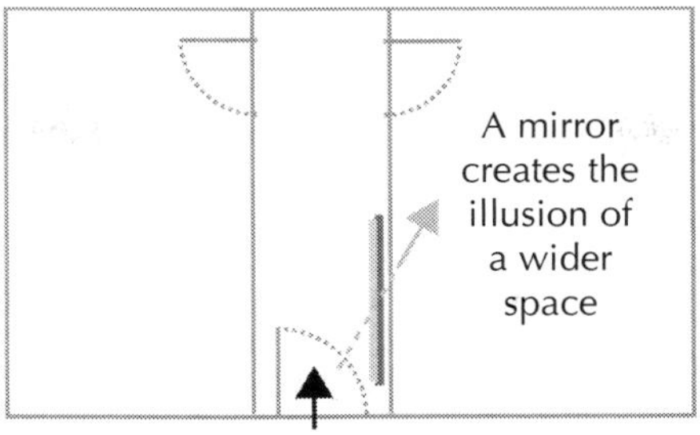
A mirror
creates the
illusion of
a wider
space

Stairs

Is *chi* flowing down the stairs and right out your front door, taking your prosperity with it? Interior stairs should end at least one body-length's distance (about six feet) from the door; ten feet or more is even better. A basket or potted plant at the foot of the stairs will help catch *chi* before it flows out the door, or you can hang a faceted crystal ball between the foot of the stairs and the door. If your entry features a chandelier, empower it (page 8) to prevent *chi* leaking out the door.

Stairs to a lower level, when close to the front door, can drain *chi* away from your prosperity power spots. If there's a door at the top of these stairs keep it closed, or hang a faceted crystal ball at the top of the stairs and empower it to keep *chi* from running down to the basement.

"Mandarin duck" stairs (where the front door opens onto a double staircase, one side leading up, the other down) confuses *chi*—and you—as it doesn't know whether to go up or down. Close off one side with a door or curtain to direct *chi* toward your main prosperity power spots.

Hallways

A hallway that cuts straight through your house from the front entry to the back door funnels *chi* right out the back, before it has a chance to nourish the home:

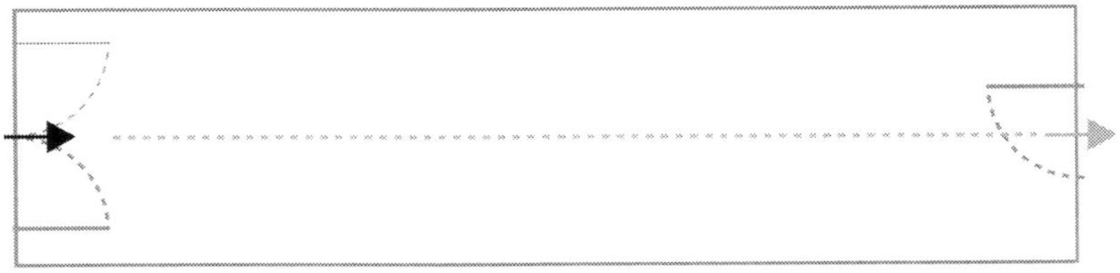

You can slow *chi* down with a faceted crystal ball, crystal chandelier, or wind chime hung halfway down the hallway or just inside the back door:

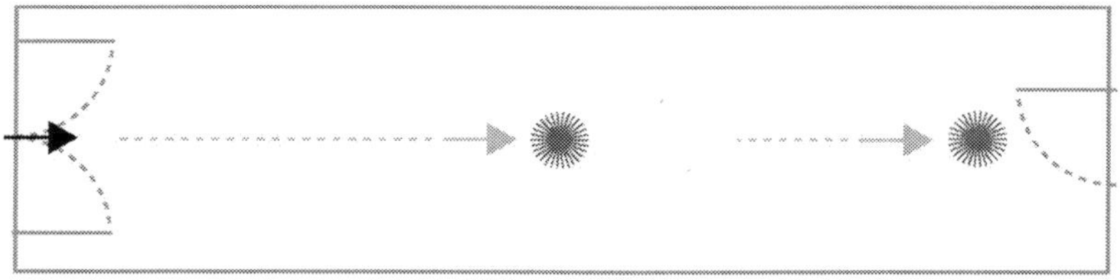

A long narrow hallway anywhere in the home will cause *chi* to move too quickly, which can increase feelings of stress or anxiety. Use three crystals equally spaced along the length of the hall, or hang a crystal outside each doorway opening off the hallway:

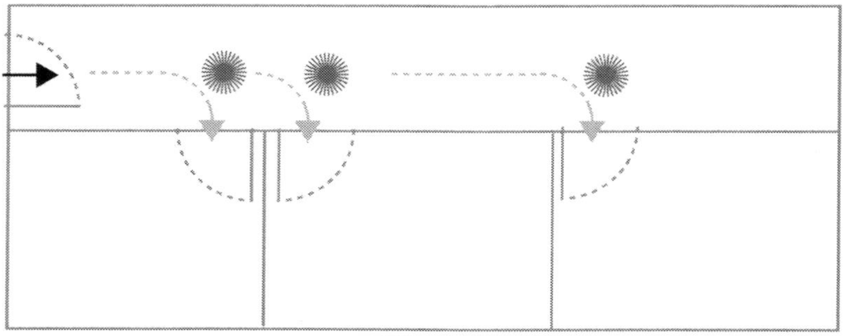

Guide Chi to Your Power Spots

Slowly walk from the front door to each of your major prosperity power spots, looking for anything that slows you down or gets in your way: a pile of newspapers, the laundry basket, exercise equipment, scattered toys, too much furniture in too small a space, etc. Deal with these now or start a list of spots that need attention and plan to correct them as soon as possible.

If any of your top priority power spots are a long way from the front door, hang a bell or wind chime in that area, or in the doorway to that room, and empower it to attract more *chi* there. You can also use either of the following two methods to direct *chi* to a power spot.

POWER LINE

Get a spool of red or purple string or heavy thread, and fastem one end to the floor or doorframe at the "mouth of *chi.*" Run the string along the wall all the way from the doorway to your prosperity power spot. Fasten the string at intervals so it won't trip anyone or get broken. If you do this neatly, tucking the string into corners, under the edge of your carpet, and behind furniture, it is not conspicuous.

When you get to your prosperity power spot, cut the string and tape that end down, too. If you want to be really precise, measure the string as you go along, and cut it at a length that is a multiple of nine feet or nine meters (use your standard unit of measurement).

Put a wealth symbol at the end of the string, such as a bowl of 108 coins, a chunk of amethyst, or a Wealth God figurine (see Appendix D for ideas). Empower the string to conduct prosperity *chi* and financial blessings into your home and bank account.

PATH OF PLANTS

Starting at your front door, place three, six, or nine plants along the route to your power spot, so that as you walk from the front door to the power spot there is always a plant in view ahead of you. It's okay to use artificial plants so long as they are lifelike and attractive. Living plants have stronger *chi,* but if they won't thrive in those spots artificial ones will be a better choice. You can also do this cure with blooming plants—look for a variety with red or purple blossoms for best effect. Empower the plants to attact *chi* to your power spot and increase your prosperity.

Principle 4

Repaint, Repair, Renew

Millionaires don't live with dust bunnies, leaky taps, weed-filled lawns or dirty windows, and neither should you. In feng shui everything is connected, so neglecting your home is a form of self-neglect. The best way to shift the *chi* of your home for a more prosperous impression is to attend to basic housekeeping and maintenance issues that may be draining your energy and abundance. In feng shui, even little things that seem like minor issues could be having a major effect on your prosperity. Here are some common problems to look out for, and why:

- A cracked walkway, sagging porch steps, loose railings, rotting threshold, or ratty doormat can all literally or symbolically trip you up and make it difficult to achieve your goals.
- Make sure the door to any power spot room opens smoothly and completely, and that the doorknob turns easily. Any *hsun gua* door that does not open easily can indicate problems accessing or benefitting from your financial resources.
- A loose doorknob in *hsun gua* can make it difficult to "get a grip on" your financial situation.
- A *hsun gua door* that does not close all the way or does not easily stay closed can mean that your private business is subject to inappropriate public scrutiny, or that some unfinished money issue needs attention.
- Problems with a closet door in *hsun gua* have the same meanings and effect as other doors, with the added difficulty that these issues may be hidden from you.

- Dirty windows in *hsun gua* make it hard to see your financial situation clearly, and can indicate clouded judgment.
- Burnt-out lights, fixtures that don't work, or inadequate lighting in *hsun gua* will all contribute to a lack of vision, energy, and initiative in pursuing your financial objectives. If you need more inspiration and insight where money is concerned, turn some lights on in *hsun gua*—the brighter the better.
- In feng shui, the kitchen and the stove are very important to prosperity. Broken burners especially indicate financial problems, so get them fixed immediately. Dirt and grime will also affect the prosperity *chi* associated with your stove, so be sure to keep the stove sparkling clean.
- Plumbing problems anywhere in the house indicate that resources are leaking away from the home. Fix them immediately!
- Minor leaks can be just as damaging as major ones, so pay attention to toilets that run a little too long after flushing and even the slightest dripping from any faucet.
- Clogged plumbing indicates clogged energy and should be corrected. When old energy has no way to get out, new energy has a hard time getting in. In *hsun gua*, clogged drains can indicate that you've been clinging too strongly to the money you've got. Pinching every penny may seem like a good idea if your financial situation is tight, but energetically it keeps new money energy from flowing in. (We'll explore this issue in more detail in Part II.)

With these guidelines in mind, it's a good idea to do a thorough inspection of your home. Start with your prosperity power spots, and make a list of anything that needs to be cleaned, repaired, or replaced. Make a separate list of maintenance issues for the areas that are not power spots, and plan to take care of them when the priority tasks are done.

Principle 5

Clean Up Your Clutter

The word "clutter" comes from an Old English word, *clott*, which means "to cause to become blocked or obscured." Like a blood clot that blocks circulation in a vein, clutter prevents *chi* from circulating through your home and life.

How Clutter Affects You

Clutter is disempowering; it saps your energy, erodes your spirit, and holds you in the past. When your prosperity power spots are filled with clutter, your financial situation may feel stuck or hopeless. Here are some specific ways clutter might be affecting your life:

- Kitchen clutter blocks your sources of abundance and makes it hard to nourish yourself and others. De-cluttering your kitchen opens up space for you to receive the financial and emotional nourishment that you need in life.
- Cluttered living and dining rooms affect family and social life. This can lead to a lack of emotional support from your family, and can hinder networking and career advancement.
- Clutter in your office slows your productivity, adds to your stress, and prevents ideas and opportunities from manifesting. If you want to attract new clients, new projects, or a new direction for your business, clean out your file cabinets and hard drive.
- Halls are the highways of your home. Clutter here creates a traffic jam that prevents connections between different areas of your life. Look at your halls to see how you feel about your life's path: are they well lit and easily navigable, or do they trip you

up? If you feel a disconnect between work and family, self and others, your needs and your obligations, it may be time to give your hallways a good clearing out.

- Bathroom clutter can indicate a lack of attention to self that goes beyond the physical. Eliminating clutter and disorder in your bathroom and transforming it into a place of refuge will help smooth your transitions at the beginning and end of each day.

- Adults' bedrooms should function as places of renewal for self and relationships. If you feel "wired and tired," creating order out of chaos in this most personal space can help you to relax and let go of the stress of the day. Then you can get a good night's sleep or enjoy some special time with your partner.

- Closets represent things that are hidden, unknown, or unrecognized. When we fill our closets with clutter, we stifle our ability to be intuitive and insightful. Cluttered closets can indicate problems that you may not be consciously aware of but which impede your progress through life, work, and relationships nonetheless.

- A cluttered attic creates a feeling of being under pressure. It's hard to feel optimistic or inspired about your financial future when there's so much stuff "hanging over your head." Ancestor issues reside up there, too, along with all those boxes and chests holding the detritus of generations. The basement and other below-ground storage areas are considered abodes of the subconscious, so watch your step and get that clutter cleaned up!

- Your car is a symbol of your mobility, independence, and ability to be self-directed in life. If there's so much stuff piled up in your garage that you can barely fit the car in there, you may be hampered or overly cautious moving forward in life as well.

Clutter Clearing Makes Room for Blessings

Clearing out your clutter gets you out of your rut and creates space for possibility. Instead of moping around worrying about your bills, you may find yourself deciding to go back to school, change your career, or start your own business. No matter how severely financial worries may be dragging you down, I guarantee you that clearing your clutter will dramatically improve your mood and energy and that then your other concerns won't seem quite so unmanageable.

People who are able to live without clutter trust themselves to make good choices. As you become more conscious of what you allow into and keep in your home, you will develop a higher level of trust in your own decisions.

Another benefit of getting rid of your clutter is that it can literally lighten you up and help you lose weight. All that stuck energy in your environment affects you on both emotional and physical levels, and encourages extra pounds to hang around. If you are feeling listless and uninspired to take action about your finances because you are overweight or out of shape, getting rid of clutter everywhere in the house should be a key part of your financial strategy.

Stop thinking of clutter-clearing as a tremendous chore, and start thinking of it as one of the most effective self-empowerment tactics available to you. Each magazine and piece of paper you recycle, every book you give to the library, every knick-knack and item of clothing you release to a new owner creates space in your life for new insight, energy, joy, and abundance to flow in. If you need immediate cash, yard sales and online auction sites are a good way to turn old energy (lingering in your home as stuff you no longer need or want) into some useful cash.

The space you create by releasing clutter will allow all kinds of gifts to flow into your life, material, spiritual, and emotional. Feng shui helps us to see that letting go of excess makes room for us to receive the "fortunate blessings" that are the essence of *hsun gua*.

If getting rid of clutter were just a matter of catching up with housework, more people would do it. If you want to deal with your clutter but aren't making any progress on your own, consider hiring a professional organizer to assist you. Or, visit www.ClutterFreeForever.com for information on my *Clutter-Free Forever!* Home Coaching Program.

Principle 6

Neutralize Negative Influences

Predecessor Chi

Before you moved into your current home or office, did you ask about the previous occupants (if any) and why they moved out? Probably not, unless you've studied feng shui, and know about the importance of "predecessor *chi.*"

It makes sense when you think about it. If the *chi* of a space affects your life, then a quick peak at how the people before you prospered (or not) in the same space provides clues about how well you might fare there. If the people who used to live or work in that space moved out because they got married, were promoted, or retired rich, you've hit the feng shui jackpot. It's a sign that you, too, are likely to prosper and be happy there.

Although feng shui is just one factor in your life experience, if the previous owners or tenants of your home or office moved out due to divorce, bankruptcy, illness, violence, or death, you'll want to do what you can to ensure the same problems don't happen to you. Even if the specific issue that led the previous occupants to leave was not caused by the feng shui of the space, the negative vibrations of trouble, stress, and unhappiness are likely to have lingered there.

Space Clearing

Space clearing ceremonies have been used for millennia to clear and protect a home or place of business. If you know or suspect that your home or office has unlucky predecessor *chi*, a thorough space clearing is called for. It's also a good idea to periodically clear the energy of your space if you have lived or worked in the same place for a long time. Hire a professional to perform the process for you, or study one of the many books available on the subject if you want to do it yourself. Some quick methods are suggested here, but for a serious predecessor *chi* situation, a more thorough and powerful method may be required.

SOUND VIBRATIONS

Sound vibrations help to loosen stuck energy. Use a rattle, bells, wind chime, or bang on a metal pot lid to shake things up. Walk through your entire house or focus on one problem area where stuff and clutter has piled up—a sure sign of stuck energy in that area. If clearing and cleaning your space is a bigger chore than you're up for right now, ring a bell all around your body and let the sound waves energize you.

CLEAN CARPETS

Rugs and carpets collect old energy along with dirt, dust, crumbs, and pet hair. Make sure to include a thorough carpet cleaning along with your other energy-clearing methods, especially if you have been using the sound cure to loosen stale or stuck *chi*.

AIR OUT THE HOUSE

If the air in your house is stale, the energy will be, too. A quick way to refresh the *chi* in your home is to open all your windows and doors for at least 15 minutes. Even if your home is well ventilated, this is a good thing to do if you have been having a run of bad luck. The best time to do this is between 11 PM and 1 AM, when the *chi* of the day is shifting. If you can do this when the air is clear and fresh-smelling and there is a gentle breeze, that's even better.

Secret Arrows & Sha Chi

SECRET ARROWS

Secret Arrows are a specific form of *sha chi* (harmful energy) caused by things that point at you or your house. The sharper and larger the point, the stronger the negative effect will be. Secret arrows are wounding on an energetic level. If you are exposed to them your health and energy can suffer.

As you can imagine, a secret arrow aimed at a prosperity power spot can injure your financial situation. This could manifest as a chronic illness that makes it hard for you to earn a decent income, migraine headaches, failed business deals, or conflicts with clients or partners, to name just a few possibilities. There's no way of knowing exactly how a secret arrow will hurt you, but you can be sure that some kind of damage will be done. Here's what to look out for, and how to protect yourself against a secret arrow's nasty impact.

SECRET ARROWS OUTSIDE THE HOUSE

One of the most common sources of secret arrows is the corner of a neighboring building that points directly at your house:

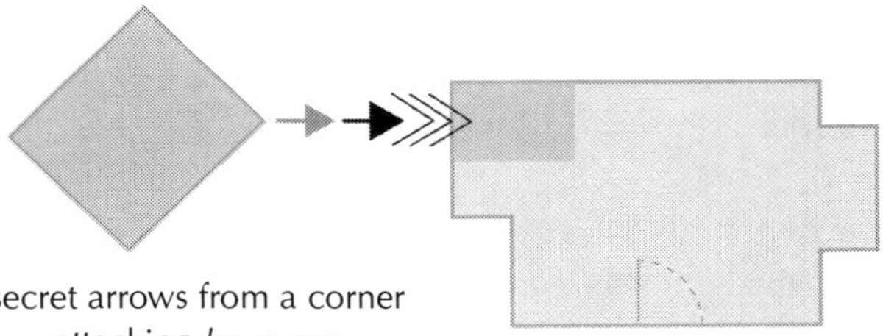

secret arrows from a corner attacking *hsun gua*

A utility pole in front of or across the street from your house can be a source of secret arrows, especially if its shadow falls across your front walkway or door during the day. Another source of *sha chi* is a narrow alley or "T" intersection that sends a strong rush of *chi* at the front door of a house.

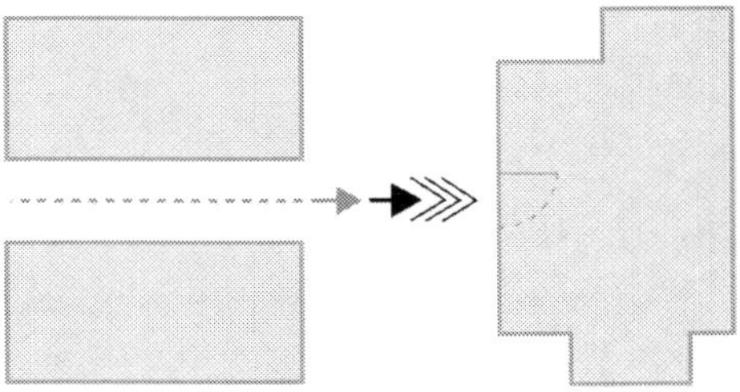

secret arrows from a "T" intersection attacking the front door

Note that for a business location, a "T" intersection can be more helpful than harmful, because it drives traffic to your door.

If anything in the area surrounding your home makes you uncomfortable in any way, chances are good it's a source of *sha chi*, and you should take precautions against it.

Use a Ba Gua Mirror for Proection

The best way to protect your home from exterior secret arrows is to deflect the energy with a mirror or other shiny surface. The traditional cure for *sha chi* aimed at the house is a *ba gua* mirror. This is a small round mirror in a red or yellow octagonal frame decorated with the eight trigrams.

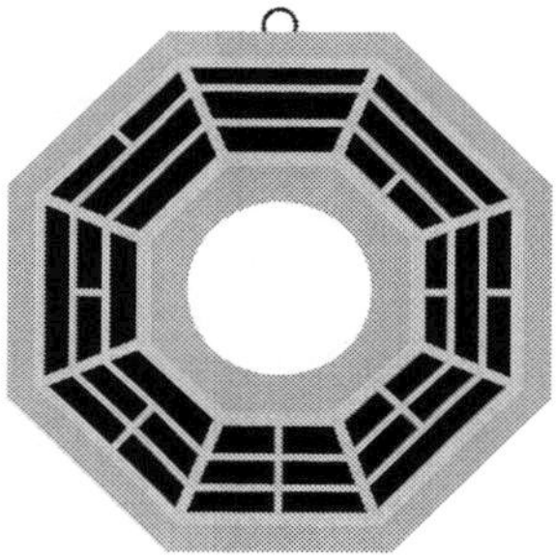

Hang a *ba gua* mirror with the three solid lines (the trigram for "Heaven") at the top, and the three broken lines ("Earth") at the bottom. Place it above or beside the front door if *sha chi* is aimed directly at the entry, or use it on the side of the house attacked by secret arrows.

In an office or apartment, you can use a *ba gua* mirror against exterior *sha chi* by hanging it on the inside of a window, facing out at the source of negative energy. Other than this use, *ba gua* mirrors should never be used indoors.

From a prosperity perspective, the most important areas to protect from exterior secret arrows are the front door, *hsun gua*, office, and your bedroom, although you should check for them in every *gua*. Secret arrows come in many guises, so take a sharp look around with feng shui eyes to see what might be aimed at your house. Check for *sha chi* by looking outward from all windows in these key areas, and take a look around from the yard as well.

While you are out checking your yard for secret arrows, keep a lookout for other sources of *sha chi* as well. Remember that anything unattractive, unhealthy, or unpleasant is a sign of negative energy. If your yard is marred by dying trees, junked appliances, a pile of wood scrap or the like, the *chi* of your home is being affected. Start with *hsun gua*, and clear out anything that has a less than beautifying effect. Bad smells are a form of *sha chi* as well, so if you notice any, inside or out, investigate the source and remove or fix it as soon as possible.

SECRET ARROWS INSIDE THE HOUSE

Secret arrows in interior spaces are caused by sharp angles or corners. The turbulent energy created at the corner may result in stress, anxiety, difficult sleep, or arguments. You can begin the work of neutralizing harmful influences by examining each of your prosperity power spots for secret arrows affecting any area where you eat, sleep, relax, or work. The sharp corner of a table, the edges of a shelf, even points or angles on a light fixture or piece of statuary can all cause a disruption in the smooth flow of *chi* nearby.

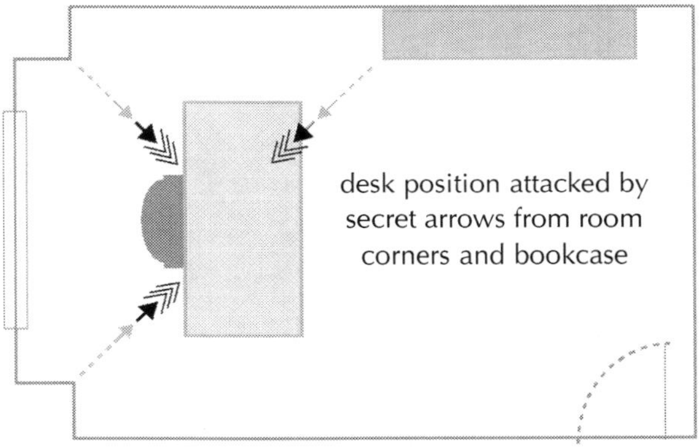
desk position attacked by
secret arrows from room
corners and bookcase

The size and height of the angle will affect how strong the negative influence is, and the more sources of *sha chi* are present in a room, the greater the total effect will be. The corner of a bookcase, for example, is not likely to be a problem if you are seated far away from it. But if there are many sharp corners crowded into a space, you'll feel their stressful, distracting effect regardless of proximity.

You can cure sharp angles in interior spaces by shielding them with a plant, fabric, or a faceted crystal ball. Hang the crystal from the ceiling with red string cut to a multiple of nine inches or centimeters for best effect.

SHA CHI IN THE KITCHEN

Inside the house you are subject to *sha chi* any time you have your back to a door. This is especially harmful to both you and your wealth in the kitchen. In many homes, the kitchen stove is positioned so that the cook faces the wall while preparing meals, leaving his or her back exposed.

If you are not entirely at ease while you cook, that unsettled energy will be communicated to the food you prepare. On a subtle level, this may affect your health, which in turn may affect your work and your income. A doorway behind you as you stand at the stove compounds the problem; this layout is thought to lead to accidents in the home.

A chef who faces into the room while cooking is in the "command position" (below). This is one of the most important principles of feng shui, and should be followed not just in the kitchen, but for your bed and desk as well.

If you stand with your back to the room while using the stove, hang a large mirror over the stove so that you can see behind you. If you can, hang the mirror so the burners are reflected in it as well. This symbolically doubles your food, and therefore, your money!

THE COMMAND POSITION

Sitting where you can't see what's going on behind you makes you feel vulnerable and tense. In addition to not being able to see who's behind you, the *chi* entering that space is hitting you in the back. If your bed, desk, couch, or stove puts you in this position, it will increase the level of stress you must deal with every day.

In feng shui, we want major pieces of furniture (desk, bed, etc.) to be positioned so that they give you a view of the doorway—preferably with a solid wall behind you for support—and are not directly in the path of the *chi* coming in the door:

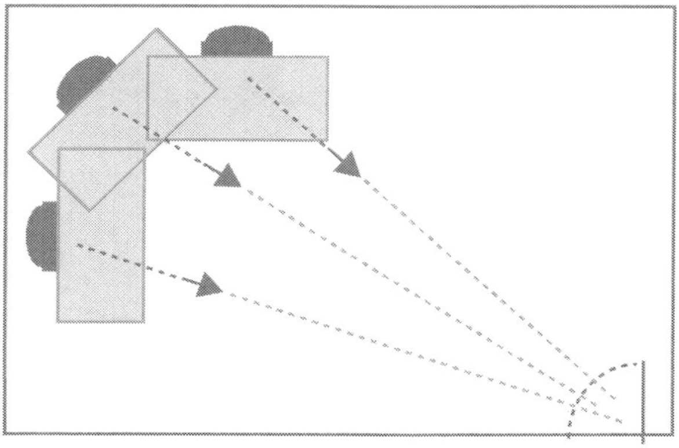

"command position" locations for desk

This is called the "command position," and it will put you more in command of your life. As you direct the flow of *chi* to your power spots, arrange your furniture so you will be in the command position. If you cannot use the command position, hang a mirror so that you will be able to see the door from where you sit or sleep:

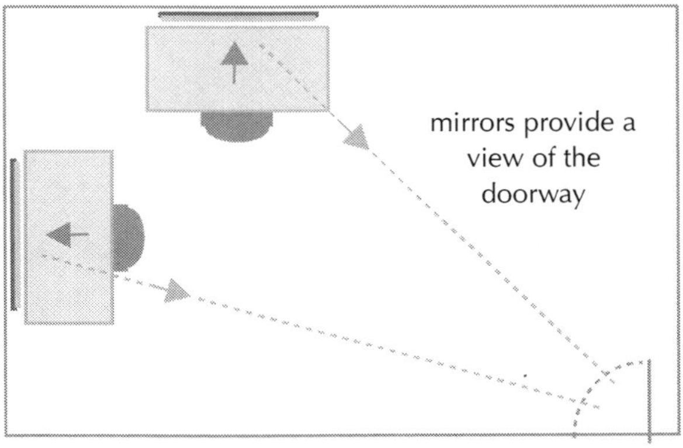
mirrors provide a
view of the
doorway

Sources of Conflict

FIGHTING DOORS

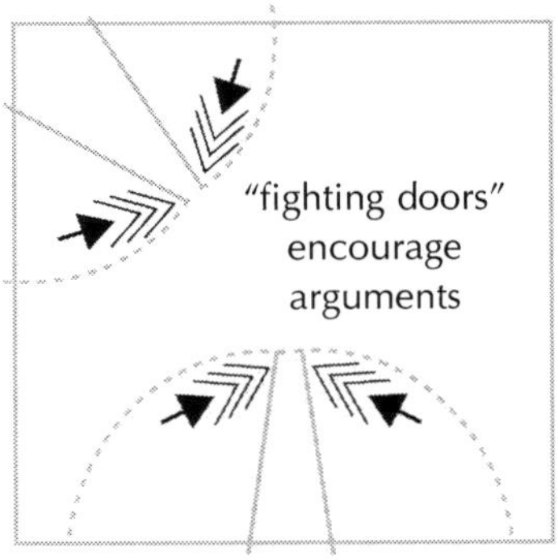
"fighting doors"
encourage
arguments

Doors that bump into each other when open lead to conflict in the home. If you and your partner tend to argue about money, look for "fighting doors" in *hsun gua*, the kitchen, and other prosperity power spots. When closet doors "fight," conflicts may be unspoken or unrecognized.

Cure fighting doors with red string or tassels. If you choose tassels, hang one from each doorknob. If using string, cut a piece long enough to tie around both doorknobs when the doors are closed. The length of the string should be a multiple of nine inches or centimeters. Tie one end of the string to each doorknob, cut it in the middle, and wrap each loose end around the the stem of the doorknob to which it is attached.

OVERHEAD SHELVES

Having trouble sleeping? Prone to headaches at work? Shelves that are too close to your head are a form of *sha chi*. The secret arrows from the edges and corners of the shelves can cause pressure, headaches, and poor concentration. Shelves over a bed can make it difficult to sleep well, due to the threat that things might fall on you as you sleep. Shelves directly over a desk can be threatening on a subconscious level as well. Knowing that the shelves are firmly attached and not likely to fall does not reassure your subconscious mind or offset the oppressive energy. If you can't move your furniture to avoid this situation, hang a faceted crystal ball between you and the shelves.

EXPOSED BEAMS

Exposed ceiling beams create pressure over the area directly beneath them. A beam over the dining table or couch, for example, can aggravate tensions in the family. A beam over a desk may make it difficult to work, or may cause headaches.

The lower the ceiling, the greater the impact will be. Keep in mind the importance of having the desk in the command position; often, there is no single perfect solution for where to place key furniture in a room. Feng shui is about making the best choices you can, given the many factors present in a room. If you can't avoid having a major piece of furniture under an exposed beam, you can lessen the impact by using light or symbols to lessen the impact:

- Chinese bamboo flutes are the traditional "cure." Hang them with red string at an angle that implies the top of an octagon:

  The root end of the wood should be at the bottom; usually this puts the mouthpiece at the top. However, if you can't tell which end is the root end, hang the flutes with the mouthpiece at the *bottom*, so air blown through the flute would travel up.

- If flutes don't appeal to you, use plants or uplights on the floor or a table beneath both ends of the beam, to lift the energy.
- Use imagery under the ends of the beam, or along the side of the beam, to symbolically lift the energy. Appropriate images include angels, birds in flight, and the like.
- Disguise the beam with fabric or a canopy over the bed
- Hang a vine, garland, or string of miniature lights along the side or bottom of the beam

CEILING FANS

Ceiling fans keep us cool and reduce air-conditioning costs. However, they also create slicing energy as they spin, which can be harmful if over your bed or desk. If you can't avoid sitting or sleeping directly under a ceiling fan, hang a faceted crystal ball underneath it, or some other image that is uplifting and protective to you, such as a bird, angel, or cherub ornament.

SLANTED CEILINGS

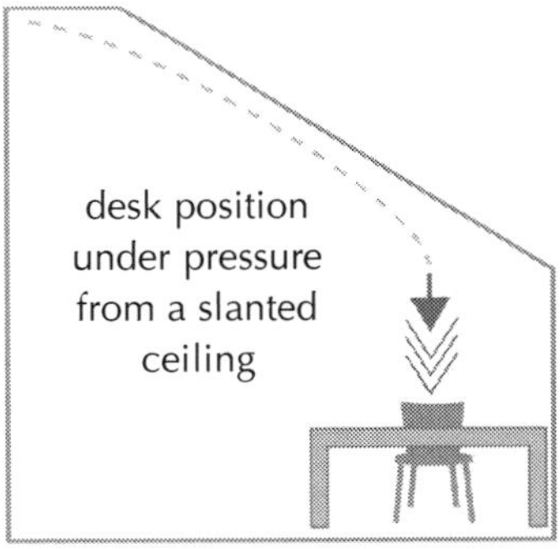

Chi flows down the slope of a slanted ceiling and puts pressure on whatever is against the lower wall. If your desk or bed is on the low side of a room with a slanted ceiling, you will be under a lot of pressure while you work or sleep.

The height of the ceiling, the angle of slope, and the overall size of the room all affect the amount of pressure created. If you cannot stand upright on the lower side of the room without bumping your head, the situation is considered severe. Even in a high-ceilinged room, the lopsided nature of the space will create unbalanced energy. This can affect you in a variety of ways:

- You may feel stressed-out, off-balance, irritable, moody, and out-of-sorts much of the time.

- You may experience uneven cash flow, a lack of steady business activity, or unusual difficulty winning new business.
- Others may perceive you as unstable or unreliable.
- Your health may suffer, or you may become depressed.
- If your bedroom or office has a slanted ceiling, it could contribute to inequality in your romantic or business relationships.

If you must sleep or work under the pressure of a slanted ceiling, here are some things you can do:

- Put a canopy over your bed, or hang a swag of fabric above the bed to disguise the uneven height of the ceiling
- Place three uplights along the shorter wall to lift *chi* on that side of the room
- Hang a faceted crystal ball overhead for protection

Financial Leaks

Leaking *chi* in your prosperity power spots can mean money is leaking out of your pocket. Plumbing, as you might have guessed, is the first place to look for potential problems.

BATHROOMS

Feng shui's association of the bathroom with ill health and harmful *chi* dates from pre-industrial times when the glories of modern plumbing and cleaning products were still far in the future. And because feng shui originated many centuries before indoor plumbing, there's no place in the *ba gua* where the bathroom is welcome.

Our modern bathrooms, however, are havens of hygiene and comfort. So long as your bathroom is clean and attractive, there's no reason to think that it's the cesspool of harmful energy that some feng shui teachings would have you believe. There's no need to panic about a bathroom in your wealth *gua* or any other key area of the home. It does not necessarily mean you are flushing away all your money, although you can protect against that just to be safe. Just keep the toilet seat down and the sink and shower drains closed (except when in use, of course), and keep the door closed as much as possible. A large mirror on the outside of the bathroom door will deflect *chi* away from the bathroom.

Make sure that your desk is not placed where there is a toilet on the other side of the wall. If moving your desk away from the wall is not possible, paint the wall between your office and the bathroom green and put up artwork representing trees or flowers. This WOOD energy will help to counteract the draining WATER energy of the bathroom.*

EXTERIOR DOOR IN HSUN GUA

If a back or side door is located in *hsun gua*, money *chi* could be leaking out that door. Make sure that the door closes and locks securely, and paint a thin red line around the inside of the door frame to keep money *chi* from leaking out of the house.

UP IN SMOKE

A fireplace in *hsun gua* can mean your finances are "going up in smoke." Keep the flue closed when the fireplace is not in use, and place a screen in front of the hearth to help keep energy from going up the chimney. Large paper fans are often sold for use as fireplace screens, but from a feng shui perspective these could have the effect of "fanning the flames."

Don't place plants near a *hsun gua* fireplace: they will symbolically feed the fire, which consumes the WOOD energy associated with *hsun gua*. Use your knowledge of the element cycles to control the FIRE energy of a fireplace in a prosperity power spot. WATER controls FIRE and feeds WOOD, so an indoor fountain or a fish tank will help to keep the fireplace energy under control.

Mirrors also represent WATER, so a mirror above the mantel can be an effective cure. Another option would be to hang a large poster or print of a water feature such as a waterfall, pond, or river above or near the fireplace.

---

* If you are not yet familiar with the five Chinese elements and how they interact, please read Appendix B to learn about these very important feng shui factors.

Signs of Poverty Consciousness

The images that surround us exert a powerful subconscious influence on our thoughts and emotions. Learn to look at your possessions with feng shui eyes, and you will discover a new dimension to your surroundings.

- *Indicators of abundance chi*: metallic colors, coins, jewelry, luxury items of all kinds, luxurious fabrics, fruits, anything full or overflowing.
- *Indicators of poverty chi*: anything empty, anything worn or torn, anything that energetically says, "poor me."

How many of each of these kinds of things you have in your home is a good indicator of your subconscious programming. It makes no difference whether or not you actually have money, or how expensive the things in your home really are. You could be struggling with debt and have few possessions, yet if you have a bowl of fruit on the kitchen table and box of pretty costume jewelry in the bedroom you have found ways to bring the energy of abundance into your home.

It works the other way, too. Even if you have lots of money, if your home is spare, your cupboards bare, and the containers in your bathroom and refrigerator are close to empty, your home is resonating with the vibration of lack.

Go to each of your prosperity power spots, and take a good look at what you see. How many indicators of abundance do you see? How many signs of lack?

Keep containers more than half full, group things together in bowls or baskets, and have at least one pretty or luxurious-looking item on display in each room, and you fill your home with a vibration of plenty.

FIRST IMPRESSIONS

As part of your campaign to reduce or remove any sources of negative energy, you should take a look at all "first impression" spaces in your home—particularly those leading to your prosperity power spots—to make sure the scene that greets you as you enter each space is inspiring and attractive. Anything dark, depressing, chaotic, violent, dirty, worn out, or unpleasant is a source of *sha chi*; when it's the first thing you see when you enter a space, it will affect your entire experience there.

Check your "mouth of *chi*" and make sure that area is as attractive and welcoming as possible. Select and arrange furniture or artwork so that you are greeted by an attractive focal point. If your front or back door opens directly into the living room or kitchen, make sure that the first thing you see is visually appealing. A sink full of dirty dishes, a messy stove, or a couch buried under a heap of toys and papers will make you feel less than prosperous each time you come home.

Once the key access areas to your home have been inspected, do the rounds of the rest of the house, and check the first impressions for each of your prosperity power spots. Remove anything that you know or suspect might have negative energy or connotations, and replace it with more inspiring and positive imagery.

Principle 7

Activate Your Power Spots

Now that you have created a path for *chi,* cleared your clutter, taken care of maintenance issues and removed or corrected sources of *sha chi,* it's time to activate your power spots with appropriate symbols, shapes, colors, and objects.

WOOD CHI

Hsun gua is associated with mature wood. All kinds of plants are appropriate here, especially those that have round (coin-shaped) leaves or red or purple blossoms.

- Outdoors, enhance *hsun gua* with evergreen trees and bushes, fruit trees, or flowering plants with red or purple blossoms. If you decide to plant trees or bushes in *hsun gua,* place nine coins in the soil beneath each one, to symbolically "grow" your money.
- Indoors, enhance *hsun gua* with large house plants, plants with red or purple blossoms, and/or bouquets of fresh or lifelike red and purple flowers.

WIND-POWERED OBJECTS

Colorful flags fluttering in the breeze are a great way to stir up *chi* in *hsun gua*. Activate *hsun gua* of your yard with a flag, banner or whirlygig. Flag poles, tree branches, eaves, and porch columns can all carry a flag or windsock. Choose blacks, dark blues, greens, and purple colors (rather than reds, yellows, or white), or include colors that represent all five of the elements.

Small mobiles and whirly-gigs can also be used as *chi* enhancements for prosperity power spots inside the home. If you use this type of cure in a place where there is not much air current, set it in motion manually from time to time as you walk by.

Wind chimes activate *hsun gua* with both sound and motion, and are a much-recommended addition to this important area. If your back yard slopes away from the house, hang a wind chime in *hsun gua* to lift energy and keep if from rolling away downhill. Small wind chimes can be used inside the house.

COLORS

Hsun gua colors are dark greens and purple. The darker greens (rather than pastels or aquas) signify mature wood, and purple is the color of supreme success and abundance. Dark green and purple paint, fabrics, furnishings, and accessories are all good additions for *hsun gua*.

SHAPES

Columns, pillars, and tall shapes are associated with the WOOD element, as are vertical stripes.

IMAGERY

Good enhancements for *hsun gua* include:

- Anything described as a wealth symbol in Appendix D, or that symbolizes prosperity to you in some way.
- Money of any kind: coins, paper currency, or any imagery having to do with money and prosperity.
- Images of things that you are grateful for: the people, experiences, and material goods that are your current or hoped-for "fortunate blessings."

NOURISH WITH WATER

WOOD is nourished by WATER, so water features and imagery are also good in *hsun gua*.

Moving water brings prosperity and good luck to the home. Water fountains and aquariums are great feng shui enhancements because they are both soothing and energizing. The sound and movement of the water activate *chi* and humidify a dry room, helping to balance *chi*. Moving water gets things going when the *chi* has been stagnant for a while (think of ice melting in the spring).

MINIMIZE ENEMIES

FIRE burns up WOOD, and METAL chops it down. Minimize the use of reds, white, metallic colors and objects, and imagery that has flaming or cutting aspects.

Candles used in *hsun gua*, such as on a Prosperity Altar (below), should be green or purple. Avoid red candles. When unlit, tall candles are better than short ones, because pillars and column shapes are associated with the WOOD element. Common sense dictates that when candles are lit, safety is always the most important consideration.

Prosperity Altar

Choose one of your best power spots as the place for a Prosperity Altar. How do you know which is the "best" spot? Start by choosing among your living room, bedroom, and kitchen. If you work at home, *hsun gua* of your office is a good location as well.

- If you wish to keep your Prosperity Altar private, use *hsun gua* of your bedroom.
- If your family will be creating the altar with you, set it up in your living room or kitchen.
- If none of these rooms offer an appropriate area, consider the dining room as well. However, if you rarely use the dining room try to find another spot, because unused rooms have low vitality.

Other considerations include the availability of an appropriate place on a table, dresser, shelf, windowsill, or countertop. Avoid any location that is next to a fireplace, stove, or bathroom as these will burn up or drain away the energy of your altar.

If possible, choose a spot where you will be able to sit quietly or meditate for a few minutes in comfort and without distractions.

WHAT TO PLACE ON YOUR ALTAR

Any of the *hsun gua* enhancements on the previous pages are appropriate for your Prosperity Altar, as are the wealth symbols described in Appendix D.

The Five Elements

Include at least one image or item to represent each of the five elements, such as:

- Fresh flowers (WOOD)
- Picture of a waterfall, or a small indoor fountain (WATER)
- Candle and/or incense (FIRE)
- Ceramic bowl or figurine (EARTH; if glazed, color will also matter)
- Natural stones and crystals (considered METAL by some, because they are extracted from the earth; others consider them an EARTH element; I lean towards using these as EARTH-type cures, but a lot depends on the color and shape of the crystal—a clear quartz crystal with sharp edges and points, for example, seems more metallic than earthy to me)
- Coins or crystals (METAL)

Make sure that the overall balance of energy leans toward WATER and WOOD, with smaller amounts of FIRE, EARTH, and METAL energy. An easy way to do this is by using a large piece of lovely green-blue cloth to cover your altar.

The Five Senses

Include at least one item that addresses each of the senses:

- *Sight*: symbolic objects and images
- *Sound*: small bell, wind chime, music box
- *Touch*: fabrics, crystals, polished stones, coins, shells, feathers, pinecones, etc.
- *Smell*: scented candles, incense, a miniature bottle of your favorite perfume, fragrant flowers
- *Taste*: fresh fruit or pictures of fruit, especially oranges; grains, especially uncooked rice; a miniature bottle of liquor

Virtual Predecessor Chi

You can bring the good vibrations of prosperity into your home with objects and images of those whose path to success and fortune you particularly admire. This could be:

- A biography or autobiography of that person
- A photograph, especially if autographed
- An object that belonged to that person

Ancestor Chi

Photographs of (or things that belonged to) older relatives whom you love or admire. They don't have to have been rich; qualities such as persistence, integrity, ingenuity, and warm-heartedness can all assist you on your path to abundance.

Spiritual Guides

Any spiritual figure, saint, angel, or deity appropriate to your religion, spiritual practice or culture.

Cash Flow Rituals

One of the most effective ways to activate *hsun gua* and increase the flow of prosperity into your home is with a cash flow ritual. Usually this will involve some preparatory steps, followed by specific actions that are repeated daily for a period of 9, 27, or more days.

Your Prosperity Altar is the best place to perform the prescribed actions, unless the instructions for a specific ritual say otherwise. Instructions for a variety of Cash Flow Rituals are provided Part III.

Principle 8

Work on Yourself as well as Your Home

As you learned in the Introduction, the concepts and practices of both traditional and contemporary Western feng shui emerge from the key understanding that everything in our experience is connected on an energetic level. So far, we have focused mostly on feng shui from the outside in: how the specific characteristics of the spaces that we inhabit affect various aspects of our lives, especially our experience of financial prosperity.

Because everything is connected, we can also approach feng shui from the inside out. When our inner environment is in harmony with the feng shui changes we have made to our exterior space, the desired improvements happen more smoothly and quickly. When you don't take care of yourself—mentally, emotionally, physically—it will be harder to fully appreciate the benefits of feng shui. If you are committed to experiencing a life of greater prosperity and abundance, be sure to include wellness practices as part of your overall plan.

Caring for Your Body

If you've begun to de-clutter your home (Principle 5), you know what a difference getting rid of clutter makes to the energy of your home. So, how about getting rid of some of the clutter in your body? Even if you exercise regularly, have never smoked, and eat a healthy diet, you are still exposed to a frightening array of environmental toxins from air, tap water, pesticides and preservatives in foods, synthetic materials and chemicals in your clothes, furnishings, and cleaning supplies.

Diet, for many people, adds to the problem; most commercially prepared and packaged foods are severly lacking in nutrients. Unfortunately, avoiding junk food and taking a daily multi-vitamin are not enough to counteract the deficiencies and toxicities of the modern diet and environment.

When our bodies are burdened with accumulated toxins, and our diets are deficient in vital nutrients and enzymes, two things happen. First, we don't digest well, so our bodies don't get the nourishment they need regardless of how healthy our diets are. Second, as a result of poor digestion, we don't eliminate well, with the result that our bodies become increasingly toxic. As much as 85% of all health problems—including precursor conditions to many degenerative diseases—can be traced to poor digestion and elimination and to the compromised liver and kidney function that accompany a toxic gut. Other symptoms of poor digestion and elimination include fatigue, depression, allergies, lack of mental clarity, lower back pain, weight gain, bad skin, and a host of other ailments including colon and other cancers.

This topic may not seem relevant to the feng shui of prosperity, but what most of us want from greater prosperity is an improved quality of life, and optimal health is an essential part of that. When we are not functioning at our best, earning a living becomes more difficult, tiring, and stressful. It's worth asking yourself how much good it will do to improve your finances if you are too stressed, tired, ill, or irritable to enjoy your new prosperity.

The key to wellness is to detoxify the body and provide your organ systems with high-density nutrition from organic sources. After years of trying—but not loving—many different products, I have finally found a brand that I love. The Amazon Herb Co. is a mission-driven organization that offers a superior product line while supporting indigenous villages and helping to protect the Amazon rainforest.

In less than two weeks their unique formulas soothed my sometimes uncooperative digestion, reduced my fatigue, helped stabilize my energy, improved my sleep, and made my "lunar cycles" much more bearable. I take the Rainforest Health Pak products daily and can't imagine going without them. The purity and density of these products just can't be found anywhere else. For more information, you can visit our associate website at www.AmazonBioEnergetics.com.

Caring for Mind & Spirit

People who have been meditating for many years often discover, when they learn about feng shui, that they have already made appropriate adjustments to their space. This is because their meditation practice has enabled them to intuitively sense what's going on energetically in their environment. A regular meditation practice will help you become more aware of your own physical and mental *chi*, and be more in tune with the *chi* of your home. The following simple meditation technique is often recommended by feng shui practitioners for clients who need help with stress, fatique, anxiety, depression, or ill health.

HEART CALMING MEDITATION

Sit with your back straight in an upright chair, or cross-legged on the floor with a cushion under your hips. Rest your hands on your thighs, or hold them in the "heart calming" *mudra*: palms up, left hand on top of right with the thumbs touching. Close your eyes, relax, and take a few deep breaths.

1. Take a long, slow, deep breath, inhaling through the mouth, and imagine that your entire body is filling with bright white light. The light fills every cell in your body, and absorbs all illness, tension, fatigue, and negativity.

2. Exhale in eight short puffs followed by a ninth long puff that completely empties your lungs. As you exhale, imagine a dark cloud of negativity leaving your body and dissolving into nothing.

3. Repeat this inhale-exhale pattern eight times, for a total of nine breaths. (I like to visualize the grey exhale becoming lighter with each breath, so by the ninth breath the exhale is clear and clean, and my body is completely free of negativity.)

4. Sit quietly for a few moments after you are done, and notice any shifts in your mood and energy.

Principle 9

Evaluate Your Results

It's important to balance a focus on what you desire with the understanding that the effects of feng shui are not always exactly what you had in mind. Increased prosperity might come from an unexpected windfall, or it could result from more clients, a greater workload, and longer hours on the job. It might even result from a situation that at first seems like bad luck, such as the unexpected termination of your job, or even an accident or sudden illness that interrupts your career. In the short term, you are devastated; looking back five years later, you see this period as a critical turning point that set you on a path to greater success and personal and financial achievement.

Seeming misfortunes that dramatically interrupt our progress are often signs that we need to change direction in order to better fulfill our life purpose. This kind of forced transformation is not uncommon among those who go on to become both professionally successful and emotionally and spiritually fulfilled.

When you experience a financial set-back or an apparent lack of results, this usually does not mean that feng shui isn't working. It's more likely that there is a life lesson to be learned (or unlearned) before you are able to fully allow and embrace prosperity. Perhaps what you think you want isn't really what you need. For example, you may have rushed to accept a promotion when what would most benefit you is a complete change of career.

When feng shui seems to trigger the end of a path, it's often because something even better is on the verge of appearing in your life. Remind yourself to see each setback as a valuable learning experience, and remember that true prosperity is worth waiting for.

Resisting Change

The single most common barrier to success with feng shui is resistance to change. Achieving our dreams almost always means stretching outside our comfort zones, so it is natural to feel hesitant about what feng shui might bring. You can gain insight into your own prosperity issues by examining how consistently you follow through with your feng shui plans (especially the cash flow rituals described in Part III), what kinds of results you see, and how you respond to the experience.

If you've made feng shui adjustments but feel that nothing is working, ask yourself these questions: "Do I really want it?"; "Am I ready to receive it?"; "Do I believe I deserve it?"

Trust that if you have an open heart and an accepting attitude, the universe will bring you exactly what you need to move you forward toward abundance.

Signs of Progress

Be alert for little signs that your money energy is shifting, such as an unexpected refund, or finding something on sale for which you had expected to pay full price. By noticing and appreciating these small miracles, you signal your readiness to receive even greater abundance. Record the good things that happen in your Prosperity Journal every day, and if you slip into feelings of lack or discouragement look around for something for which you can say "thank you."

Shifts in Consciousness

Measuring, judging, and comparing is not the best way to evaluate your success with feng shui, especially when your goals are focused on money. Comparing what we have to how much more others have makes us feel small and disconnected from Source. This blocks abundance from flowing into your life just as surely as the clutter that results from not caring for your home blocks the flow of *chi* into your space.

As you evaluate your feng shui results, it is important to notice what you are receiving, regardless of whether or not it is what you desire and no matter how insignificant it may seem. If you can notice a coin on the sidewalk, see it as a sign that something is being provided to you, and respond with pleasure and gratitude for something as small as a penny, you turn your thoughts and feelings toward receiving abundance. If, instead, you mope around muttering to yourself that nothing ever goes right for you and how feng shui isn't working, you may walk right past many of life's gifts without even noticing them.

These little gifts are tests of your readiness to receive. When you are open to receiving, and take the time to say "thank you" even for pennies found on the sidewalk, you make it possible for more and greater things to come to you. When you look for abundance, beauty, and good fortune all around you, you vibrate with joyful appreciation for the generosity and support of the universe, and encourage more blessings and good fortune to come your way.

> Feng shui corrects energy blocks in your space, but the energy blocks in your head and heart can only be cured by working from the inside out, as we explore in more detail in Part II.

Part Two
The Inner Path

In Part I: The Guiding Principles, you learned to apply the fundamentals of contemporary feng shui to your prosperity power spots in order to create an environment that attracts, welcomes, and supports financial success. In this section, you will learn how to use every area of the ba gua as stepping stones to greater wealth and abundance.

Prosperity Feng Shui from the Inside Out

The nine Fast Feng Shui Principles presented in Part I are based on the premise that everything is connected energetically, and that whatever is going on the space around us will affect us in some way. Feng shui practiced in this way works from the outside in: by improving the *chi* of our external environment we aim to improve our experience, whether in subtle or dramatic ways.

There are two potential drawbacks to feng shui, especially for beginners. The first is that in focusing on one key application, such as prosperity, it's easy to look for the *gua* that matches that concern—*hsun gua,* in this case—and to give that area all of our attention, forgetting that every part of the *ba gua* is an important factor in the *chi* of our home.

The second potential drawback is that in focusing attention on our external space we may overlook the fact that our thoughts, feelings, and beliefs are what ultimately drive our decisions and actions. The feng shui changes that we make to our space can influence how we feel (hopefully for the better), but these changes alone usually cannot offset the influence of the deeply held beliefs and unconscious attitudes that so often rule our behaviors.

In this section, you'll take your feng shui practice to the next level by exploring how all the *guas* can contribute to an improved financial experience. You'll also discover what the *ba gua* has to teach us about eight key attributes of a prosperous mentality, and how to put them into action in your life.

This is feng shui practiced from the inside out, and it's the secret to your financial success and happiness.

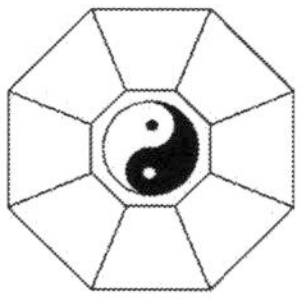

~ The Tai Chi ~

Start From the Center

Whatever is going on in the *tai chi* (the center of the *ba gua*, and the center of your home) affects all of the other *guas*. To get a sense of the potential power of this space, think of homes you may have seen in magazines or at the movies that feature a central courtyard filled with lush foliage, beautiful flowers, and perhaps a water feature such as a lily pond or a fountain. The tranquil beauty of such a space fills the entire home with an abundance of positive *chi*.

Most of us live in simpler abodes, but the basics still apply. Ideally, the *tai chi* of your home is clean, uncluttered, well-lit, and pleasantly furnished. Take a moment now to look at your floor plan and identify the physical center of your home. What's happening architecturally in that area? Is it a hallway, part of the living room or kitchen, or is your *tai chi* occupied by a bathroom, closet, or staircase?

Walk over to that area now. Is the space pleasant and attractive , or is it cluttered, dark, maybe a little grubby? If there's a closet or bathroom in the *tai chi*, is it clean and tidy or is it a jumbled, disorganized mess? Interior walls that meet in the *tai chi* may split the area among several different rooms; what's going on in those corners? If there's a staircase in your *tai chi*, are the steps piled with stuff? What condition is the carpet, runner, or wood finish in? Is the stairwell well-lit? What condition is the paint or wallpaper in?

Think of three ways that you can create a more prosperous and attractive atmosphere in the *tai chi*. For example, replace that worn area rug with a new one, use a higher-wattage bulb in the fixture, and touch up the paint to cover the scuff marks. A bathroom or closet in the *tai chi* will benefit from a full-length mirror on the outside of the door. Place a wealth symbol where it will be reflected in the mirror. Note these plans in your Prosperity Journal, and add appropriate items to your task and shopping lists.

Now look for an opportunity to place some kind of wealth symbol in the *tai chi*. This could be a piece of art for the wall, a figurine on a shelf or side table, or a bowl of coins tucked into a bookcase, to name just a few options. If your *tai chi* is very small, a faceted crystal ball hung from the ceiling will help improve the energy of the space.

Your Core Beliefs

When you look at the *ba gua* from the inside out the *tai chi* represents your core beliefs. This is because your belief system, whether conscious or not, affects all aspects of your life—just as the condition of the *tai chi* of your home affects the entire structure.

Our subconscious beliefs about money often conflict with what we think we want, and they can be extremely effective in keeping us from realizing financial success. For example, perhaps you say that you wish to be wealthy. But, hidden inside, what you really feel is that you don't deserve to be rich. As a result, you repeatedly make choices that cause you to earn less, accumulate debt, and make unwise investments.

These limiting beliefs are usually formed during childhood. Perhaps a parent or authority figure often said something like, "Asking for more is greedy. Just be thankful for what you've got." That message is now firmly planted in your subconscious mind, limiting your ambitions and keeping you from achieving your financial potential.

Here is a list of some common inner messages many of us have acquired about money and wealth. Check off any that resonate with you, or add additional ones of your own. Use your Prosperity Journal to explore where these beliefs may have come from. Think in terms of how your family talked about money (or avoided talking about it) when you were young, and see if you can remember specific childhood experiences that may have shaped your opinions.

False Money Beliefs

- ☐ I have to work hard in order to make money
- ☐ Money corrupts
- ☐ Rich people can't be trusted

These eight areas of the *ba gua* form four dynamic pairs, each pair revealing related aspects of the essential attitudes that determine our ability to fully experience abundance in all its forms:

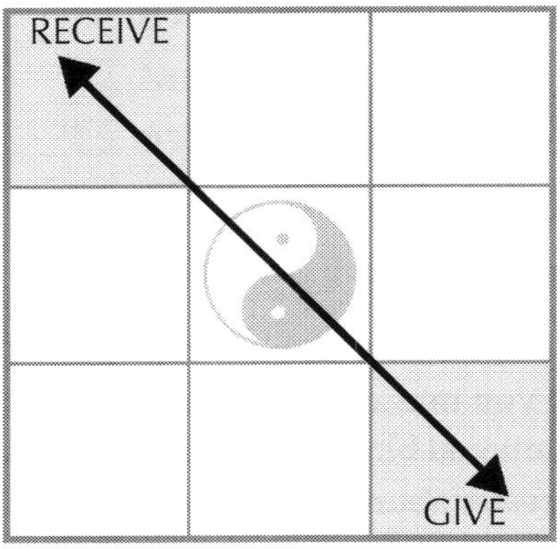

Allowing money to flow

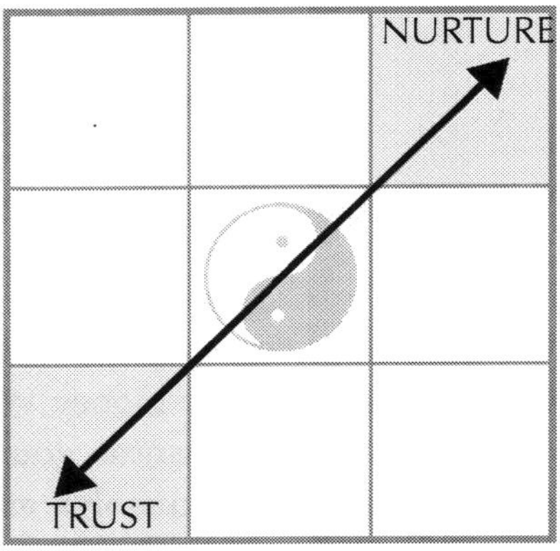

Giving up control

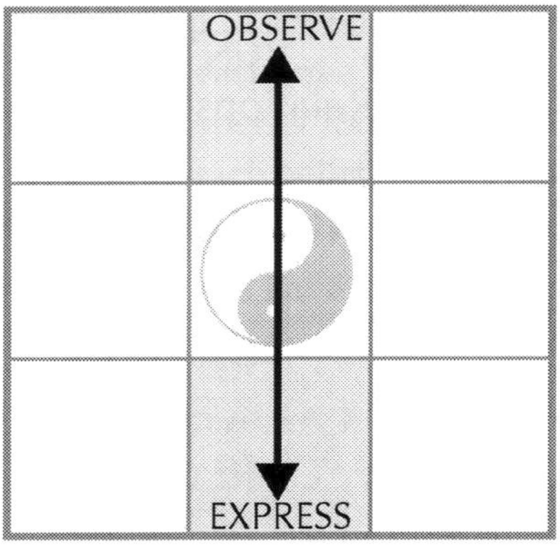

Recognizing abundance

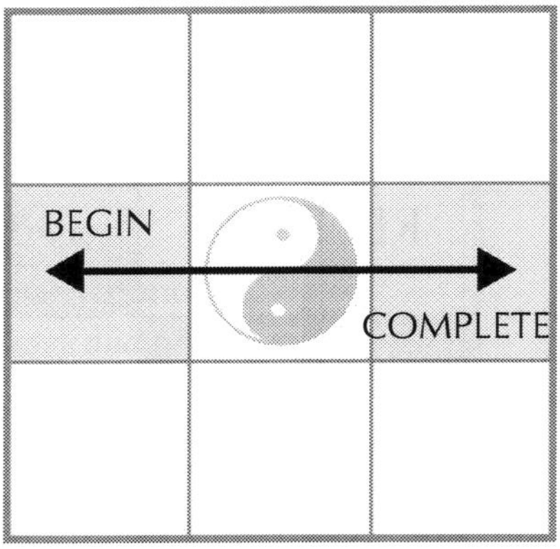

Taking appropriate action

The eight *guas* are stepping stones that guide us to a fuller understanding of how to achieve prosperity from the inside out. Embracing prosperity means stepping into your power, and mastering these key money issues is your secret to financial success. By combining outer feng shui work on your space with inner transformations inspired by the *ba gua*, your ability to attract and manifest money will be unleashed.

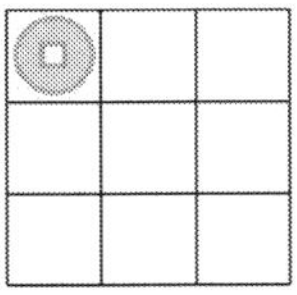

Hsun Gua ~ Fortunate Blessings

Step 1. RECEIVE

Hsun gua, commonly called the "wealth" area of the *ba gua*, is more accurately named "fortunate blessings." Just as true abundance is about more than just financial wealth, the energy of *hsun gua* encompasses all of the good that enriches our lives: friends, family, experiences and things, as well as money.

In Part I, you learned how to apply the Fast Feng Shui principles to money issues, which naturally puts a lot of attention on *hsun gua*. If you are caught up in reading through this book to the extent that you have not yet sprung into action, this would be a good time to start. Grab your Prosperity Journal, or a pad of paper and a pen, and check out what you find in all the *hsun gua* corners of your home. In addition to the usual *sha chi* suspects (dirt, clutter, and untidiness, as well as secret arrows and anything worn or shabby) what else is going on in *hsun gua*? What catches your eye in these areas? Be alert for imagery (artwork, photos, symbols) that implies scarcity, poverty, or difficulty in any way. For example, a ship under full sail on calm seas is a positive image, but a ship caught in a storm or involved in a naval battle is not the kind of symbol you want to have in this area.

Removing inappropriate objects and imagery from *hsun gua* makes space for feng shui cures and wealth symbols. But what else might you consider a "fortunate blessing?" Your family and friends, your health, a job you love? Of all the people, things, and experiences that have already filled your life, for what do you feel especially grateful? Place something in *hsun gua* (a photograph or memento) as an expression of your gratitude and a reminder that prosperity in its broadest sense implies satisfaction with all areas of your life, not just money. (For more ideas on how to activate *hsun gua*, see pages 42-46.)

Opening to Receive

On the outer level, *hsun gua* is about the blessings that we receive; on the inner level, it's about how open we are to receiving those blessings. Most of us, when we are in need of money, assume that we are ready to receive it—preferably in vast quantities, and the sooner the better! The problem is that our focus remains on what we lack, so that's what we attract: more lack, more wanting, more feeling anxious about money. When you feel anxious about money you feed the state of not having enough with your mental and emotional energy.

Lack and want are constricting emotions that get in the way of your ability to receive. Our awareness of not having enough is strongest when we envy what others have. It is impossible to feel envy if you are content with what you have, so envy is a sign that you are experiencing lack—even if you appear to be prospering. Envy makes us acutely aware of what we don't have, and it pushes our prosperity further away.

Here's a good way to turn the negative energy of envy around to work in your favor: any time you feel envious, take a deep breath and say to yourself, "Whatever good happens to others can also happen to me." Imagine that you have what you envy: see yourself driving your new Mercedes, or owning your own home, or wearing designer clothes, or writing checks to pay all your bills in full knowing you have plenty of money in the bank.

Hold this mental image for as long as it takes for you to feel "I have" instead of "I want." This means you have to let go of *wanting* it, and pretend that you already *have* it. Do this a dozen times a day if you need to, and soon you won't feel as envious anymore. Someone drives by in a shiny new Mercedes and it lifts your heart instead of sinking it, because you are confident that you'll be driving a new Mercedes of your own someday.

This is what opening to receive feels like. You know what you want, and you feel good because you trust that it will come to you. No matter how dire your present circumstances may be, you know that the future will be better. The more you can feel good about anything having to do with money—even if it's just for a few seconds at a time—the more you flex your receiving "muscles" and start allowing good things to come your way.

THE WEIGHT OF MONEY

In talking about positive and negative feeling states, keep in mind that "feeling" refers both to emotion and to sensation. The physiological affects of emotions are very real, as you can experience for yourself in the following exercise. To do this, you will need some kind of weight, so find a 5- to 10-lb. free weight or a jug of detergent from the laundry room or anything that you can lift with one hand with some exertion but without straining.

Now think of a positive money experience you had in the past or that you hope to have in the future. This should be a specific scenario of joy, excitement, and appreciation. Make it a big one! If you can't think of anything really good, imagine that you've just won the lottery, or whatever gets you really happy and excited about money. Got something in mind? Good. Now think of a time when you felt envy or lack about money. The more specific your memory, the better. This may be:

- The envy that swept over you when your "dream" car passed you on the highway today as you chugged along in your old clunker, hoping it won't need more repairs anytime soon.
- Overhearing someone talk about a recent trip to the Caribbean—the kind of vacation you couldn't possibly afford to take.
- How you felt when you opened your credit card statement and saw that you can barely cover the finance fee this month.

Your own experience may be something very different from these, and that's fine. Work with whatever situation comes to mind for you. Now you're ready to discover how your emotions affect your strength:

1. Stand with your feet about hip-width apart and take a couple of deep breaths to relax and clear your mind.
2. Focus on your *negative* money experience for at least 5-6 deep breaths. Get as fully into the imagined experience as you can, until you start feeling really yucky about money.
3. Pick up your weight and do a few slow biceps curls. Focus on getting a clear sense of how heavy that weight feels to you and how much exertion it takes to lift it.

4. Now focus on your positive money experience for a few deep breaths. Stay in that imagined situation until you really feel good and there's a big smile on your face.

5. Try lifting your weight again. It should feel lighter this time: that's the effect of a positive emotion on your strength and vitality!

Now you know the powerful effect your mental state can have on your physical energy. When I talk about being open to receive, I mean that your energy about money should be light, confident and cheerful, no matter how dire your immediate financial situation appears to be. When money worries or too many bills weigh you down, deliberately choose to focus on thoughts of abundance instead.

Getting into a positive feeling-state about money can be difficult if you don't know how you're going to pay the rent next month. If you've been in the habit of dooming-and-glooming your money situation it may take some time and practice to shift gears. Here's a meditation and visualization exercise that can help you to do that.

Experiencing the Inner Aspects of Hsun Gua

PREPARATION

Sit quietly with your eyes closed, and think of the negative situation you used for the "Weight of Money" exercise. See if you can identify a place in your body where you experience that memory as a physical sensation. This could be something like a sick feeling in your tummy, tightness in the chest, a clenched jaw, or hunched shoulders. Mentally scan your body to see what comes to your attention. (If you can't pick up any physical clues, that's okay.)

RELEASING

We're going to use a variation of the Heart Calming meditation that you learned in Part I. This time, the focus is on releasing the negative feelings about money that block your ability to receive.

1. Sit comfortably with your hands in the Heart Calming *mudra* (palms up, left hand on top of right, with the thumbs touching).

2. Take a long, slow, deep breath in through the mouth. As you inhale, direct the breath toward the area of your body where you physically feel envy or lack, and imagine it bathed in brilliant white light. (If you did not identify a specific sensation, allow the light to fill your entire body.) Imagine the light absorbing all feelings of envy or lack

3. Exhale in eight short puffs followed by a ninth long puff that completely empties your lungs. Imagine all your negative feelings about money being expelled with the breath.

4. Repeat this inhale-exhale pattern eight more times.

5. Sit quietly for a few moments after you are done, and notice any shifts in your mood and energy. The areas where you hold money tension should feel more relaxed.

   Continue by doing the following visualization.

VISUALIZATION: "MONEY SHOWER"

Release the Heart Calming *mudra*, and stand up, with your arms at your sides with the palms up. Imagine a rain of pennies (or the smallest coin in your local currency) falling all around you. This is a magical rain of pennies, so any that touch you as they fall do so with just the gentlest of kisses. They cannot harm you or cause discomfort in any way. Know that these pennies are a gift to you from Heaven and an expression of Divine love being showered upon you.

As the pennies start to pile up on the ground around you, imagine that now it is raining nickels… then dimes… then quarters (or your local equivalent). The more clearly you can see each type of coin, the better.

Now imagine $1 bills falling all around you… and $5 bills, $10s, $20s, $50s, $100s… the money can fall as slowly or as quickly as you like, so long as you clearly visualize each denomination before moving on to the next. This money is all a gift for you. All your needs are met. All your money worries are over.

Now add some checks into the mix, made payable to you for large amounts of money. Be sure to visualize your name clearly visible as the payee on at least a few of these checks. Know that you don't have to do anything to deserve or earn this abundance. It is yours just for being.

Stay with this visualization until you feel joyful and provided for. You may feel a slight sensation of heat in the area of your heart, or in the "third-eye" area between your brows. When you are ready, fold your hands over your heart and say "thank you!" three times.

Repeat this visualization as often as you like. If this section has been particularly relevant to you, I recommend that you practice this visualization daily for at least nine days, to help shift your energy.

JOURNAL QUESTIONS

- Are you sometimes uncomfortable receiving gifts, or asking for or getting a raise?
- If so, what thoughts or feelings accompany that?
- What specific past experiences might have influenced this reaction?
- What percentage of your thoughts about money are positive, and how many are negative (anxiety, worry)?
- Do you worry about money more than you really need to? (for example, feeling anxious about money even though you have more than enough to pay the bills and feed your family.)

The Power of Appreciation

If you are longing for prosperity, the single most important thing you can do is stop wanting and worrying and start saying "thank you, thank you, thank you" for all that you have already received and all that you are about to receive. The act of giving thanks and expressing gratitude opens your heart and allows prosperity to fill your experience.

Action Steps for Hsun Gua

- Say "yes" whenever you are offered something. If you see a penny on the sidewalk, pick it up and say "thank you." If you pass up little gifts, you make it harder for larger gifts to manifest for you.

- If you have not yet begun to keep a gratitude journal, this would be a wonderful time to start. Simply write down—preferably daily—whatever you feel grateful for today. There's no right or wrong way to do this, although one of my favorite methods is to make a list each night of "Top 10 Things I Appreciate Today." Sometimes this is big things, like receiving a large check in the mail, and sometimes it's little things, like finding a shady parking spot, or having time to go for a quick swim before dinner.

- If you're having a difficult day and gratitude seems out of reach, sit quietly and use the Heart Calming method for a few minutes. When you feel more tranquil and relaxed, focus on your heart. Feel how steadily it beats. Ba-bum, ba-bum, ba-bum. With each heart-beat, think "thank you." It doesn't matter if you don't mean it yet, or if you aren't sure what you are thinking "thank you" for, or who you are directing it to. Just keep repeating "thank you" to yourself, either in your mind or with your voice, in time to your heartbeat, until it feels comfortable and natural. This practice may trigger an emotional release, so it's okay if you laugh or cry or choke up a little. Stay with this until you feel gratitude in your heart. It doesn't have to be for anything, just notice that the feeling is there and stay with it for as long as you can.

Giving to others is a very powerful demonstration of thanks and gratitude. It's the inner aspect of *chien gua, hsun gua*'s dynamic partner.

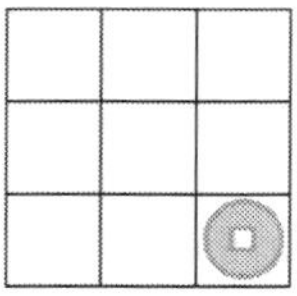

Chien Gua ~ Helpful Friends

Step 2. GIVE

Chien gua, the area of "helpful friends" and "travel," also symbolizes the role of the father. This area is associated with the METAL element; its colors are white, grey and metallics. Metal objects support the energy of *chien gua*, as do EARTH cures such as ceramics, stones, and colors such as browns and terracotta. Avoid having too much WATER, WOOD, or FIRE energy in this area, since these elements will weaken METAL.*

The helpful friends aspect of *chien gua* includes mentors, support networks, and benefactors. Perhaps you could use the assistance of a loan officer, credit counselor, tax attorney, career or business advisor or personal coach to help you find ways to increase your income, manage your debt and expenses, or learn better money-management habits. If so, make a list of the qualities—professional and personal—that your ideal advisor(s) would embody, put it in a red envelope, and place it in *chien gua* of your home or office. Hang a metal wind chime or brass bell over the envelope to activate your cure.

Another good way to enlist the energy of *chien gua* in support of financial success is to create your own virtual Board of Directors. This can include people whom you trust and respect, as well as public or historical figures whose accomplishments, leadership, personality, or lifestyle you admire. Glue photographs of these advisors to a piece of poster board or the inside of a file folder. Label each photo with the person's name and the key qualities for which you chose him or her for a seat on your Board. Keep this montage in *chien gua* of your home or office, or in a drawer in *chien gua* of your desk.

---

* For more on interactions among the elements, see Appendix B.

Think about how the travel aspect of *chien gua* might be relevant to your financial goals. Take a look at your 108 Desires list, and see if any are related to travel in some way. Perhaps you'd like to:

- Travel more often for business, or be assigned to the Paris account.
- Achieve Platinum Ambassador status with your network marketing company and win the Alaska cruise this year.
- Take your kids to Disney World next summer.
- Have a vacation home.
- Spend Christmas in Aspen or in Acapulco this year.

Find an image or symbol that represents your goal— such as a photo of the Eiffel Tower (Paris), or a Mickey Mouse snow globe (Disney World)—place it in *chien gua*, and empower it to help you reach your travel destination.

Giving Creates Space for More to Come in

When we approach *chien gua* from the inside out, we are reminded to take on the role of benefactor by giving generously to others and doing what we can to support them on their paths.

Some form of giving is an integral part of prosperity. For example, many people think of Bill Gates, founder of Microsoft, as someone who enjoys immense wealth, without realizing or remembering that he is also among the world's greatest philanthropists. Most people who are blessed with wealth feel a desire to give back in some way. When you give—whether to an individual, a charitable organization, or to your church—you embody this important aspect of wealth and place yourself in the company of millionaires and billionaires around the globe.

Giving is the natural counterpart to receiving. In order for you to fully experience abundance, money needs to flow *through*, not just into, your life. Imagine that you are standing on a riverbank with an empty bucket in your hand. You fill your bucket from the river, but if you believe that one bucketful is all you are allowed (or all you deserve) you may hesitate to use it, for fear that once it's gone your bucket will be empty forever.

This is a common way of thinking, but it's backward. The truth is that the resources of Spirit are limitless, and the only one who puts limits on how much you can receive is you. If you use what's in your bucket to water the garden, fill the dog's water dish, or make soup for dinner, you create room in your bucket to receive more. If you hoard your water, on the other hand, you restrict yourself to that one bucketful. Meanwhile, your flowers droop, your dog whines and pushes his empty water dish around the floor, and you don't eat. Giving as consistently as you receive is essential to a full experience of prosperity.

Now, before you email me to explain that you don't have anything to give because: a) you are too poor already; b) your family comes first, and it would be irresponsible not to save for retirement or for college tuition; or c) you just don't want to—you earned it and you plan to keep it—let me put this in perspective.

There's nothing wrong with taking care of yourself and your family first, so long as you have some kind of caring left over for others. If you can't give money, perhaps you can be generous with your time, skills, or compassion. The next time you have a penny to spare, put it in one of those donation canisters at the supermarket check-out counter. It may not be much, but added to everyone else's pennies it's enough by the end of the month to make a difference to your local animal shelter or whatever organization is being supported.

Sticking to a tight budget because you are saving to make the down payment on a house shows you've put some careful thought into your financial priorities. Accumulating a "rainy day fund," contributing to your 401K plan, and setting up a college fund for your kids are mature, responsible behaviors and I encourage you to practice them. What blocks prosperity is not responsible saving, but compulsive penny-pinching. Hoarding happens when lack of trust in the future drives you to deny yourself, your family, and your community in favor of putting aside more than you reasonably might need. It puts money before people, which is not where it belongs.

It has often been said that money can't buy happiness, but I don't believe that's true. Like love, money is not fully rewarding—or even useful—if it only flows one way. If you are fortunate enough to have a little extra coming in every month, try giving some of it away; you'll discover a very special kind of happiness that only comes through sharing your fortunate blessings with others.

A Few Words about Tithing

A "tithe" is a tenth part. "Tithing" means to give 10% of your income to God, in the form of a donation to your church. Any church or spiritual group to which you belong is a fine place to start giving regularly, at whatever level is within your means. If you don't belong to a church, consider giving to a charity whose mission you believe in. I like to divide my giving among a variety of charities that support my local and global communities and that serve both environmental and social needs.

Committing to give a certain percentage of your income enables you to give consistently as your income rises (or falls). The more consistently you give, the more you will benefit from the energy of giving. How much and where you give is less important that the spirit with which you give, so it's fine to give just 1% if that's all you can afford. As your circumstances improve, you may feel inspired to increase that portion.

Giving should be done as a gesture of gratitude, not obligation. You should give because you want to, not because I recommend it or because you expect to get something in return. If you aren't ready to embrace the practice with an appropriate frame of mind, leave it for another time.

Mentoring & Father Figures

Sharing knowledge, wisdom and experience is reflected in the qualities of *chien gua* associated with mentors and fathers. What did you learn about money from your father? (If your birth father was not around during your childhood, think about others who may have helped fill that role, such as a step-father, grandfather, brother, uncle, teacher, or family friend.)

Get out your Prosperity Journal, and answer the following questions. Keep these questions in mind over the next few days as well, and be alert to any additional memories or insights that may arise.

JOURNAL QUESTIONS

- Did your father talk openly and calmly about money, or did he avoid the subject or become irritable when it came up?
- Did he say things like "Money doesn't grow on trees," "A penny saved is a penny earned," and "Don't count your chickens before they are hatched," or did he have an "It's only money" attitude?
- How well did your father handle money?
- Did he ever make you feel ashamed about money in some way when you were a kid? If so, how has that affected how you handle money now that you are an adult?
- Are there any ways in which you rebel against your father in how you handle your own money?
- Which of your father's money lessons have been helpful to you as an adult and which, if any, have you had to unlearn?
- The energy of a father or mentor is of competence, reliability, maturity, and mastery. In what ways does your ability to handle money reflect these qualities, or are they underdeveloped?
- If you have children of your own, how do you fulfill the money mentor role with your own kids?
- What are three specific things you can start to do right away in order to improve your mastery of money?

Experiencing the Inner Aspects of Chien Gua

PREPARATION

Sit quietly, with your eyes closed, and think of a time when you've had a negative experience around giving. Possible situations might be:

- Being forced to give as a child when you didn't want to
- Feeling guilty about not giving when you could have done so
- Giving something that was rejected or received ungraciously

Keeping your situation in mind, can you identify a place in your body where this memory triggers tension or discomfort in some way?

RELEASING

Again we will be using a variation of the Heart Calming meditation, followed by a few minutes of visualization. Here we focus on releasing negative feelings about giving.

1. Sit comfortably with your hands in the Heart Calming *mudra* (palms up, left hand on top of right, with the thumbs touching).
2. Take a long, slow, deep breath in through your mouth, directing the breath toward the area of your body where you feel tension. Imagine this area bathed in a brilliant white light. (If you were not able to identify a specific body location, allow the light to fill your entire body.) Imagine the light absorbing any reluctance to share what you have, or any guilt or embarrassment you may feel as a result of a past giving experience.
3. Exhale in eight short puffs followed by a ninth long puff that empties your lungs. As you exhale, imagine all your negative feelings about giving evaporating.
4. Repeat this inhale-exhale pattern eight more times.
5. Sit quietly for a few moments after you are done, and notice any shifts in your mood and energy. The areas where you hold money tension should feel more relaxed.

VISUALIZATION: "RIVER OF ABUNDANCE"

Lie comfortably on your back, either on your bed or on a rug or carpet on the floor. You may place a cushion under your head or behind your knees if you like. With your arms at your side and your palms up, take a few moments to relax deeply.

Imagine a stream of light flowing into your left palm. (You may "feel" this with your imagination or visualize it, whatever works for you.) The light moves up your left arm, across the center of your chest, then down your right arm and out the palm of your right hand.

Stay with this imagined experience for a few moments, focusing on the flow of energy in your left palm, up and through your heart area, and down and out your right hand. Know that this river of energy is never-ending. As it flows out from your right hand, it pulls more in through the left. This is your endless source of abundance, the divine source of prosperity and well-being. It can never be diminished.

After a few minutes, raise your hands and cross them over your heart center, allowing the light to fill your entire body. When you feel ready, release your hands and relax for a while before opening your eyes. Repeat this visualization as often as you like.

Action Steps for Chien Gua

Choose one of the following methods to practice for the next 30 days, using your Prosperity Journal to record any emotions or insights that come up as a result:

- Give away a little bit of money every day. A penny is enough. Drop it in a collection jar, give a tip to the barrista at your coffee stop, or leave a quarter on a shelf at your grocery store for someone to find. Be creative and anonymous.

- Give something each time you are asked for money, instead of saying "not today." Give to kids raising money for their sports team, to panhandlers on the street, and send a few dollars to charities whose solicitation letters arrive in the mail. (This doesn't mean you should give to scam artists and bogus solicitations. Only genuine requests count here.)

- If your career provides regular cash income (such as tips), choose a percentage between 1% and 5% to give away over the next 30 days. Each day, count out the appropriate portion of what you have received, and give that away within 24 hours.

- If you absolutely cannot give money at this time, donate at least one hour a week to a worthy cause or organization.

True giving happens with no thought of reward. It is directed by kindness and a genuine desire to share our good fortune and be of service to others, an attitude that epitomizes the quality of "nurturing" associated with our next step toward prosperity, *kun gua*.

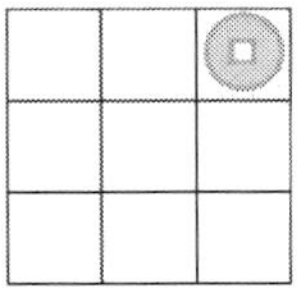

Kun Gua ~ Relationships

Step 3. NURTURE

Kun gua, most commonly known as the "relationships" or "marriage" area, has to do not only with partnerships of all kinds (including both love and business relationships) but also with motherhood. *Kun gua's* element is EARTH, and its colors are pink, red and to a lesser degree white. Ceramic objects, stones and crystals are all appropriate in *kun gua.* Candles and other FIRE cures are supportive *kun gua,* while too much WATER, METAL, or WOOD energy will have a weakening effect. Plants can be used here if they have red, pink, or white blossoms. Luxurious fabrics and textures, such as velvet, satin, and chenille, are all well-suited to *kun gua.*

Take a few minutes to review your list of 108 Desires for any that reflect the partnership or motherhood aspects of *kun gua.* For example, perhaps your long-term financial goals are tied to making partner at your firm within the next few years, or maybe you are in the midst of a divorce and negotiating for a more favorable settlement. You may dream of opening a business that will require connecting with the right partner or investor, or you may be trying to figure out if the family budget will allow you to work part-time and see more of your kids.

Take a look at the *kun gua* areas of your home, being alert for signs of discord or *sha chi,* such as:

- A pair of lamps or candlesticks, one of which is broken
- Pairs of things that are separated from each other, rather than being placed together
- Images that show people or animals in conflict or competition

If your finances are affected by a love or business relationship that is ending—or that you would like to end—remove all documents and other items relating to it from *kun gua* of your home or office. Discard them if you can, or store them in the garage or by a back door, with the intention that this person will soon be out of your life.

To help attract a new partnership relevant to your financial goals, make a list of the skills, experience, and qualities you are looking for. Write "My Perfect Business Partner"—or whatever best describes your need—at the top of the page. Or, type your list in the form of a "help wanted" ad as it might appear in the classifed section of a newspaper. Put your list or ad in a red envelope or folder, place it in *kun gua* of your home or office, and empower it using the IVAG method (page 8).

Nurturing Kindness

To nurture something means to care for it with kindness, helping it stay healthy and strong and guiding it to successful maturity. When loving kindness is missing from our lives—when we neither nurture nor feel nurtured—the result is an inner emptiness which we often try to fill with compulsive shopping or a relentless pursuit of money. We forget that true prosperity depends as much on joyful appreciation of blessings in all aspects of life as it does on amassing lots of things or earning vast sums of money. The loving kindness of family and friends provides emotional prosperity, which is part of a deep experience of abundance.

Dr. Wayne Dyer, in his book, *Intention*, describes how an act of kindness triggers the release of serotonin (a brain chemical that makes us feel good) not only in the person receiving that kindness, but also in the person acting kindly and in people who observe the kind act. Each of those people touched by the biochemistry of kindness are more likely to be kind in turn, causing a ripple effect that reaches into the quantum field and affects all of us.

Exploring *kun gua* from the inside out, we look at how we use money to nurture ourselves and our families, and at how well we nurture our resources. When we embody "nurture," we become wise caretakers of our financial assets, spending and investing with care and attention, and guiding our investments to grow and flourish.

The Effects of Neglect

When we give inadequate attention to nurturing our selves, our family, or our money, we devalue that which we neglect. Neglectful attitudes are revealed when we say things like, "It's only money," "I have no idea how much I have in my retirement fund," "I never balance my checkbook; with so many ATM and electronic transactions, who can keep track?" or, "It's crass to care about money. I'm above that."

Remember that *chi* flows where your attention goes. If you don't pay attention to your money the inevitable result is that you won't have very much of it. Taking care of whatever money you have through simple tasks such as filing receipts, balancing your checkbook, and paying your bills on time shows the Universe that you can handle more. Do whatever you can to demonstrate that you value and honor money, and chances are you'll receive more of it soon.

Money and Mother-Figures

Nurturing is reflected in the *kun gua* qualities of mothering and care-giving. Open your Prosperity Journal and answer the questions below. (If your birth mother was not around during your childhood, think about others who may have helped fill that role, such as a step-mother, grandmother, sister, aunt, teacher, or family friend.)

Keep these questions in mind over the next few days as well, and be alert to any additional memories or insights that may arise.

JOURNAL QUESTIONS

- What attitudes or beliefs about money did you learn from your mother?
- Which of your mother's money lessons have been helpful to you as an adult and which, if any, have you had to unlearn?
- Did your mother talk about money in ways that were different from your dad? What were her favorite money sayings?
- The energy of a Mother figure is of nurturing and care-giving. Are those qualities appropriately reflected in how you spend your money, or are you too restrictive or carefree in this area?

- How well do you nurture your money?
- What are three specific ways you can be more nurturing to yourself in how you use or manage your money? This could mean spending more, budgeting differently, or spending less as you look for balance between self-neglect and overindulgence.

Letting Go of Anger

When someone harms us or our loved ones—physically, emotionally, or financially—anger is a natural reaction. They've hurt us and we want to hurt them back. The problem is not so much that we experience the impulse to anger, but that we hold on to it for far too long, nursing our grudges instead of minding our emotions. Focusing on how you were wronged keeps your energy stuck in the past and makes it more difficult for things to go well in the future. You start to anticipate reasons to be angry before they happen, and before you know it you are in the habit of assuming the worst of people.

Unfortunately, the person most damaged by this is you. Anger, like any form of stress, triggers the release of the stress hormone cortisol, which literally bathes your brain cells with acid. It causes disharmony throughout the autonomic nervous system, impairs mental function, and suppresses the immune system. In fact, it can take your immune system several hours to recover from just a few minutes of anger.

Positive, heart-centerend emotions such as care and appreciation, on the other hand, have the opposite effect. They bring the nervous system back into balance, lower blood pressure, and increase cardiovascular efficiency.*

If you have been harboring anger or resentment against someone over money—no matter how well deserved it may be—part of your path to prosperity will involve learning to treat yourself with greater loving kindness by letting go of these toxic emotions. Two remarkably simple yet effective methods for coping with negative feelings are The Sedona Method® and the HeartMath Solution (see the Resources section at the back of the book for details).

---

* *The HeartMath Solution,* by Doc Childre and Howard Martin, provides a fascinating overview of current research on the biochemistry of emotions.

Experiencing the Inner Aspects of Kun Gua

PREPARATION

Sit quietly, with your eyes closed, and think of a time when you've felt resentful or angry about a financial situation, or about an incident that ended up costing you money. Typical situations include:

- Feeling angry at someone who cheated you, or who owes you money and has not paid you back in spite of repeated promises.
- Feeling angry at the idiot who backed into your car in the parking lot, causing damage that cost hundreds of dollars to repair.

See if you can identify a place in your body where your memory of that experience becomes a physical sensation.

RELEASING

Again we will be using a variation of the Heart Calming meditation, followed by a few minutes of visualization. Here the focus is on releasing feelings of anger or resentment about money.

1. Sit comfortably with your hands in the Heart Calming *mudra* (palms up, left hand on top of right, with the thumbs touching).
2. Take a long, slow, deep breath in through the mouth, imagining that brilliant white light is filling your entire body. Visualize this light bathing every cell in your body in loving kindness and absorbing all harsh or stressful feelings.
3. Exhale in eight short puffs followed by a ninth long puff that empties your lungs. As you exhale, imagine all your hard feelings dissolving into nothing.
4. Repeat this inhale-exhale pattern eight more times.
5. Sit quietly for a few moments, and notice any shifts in your mood and energy. If you identified a specific area where you feel or hold anger, check to see if it now feels more relaxed. If you still feel tension there, repeat the inhale-exhale pattern for nine more breaths, focusing the white light on that area.

VISUALIZATION: "CIRCLE OF LIGHT"

Lie on your back as you did for the "River of Abundance" visualization in the previous chapter. Arms are by your sides, palms up. Relax.

Focus as you did before on experiencing a steady stream of light flowing into your left palm, up your arm, through your heart center, down your right arm, and out through your right hand. Stay with this simple flow of energy for a minute or so, and relax into it.

Now imagine that there is someone lying on either side of you. You don't have to know who these people are, but you can imagine they are people you know and trust if that is more comfortable for you. Visualize the river of light flowing through these others, too. The light flows from your neighbor on the left, through you, then on to flow through the person on your right. You are linked together in an endless current of receiving and giving.

Imagine now that you are just one link in a vast circle of beings, all connected by this river of light. Feel how the energy connects all of you, and that whatever you send out eventually circles around to you. Allow your heart center to open, so that the light that flows through all of you is pure love and kindness. Feel it nurture and soothe you.

Stay with this image for as long as you like. When you are ready, take your time getting up, and try to stay in a quiet space in your home and in your mind for another 10-15 minutes. Use your Prosperity Journal to record any feelings or insights that you would like to capture from this experience.

Action Steps for Kun Gua

- Treat your money with care: pick your purse up off the floor; clean out your wallet; gather your loose change together and find an attractive bowl or jar to keep it in; balance your checkbook; file your account statements; read that report from your stockbroker; stop dumping your receipts in your underwear drawer. If you were money, would you want to come live in your house? Show your money that you care for it.

- Practice daily acts of kindness. Let another driver in ahead of you. Stop to let a pedestrian cross the street. Hold the door open for someone. Take a moment to smile and say "thank you" as you accept your shopping bag from the cashier. Say "good morning" to whoever is in the elevator when you step on. Say "thanks, honey" to your spouse or kid when they take out the trash or feed the dog. When you act with kindness towards others throughout the day, you invite the Universe to treat you with kindness in return, with the result that pleasant surprises will start to manifest for you more and more often.

There's one more aspect of *kun gua* that is worth mentioning here: the quality of "yielding." We see this in action when we place our own concerns aside in order to yield our attention to our child, for example. Yielding means to give up control—even if just for a moment—and let someone else's needs or insight or priorities guide you. This kind of conscious yielding is what we do when we place our trust in a wiser, higher power, as we explore in the next step on our path to prosperity: *ken gua*.

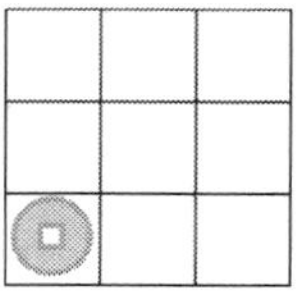

Ken Gua ~ Knowledge & Spirituality

Step 4. TRUST

Ken gua is the area associated with knowledge and academic learning. The element for this *gua* is EARTH, and the colors associated with it are brown and light blue. FIRE and EARTH-type objects are appropriate here; too much WATER, WOOD, or METAL will weaken *ken gua*.

On a mundane level, *ken gua* prompts us to ask whether increased knowledge would help us achieve greater mastery of our money. If you have been a less-than-stellar steward of your finances, perhaps it's time to learn how to create and stick to a budget, balance your checkbook, repair a damaged credit rating, invest in a mutual fund or read a financial statement.

Ken gua also has to do with acquiring greater self-knowledge through meditation, personal growth work, or therapy. In this sense it represents the archaeology of the unconscious mind. If your financial history hints at patterns of poverty consciousness or self-sabotage, the inner work of *ken gua* will be essential to achieving lasting financial improvement. Here are some ways you can use *ken gua* to support your quest for greater knowledge and self-awareness about your money habits:

- A bright light can "shed light on the topic" if you're dealing with complicated finances or faced with making difficult decisions.
- A gently moving mobile in *ken gua* will stir up new understanding, when you need to see things from a different perspective.
- Figurines or images of spiritual masters or deities, displayed in *ken gua*, support a quiet, introspective mind.

- Natural crystals (for your desk or bookshelf) or a faceted crystal ball hung from the ceiling enhance clear thinking.
- *Ken gua* is a good place to keep words of wisdom—such as books and audio programs—about prosperity consciousness, personal finance, deliberate creation or other topics you are studying.

Listening to Intuition

On a metaphysical level, *ken gua* represents our spiritual life and the quest to understand life's mysteries. It is at this deepest level that we find the inner quality of *ken gua*: trust. Mastery of this step requires that we let go of our doubts, relinquish our ego's desire to be in control, and turn our quest for prosperity over to a power greater and wiser than us.

Ego rules our conscious mind and tries to rule everything else we do. A key step in self-awareness is to recognize that the ego is just one aspect of the totality of who we are, and that we do not have to give in to its demands all the time. The most powerful demand of the ego is to be in control. When we don't feel in control of the circumstances in our lives, we respond by worrying about how things are going to turn out and by trying to figure out how we should go about fixing what's wrong or bringing about our desired outcome.

God nurtures us by indulging this desire to figure things out for ourselves, like a patient parent observing a young child trying to tie its own shoelaces, prepared to wait it out until the shoes are fastened or the child gives up and allows Mom or Dad to take over. Left to ourselves, we fumble with the laces of our lives until we appear to have achieved something resembling a knot, and then we stumble onward, loose ends flapping around our ankles threatening at any moment to trip us up. We forget that sometimes the better course of action would be to just sit down on the curb and say, "help!"

Ken gua reminds us to "let go and let God"—to get out of the way and stop trying to manage the who, what, when, where and how of our lives. Often what we really need isn't to get our sneakers tied but to see that the sneaker is the wrong shoe for the road and set it aside, trusting that the Universe will hand us a better shoe.

That "better shoe" is often delivered through our intuition, either as an "aha!" moment or through a gut feeling to take one course of action over another. An impulse to stop at this coffee bar insteadof the usual one, for example, may lead to a chance encounter with someone who contributes to the solution of your problem.

Worry is an agitated, obsessive energy that prevents you from getting into the relaxed, open state of mind where you hear the voice of intuition. The way to let go of worrying is to recognize that once you have decided what you want, the how, when, and where of it are up to the Universe. When you truly get this, you are able to let go and trust. You trust that things will turn out all right. You trust that new ideas will come to you if you stop trying to force them. You trust that the right people will enter your life at exactly the right time. You trust that the right opportunities will appear when the time is right—and you accept that it might not be today, no matter how impatient you feel. You trust that—creative and brilliant and wise as you are—there are incredible possibilities out there that you can't even begin to imagine.

When we live in doubt, we preoccupy our minds and divert our energy from a more soul-directed life. Trust has a profound effect on your ability to experience one of the greatest blessings of prosperity: a deep feeling of inner security that does not depend on having money.

Money & Spirituality

Money in itself is not evil, dirty, crass, or unspiritual. Money is nothing more than a medium of exchange, and its spiritual value depends on what you do with it. When you have embraced the lesson of *chien gua* (giving) the prospect of becoming wealthy takes on a new dimension. Just think of all the good you could do in the world!

Imagine for a moment that you are rich beyond your wildest dreams. You have everything you have ever wanted, and more money than you can possibly spend. You don't need or want another vacation home or luxury cruise or expensive car. You've had lots of fun spending money on yourself and your family, and now you are ready to give some away. To this end, you have established a charitable foundation with an endowment of twenty million dollars to give away.

What will the purpose of this foundation be? How will you use $20 million to do good in the world? Think of three ways you could make the world a better place. What kind of good would you like to do?

Experiencing the Inner Aspects of Ken Gua

Think of a time when you have felt anxious because you couldn't see a solution to a difficult situation—preferably one in which money was involved. Try to identify a specific area where your desire to control the outcome manifests as a feeling of tension in your body.

RELEASING

Again we will be using a variation of the Heart Calming meditation, followed by a few minutes of visualization. Here the focus is on letting go of feeling that you have to come up all of the answers yourself.

1. Sit comfortably with your hands in the Heart Calming *mudra* (palms up, left hand on top of right, thumbs touching).
2. Take a long, slow, deep breath, in through the mouth, directing the breath toward the area where you feel tension. Imagine this area bathed in a brilliant white light. (If you were not able to identify a specific body location, allow the light to fill your entire body.) Imagine the light absorbing your need to figure out how to solve your money problems yourself.
3. Exhale in eight short puffs followed by a ninth long puff that empties the lungs. Visualize your need for control dissolving.
4. Repeat this inhale-exhale pattern eight more times.
5. Sit quietly for a few moments, and notice any shifts in your mood and energy.

VISUALIZATION: "YOU'LL SEE IT WHEN YOU BELIEVE IT"

Think of a specific experience from your 108 Desires list, such as getting out of debt, buying a new car, moving to a better neighborhood, or going back to school. Imagine that this has already happened for you. What will you experience when this dream comes true? Create a vivid, detailed scene in your mind by answering the following questions:

- Where am I?
- What time of year is it?
- What time of day is it?
- What am I doing?
- Who else is here?
- What do I see, smell, taste, touch, and hear?

For example, if your dream is to get out of your cramped apartment and move into a spacious home in a nicer neighborhood, you might visualize driving up to your new home, and walking through the front door. Good details to include would be what your house looks like, the size of your yard, details of the landscaping and front walk. You might notice the warmth of the sun on your skin, the fragrance of flowers, and the sound of birds or a neighbor's lawnmower.

If your dream is to buy a sports car, visualize in detail what that car looks like parked in your driveway, then imagine getting into it, starting the engine, and going for a drive. You might notice the sound of the engine when you accelerate, the comfort of the leather seats, and that wonderful new car smell.

Be alert as you imagine your scene to any doubting thoughts or negative self-talk that may come up, such as, "Who am I kidding? That's never going to happen!" or "Owning a home is way out of reach for me." If something like this happens, shift your focus back to your breath for a few moments. With each inhale, say to yourself, "I believe in miracles." As you exhale, say "I release my doubt."

Once you have imagined a very detailed scene, using all of your senses, take another minute or so to focus on how you feel. Your scene should feel good! You should be smiling and happy and excited about finally having what it is you want. Label that good feeling, by thinking of a word to describe it, like "happy" or "delighted" or "excited." Now summarize the experience for the benefit of your subconscious mind by saying something like, "I am so excited to finally own my own home!"

When you are ready, bring your attention back into the present moment. Try to stay in a calm, quiet space for a few minutes before going on with the rest of your day.

Use your Prosperity Journal to record any feelings, resistance, or insights that came up for you as a result of this exercise.

Action Steps for Ken Gua

- Spend 3-5 minutes every day feeling good about what you want, as though you have already received it. Close your eyes and revisit your imagined scene (or create a new one), and get into that feeling-really-good state of mind. When you connect the thing or experience that you desire with a strong experience of feeling good about it, you send a message to the Universe that you have complete trust and confidence in that outcome.

- Turn your problems over to God. Look around your house for a reusable container, such as a glass jar, coffee cannister, or shoe box. Label it: "THINGS FOR GOD TO HANDLE."

  When something is causing you concern, write a brief note to God including: 1) a description of the problem; 2) a request for help; 3) the words "thank you."

  For example: *Dear God, I need new tires for my car. Please make these available to me at a price I can afford. Thank you.*

  Keep it simple; the point of the God Jar is to delegate the details!

  Put your note in the jar and stop worrying about it. Don't take it out and reread it, and don't keep adding more notes about the same problem. Trust means you don't need to ask more than once! If your God Jar fills up, you can either empty it out (toss or burn the notes) or start a new jar.

When you learn to delegate your problems to a higher power with faith and trust, you free up a huge amount of mental and emotional energy that used to go toward worrying and controlling. All of that energy is now available for more fully expressing your true self in the fulfillment of your soul's purpose, which is the task of our next step on the path to abundance: *kan gua*.

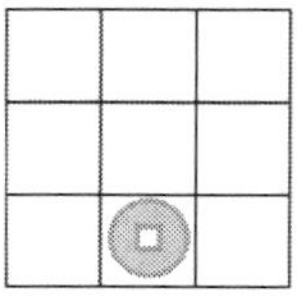

Kan Gua ~ Career

Step 5. EXPRESS

Kan gua is about "career" and "communication." Its element is WATER, and its colors are black and dark blue. Water fountains and images of rivers and waterfalls are good enhancements for *kan gua*. If you are redecorating, choose curvy, irregular shapes and patterns for fabrics and furnishings in this area.

On a mundane level, *kan gua* helps us deal with such challenges as finding a job (or a better job), gaining a promotion, and negotiating a pay raise—important factors in financial well-being. Look at what's going on in *kan gua* of your office to see if you are being held back. Clutter here will keep you overwhelmed with current obligations, so you don't have time or attention to pursue anything new. A bookcase or file cabinet in this position crammed full with binders, documents, or reference materials from past projects will hold you at that level.

If you want a new job, new responsibilities, or new opportunities for growth, make sure that at least 25% of the shelf and storage space in *kan gua* is open and available for new energy—things, projects, connections—to come in. If you do not yet have your "dream job," collect images or symbols that represent what that position would be for you, whether that's a promotion within your current organization, or the opportunity to start a business of your own. Place these on a shelf or in a picture frame in *kan gua* of your office. If you'd prefer these not to be on display, keep them in *kan gua* but out of sight.

Imagine the *ba gua* stretched to cover your desk: *kan gua* is in the center front, where you sit. Does your desk feature a shallow center drawer? If so, clean it out. Of all the storage areas in an office, this is the most likely to turn into a junk drawer. Get rid of the stuff you don't use, and tidy the rest with a drawer organizer of some kind.

Living With Purpose

Kan gua prompts us to examine how we express who we are through both our work and our words. By "work," by the way, I mean whatever you do with your time and attention, whether that's a traditional job, household management/child care, or volunteering.

It's difficult to feel prosperous when you don't enjoy what you do for a living, no matter how well-paid you may be. If your work involves something you love, on the other hand, and brings a sense of fulfillment, you will feel as though you are being paid to play instead of work, and what could be more prosperous than that? This is the aspect of *kan gua* that has to do with finding your life path and expressing your soul's unique purpose through what you do.

If you would continue to do whatever it is that you do for "work," even if you no longer needed the money, then you have found your life path. Many people, unfortunately, either have not connected with their inner sense of purpose, or feel trapped working for money while trying to pursue purpose on the side.

"Do what you love, and the money will follow," like many popular sayings, sounds a little too simplistic to be true. There is a great deal of truth in this, however; the trick is that "do what you love" is not always easy at all, because it requires first that you connect with a sense of unique contribution. Doing what you love is not necessarily the same as doing something fun for a living, or having a cool job. When you work with purpose, you have an inner certainty that you are meant to take this path. Persistence in the face of adversity seems like the only reasonable option. You are guided by intuition, and are willing to get out of your own way by giving up control of what, when, and how to a higher power. You trust that you will be guided and supported in unexpected ways, because that is what happens when you find your path and open your heart.

What if you don't have a clue what your purpose is? Most likely, you haven't made discovering it a priority objective. Some people know from a very young age what they want to do with their lives. Others find their path much later in life. Any quieting, centering practice (such as yoga, meditation, or long walks) that helps you get in touch with your intuition will be helpful.

If you have a sense of purpose, work hard, trust your intuition, and try to do everything right, yet are still not thriving, usually one of three things is going on:

1. Your sense of purpose is coming from your head, not your heart; you are doing what you believe you "should" or "need" to do, not what your soul wants you to do.

2. You need to get out of your own way; subconscious beliefs that you do not deserve success, or that wealthy people are unspiritual, or that being successful will bring more responsibility or attention than you will be able to handle—or whatever your personal money bugaboo is—are certain to hold you back.

3. You are approaching things backwards…

Acting As If

The key point of, "Do what you love and the money will follow," is that you shouldn't use lack of money as a reason to postpone becoming the person you want to and are meant to be. But most of us do just that, much of the time. Our vision of a desired future is burdened by a very clear idea of all the things we need to have or do first.

Have you ever said to yourself something like this?

- *When I get that promotion, I'll be able to afford a vacation, and then I will finally be able to relax and **have some fun**.*

- *When I have more money, I'll be able to pay down my credit card debt, and then I will **feel more secure**.*

- *Some day I will be able to afford a home of my own in a good neighborhood, and then I will really **be happy**.*

Notice that no matter what goal or desire you focused on, the thought process is the same: before we can feel what we want to feel, we think we have to have something that we haven't got. "Well, duh," you may be thinking, "that's pretty obvious, isn't it?" Actually, it's backwards thinking. The reason this is backwards is that how we feel is one of the few things in life that is actually within our control. It doesn't always seem that way, but it is. One very powerful way to attract what you want into your life is to act as though you already have it—even if only in your imagination.

If you believe that having more money will make you happy, or help you feel more secure or more relaxed, then the most powerful thing you can do to turn your financial situation around is to find ways to start feeling happier, or more secure, or more relaxed right now, rather than putting it off until you have the money you want. Figure out how you want to *feel*, and use the power of your imagination to start feeling that, and you will attract the outer circumstances that support it.

The saying, "to be happy, act happy" is another trite phrase that is actually full of wisdom. You can experience this yourself, by pretending that you are in an acting class and that you have been asked to model someone who is depressed and anxious about money. Try doing this right now. See if you can convey through posture and facial expression that your life is hard, you feel worn down, and you've lost all hope that tomorrow will be any better. Stay with this for a minute or so, then notice how you feel.

If you just tried this, you probably noticed that after adjusting your posture and expression to *appear* discouraged, you started to feel that way a little, too.

Now take a moment to model a happy optimist. Life is good, your wallet is crammed with $100 bills, you just got a fabulous new car, and tomorrow is going to be even better! How does your posture change? What happens to your head and arm positions, your facial expression? What happens to how you feel?

Standing tall with your shoulders back, head held high and a big smile on your face triggers changes in your brain chemistry. That's right: smiling, even when you don't feel like smiling, can actually lift your mood biochemically.*

"Acting as if" means that to be prosperous, you need to feel prosperous! (If that's too much of a stretch, aim for feeling that it is possible for you to someday be prosperous.) This doesn't mean to run out and buy a house, car, or clothes you can't afford. It means to walk, talk, and

* If you've been feeling down lately, I suggest setting a timer or the alarm function on your watch to ring once an hour as a reminder to sit (or stand) tall, shoulders back, and relax into a smile for a few minutes.

feel as though everything is okay, that all your needs are met, all your bills paid, and every aspect of your life is provided for, no matter how much or how little of that is actually present for you today.

If feeling prosperous—or even the possibility of being prosperous—is very difficult for you, you may have to start by monitoring how you think, which means paying attention to the words you use, both in your self-talk and in what you say to others.

Talk Yourself Rich

Your words help to create your reality. Does your language reveal a belief that money is hard to get, or that you'll never get enough of it? What do the casual comments you make throughout the day reveal about your expectations from life? Watching what you say about money is just as important as watching what you think or what you do.

Pay attention for the next few days to how people around you talk—about sports, about health, about love, about money, about anything. Happy people are not optimistic talkers because they are happy; they are happy because they think and talk positively. People whose language reveals a "poor me, life is hard" outlook are not negative *because* they are unhappy; they are unhappy at least in part because they are in the habit of thinking and talking and feeling down.

Take a moment to mentally review the past week. When you were asked, "How are you today?" or "How are things in the marketing department these days"—or whatever fits your situation—how did you respond? Did you say something like: "We're swamped," "Same old, same old," "It's a mad-house around here these days," or "As well as can be expected,"or did you say: "I'm doing great, thanks!" or "Life is good!" or even, "Can't complain!"?

If you are hoping for better than "same old, same old" in your life, use the power of your words to claim constant improvement. Next time someone asks how you are, try saying, "I'm doing great, thank you!" instead.

Here's a wonderful phrase you can use whenever you hear yourself (or a family member) says something less than prosperous: "It's a good thing we're rich!" And the best thing is, you don't have to be rich to say it.

For example, if your spouse says, "Wow, our electric bill is really high this month" you reply, "It's a good thing we're rich!" Or, if you catch yourself saying, "I can't believe we just spent $185 on one cart of groceries," just add on, "...it's a good thing we're rich!"*

Ever since we've been using this phrase around our house, it's been just a little harder to worry about money, and however high our grocery bill gets our income somehow rises to support it.

Try this the next time you have a moment of sticker shock or money panic. Your logical brain may know it's not true, but your subconscious brain is easy to fool. And if using this statement seems absurd, that's fine too, because anything that makes you laugh will lighten your mood—an important step to experiencing increasing abundance.

Experiencing the Inner Aspects of Kan Gua

If you have not yet connected with a sense of purpose about what you are doing with your life, here's a meditation to help you open to intuitive guidance.

First, see if you can identify a place in your body where you feel lack of purpose or frustration as a physical sensation.

Use the Heart Calming method to inhale white light either into the place where you feel blocked or to fill your entire body, and exhale your tension, frustration, or sadness.

Remember to take long, slow inhales through the mouth, and to exhale in eight short puffs followed by a final long ninth puff until your lungs are completely empty. Repeat for a total of nine breaths.

Continue to sit comfortably with your eyes closed, breathing naturally through your nose. Place your attention on your heart center, and ask to be guided to your right path, or for clarity about your purpose, or to be shown a sign of what direction you should take—whatever request or question feels right to you right now.

Pay attention to any ideas or images that come to you: they may be pieces of your answer.

---

* Credit goes to Mike Dooley for this wonderfully affirming phrase. For more of Mike's inspirations, I recommend his audio program, *Infinite Possibilities: the Art of Living Your Dreams*. See the Resources pages for details.

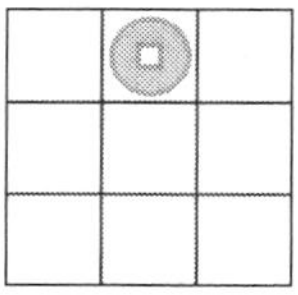

Li Gua ~ Fame

Step 6. OBSERVE

Li is the area of "fame" and "reputation." When applying feng shui to our homes, we look to *li gua* to improve how we are seen by others and to ensure that we get the recognition we deserve.

The element of *li gua* is FIRE, which adds "illumination"to the meanings for this area. Candles and lights are good in *li gua*, as are plants and flowers, which represent the WOOD element that nourishes FIRE. Avoid having too much WATER energy in *li gua*, as it will put out *li*'s FIRE. EARTH and METAL are also not recommended here.

Would enhancing your reputation or increasing your visibility— or that of your company or product— help you achieve your financial goals? If so, look for creative ways to enlist the energy of *li gua*, such as:

- Hang a bird feeder in *li gua* of your yard. Birds visiting the feeder will stir up the energy of this area.

- Put a telephone or your fax machine in *li gua* of your office to help "get the word out" about your products, services, or business.

- Place an image, object, or award in *li gua* to represent what you want to be known for: reliability, great service, innovation, etc.

- Add real or symbolic money to *li gua*, to help you become known as someone with money.

Li gua is a key area for vigilance against clutter (unless you want to be known as a slob), and anything outdated. It was great that you won that journalism award—back in 1985. Get some attention for what you're writing today by making up a new award on your computer, with next year's date on it. Put it in a red frame and hang it in *li gua*.

Look for Signs of Abundance

Symbolically, *li gua* represents how we envision our lives and perceive the world through the filter of our beliefs and attitudes. One of the most powerful—and simple—ways to make your daily life experience more positive is to consciously choose where you place your attention. If you want to experience greater abundance, start to notice the abundance that is already all around you, rather than focusing on signs of scarcity that may also be present.

For example, from my lanai in Hawaii I can look at the guava tree, which was laden with fruit two months ago, and notice that now it has none (scarcity), or I direct my attention to a crop of late-season mangos ripening on the mango tree (abundance). I can also notice that the little green birds eating those mangos are truly experiencing abundance by sinking their beaks into a sweet, juicy fruit about 10 or 12 times their size. Their thoughts, if they have any, must be something like, "Mmmm... mango!" not, "Uh oh, where did all the guavas go?"

Choose to see abundance all around you every day, no matter how inadequate your financial means may be right now. Each time you feel lack, look for something that you can enjoy instead. Here are some ideas for learning to place your attention on abundance, rather than scarcity:

Instead of focusing on...	Choose to see...
How much it will cost to fill your car's gas tank.	The abundance of gas stations and choices available to you, and how easy it is, when you need more gas, to get it.
How much you just spent at the grocery store	The abundance of fresh, healthy foods available at your local supermarkets.
Your credit card balance	All the wonderful things and services you have been able to enjoy on credit.
The meager size of your bank account	The dollars that do flow into your life, in the form of your paycheck, discounts, gifts, and rebates on items you purchase.

NOTICE WHEN MONEY SHOWS UP

Have you ever seen a coin on the sidewalk and decided not to bother picking it up because, well, it's just a penny?

I used to do that. "I'm doing all right," I would think. "I don't need to pick up a dime. I'll leave it for someone less fortunate than me to find." I thought I was making a small gesture of generosity and affirming my own prosperity. But what I was really doing was rejecting a small gift of abundance from the Universe, and sending a message not to bother putting more money my way.

Now that I have a better understanding of how prosperity really works, I make a point of noticing *any* kind of money that comes to me. A penny in the parking lot, great! An email telling me I've earned a 25-cent commission on a website referral, wonderful! A $5 gift certificate to Amazon.com, fabulous! My preferred brand of toothpaste on sale this week, terrific!

No matter how small the amount, whenever any kind of money comes to me, expected or not, I take a moment to appreciate it and to say "thank you!"

The more you notice and appreciate all the different ways money comes to you, from a dime on the sidewalk, to your regular paycheck, to free time left on a parking meter or winning $2 on a lottery ticket, the more prosperous you will feel. And the more prosperous you feel, the more you encourage more abundance to come your way.

My grandmother was fond of sayings like, "Find a penny, pick it up, and all the day you'll have good luck." This bit of folk wisdom explains the truth that when you gladly receive even small of gifts, you position yourself to experience more and greater lucky moments. People who choose to view the world as abundant and supportive are more open to luck and opportunities, because they have no resistance to good things coming to them in unexpected ways. When you view events and people with pessimism and low expectation you will see and experience more reasons to feel the world is a hostile and difficult place.

Choose to perceive yourself as someone to whom money flows and to whom lucky things happen, and you will see and experience more and more reasons to feel happy and prosperous.

Acting As If

When you see a wealthy person on the street, or in a restaurant, or on TV or in a movie, how do you know that person is rich? What are the visual clues that to you mean someone is wealthy? Your list will probably include:

- Drives an expensive car
- Wears designer clothes
- Eats in fine restaurants
- Lives in a fancy house
- Take expensive vacations

and so on.

Can you think of at least three ways that rich people live that you can emulate in a small way—without spending money you don't have? Note your ideas in your Prosperity Journal. Here are a few examples to get you started.

- Observation: *Rich people drive expensive, well-maintained cars.*

  Emulation: If you have a car, keep it clean, polished and well-maintained. Don't wait until you have a fancy car to act like you have a fancy car. By taking excellent care of your budget-mobile, you show the Universe that you can take care of a luxury car.

- Observation: *Rich people are well-groomed and nicely attired.*

  Emulation: We may joke about Donald Trump's hair style, but at least it is always neatly brushed. Pay attention to grooming, and dress as well as you can within the limits of your budget. Hot young actors may get away with looking grubby and unshaven for their appearances on the Late Show, but I suggest you model your style after Jay Leno or David Letterman instead: they always look "like a million bucks." Even if you habitually wear jeans and T-shirts every day, you can at least wear clean, unwrinkled, jeans and T-shirts that are in good condition.

- Observation: *Wealthy, successful people tend to be slim and fit.*

  Emulation: So what if you can't afford a personal trainer and a private chef? Do what you can to look as good as you can with what you've got. If you've been thinking about losing a few pounds or getting into better physical shape, why not start now? Think of it as your "I 'm gonna look like a millionnaire" plan, rather than "going on a diet" or "working out." Looking better will help you feel good physically and feel better about yourself. And feeling good—about how you look, about how you feel, about anything—helps you succeed in life.

- Observation: *Rich people live in expensive homes—clean, tidy, uncluttered expensive homes.*

  Emulation: You may not be able to afford a maid, but that's no reason to live in an unclean house. Show the Universe that you can keep the Formica™ in your tiny kitchen sparkling, and you're one step closer to having a marble counter in a fancier house someday. If you hate to clean house, see if you can find room in your budget for a few hours of maid service twice a month. It may not take much more than brown-bagging your lunch instead of eating out, and cutting back on DVD rentals.

Free Yourself From Limiting Beliefs

If you do not believe that you deserve to prosper, financial well-being will elude or desert you. Many people want to prosper, but are burdened by feelings of guilt, shame, or embarrassment that prevent them from believing that they deserve success. When you feel guilt or shame about past experiences—whether related to money or not—it is very difficult to achieve the high-energy states of trust and receptivity that we have talked about in previous chapters as being keys to a prosperous life.

Money issues having to do with self-worth are often hidden to our conscious awareness. You may think you deserve to prosper, while your subconscious mind has other ideas. Here's how you can use a simple muscle-testing method to discover whether your subconscious beliefs are aligned with your conscious goals and desires.

Version A: With a Partner

1. Hold one arm out to the side at shoulder height, parallel to the floor. State something about yourself that is true, such as "My name is Kelly," or "I weigh 135 pounds," or "I drive a blue Corolla."

2. Your partner presses down on your arm while you resist. The idea is not for your partner to force your arm down, but to enable both of you to gauge your strength.

3. Rest your arm for a moment, then hold it out again in the same position. Now, make a statement about money, such as "I want to be rich," or "I deserve to be wealthy."

4. Again, your partner presses down on your arm while you resist. If your subconscious mind agrees with your statement, your arm will stay strong, similar to the "true" statement you first made. However, if your subconscious mind does *not* agree, you'll discover that your arm strength has weakened. The results may surprise you!

Version B: On Your Own

1. If you don't have a partner, use a free weight as we did in the "Weight of Money" experiment on page 63. Holding a moderately heavy weight in one hand, first make a true statement about yourself, then lift the weight to gauge how difficult (or easy) that is for you.

2. Rest your arm for a moment, then make a test statement ("I want to be rich," "I deserve to have money," etc.) and lift the weight again.

3. If you can lift the weight as easily the second time as you did the first, your subconscious beliefs are in agreement with your test statement. If your arm feels weaker, though—or the weight much heavier—that's a sign of conflict between what you say and how you really feel.

If you uncovered a subconscious block with this method, there's no need to be discouraged. Awareness is the first step to changing your beliefs. You may even want to repeat the muscle testing for other test statements, such as "I really want the promotion," or "I am ready to be wealthy." Notice that just changing one key word in a statement can change the muscle-test result. The more disconnects you can uncover between your conscious goals and subconscious beliefs, the more progess you can make in clearing them.

Experiencing the Inner Aspects of Li Gua

At some point in your past, something happened that established that limiting belief. It's likely to be an incident that your logical mind would dismiss as unimportant—a minor situation that was not worth remembering. And yet your subconscious mind learned something that has been affecting your experience ever since.

Journaling, meditation, and emotional release work can all help deepen your understanding of the roots of limiting belief systems. One simple technique that can be very helpful is to sit or lie comfortably, relax, and quiet your mind with the Heart Calming technique for a few minutes.

When you're relaxed, ask your subconscious to provide a memory of where this limiting belief started. Don't try to figure out what this is; just allow an image or idea to come to you. Stay with this for a few minutes, and if nothing arises, let that be okay and try again tomorrow.

For example, a memory might arise of when you were eight years old and your mother gave you some money to take to your boy- or girl-scout troop meeting after school. Sometime before you got to the scout meeting, you misplaced the money. When you got home, your mom responded with annoyance, anger, or disappointment.

"Not a big deal," your logical adult mind says, as you reflect on this experience. "These sorts of things happen when you're eight. It's part of growing up. You learn to be more responsible."

But that's not what your subconscious mind learned. Your subconscious learned, "I can't be trusted with money," "I can never have a lot of money, because I'll lose it," or "If I have money, someone ends up being angry with me. It's not worth it."

Once you have remembered a root incident, write a paragraph in your Prosperity Journal describing what happened, including how other people reacted and what emotions you felt. Also make note of the subconscious belief statements that may have come out of it.

Now you can use the scripting and visualization techniques you've learned in the previous chapters to rewrite this incident so that you only learn positive messages from it. For example:

> I'm eight years old, and Mom gives me a $20 bill to give to my scout leader for our field trip next weekend.I feel very gown up being trusted with so much money. I put the bill in my pocket, and notice that it feels worn and soft.
>
> ORIGINAL MEMORY: But when I get to the scout meeting, it's gone! I can't find it! I feel panicky and embarrased.The other kids laugh at me and I have to try really hard not to cry. When I get home, Mom is upset and yells at me. I hate money!
>
> RESCRIPT: *At the scout meeting, I give the money to our troop leader, and learn all about the field trip. It's going to be really fun! When I get home, Mom asks if I remembered to give them the money and she tells me I did a really good job. "You're a good money manager, honey," she tells me, and gives me a hug.*

The purpose of rescripting is to create an outcome in which you feel good about what happened. This may require imagining the other people involved doing and saying unlikely things; that's okay.

Now make up one or more affirmations that turn the original negative beliefs around, such as: "I am an excellent money manager," "I can be trusted with vast amounts of money," or "I enjoy having lots of money." Read your new scene aloud, then take a few minutes to visualize it in your mind, focusing on feeling good about how it all turned out. Finish by reading your affirmations aloud.

Repeat this reading, visualization, and affirmation process every day for 30 days to reprogram your subconscious beliefs about money. If more key memories arise during the 30 days, use the rescripting method to revise them into positive experiences. Every day, choose one of your scenes to practice with for five minutes or so. You don't have to go through every scene every day, one is enough.

Action Steps for Li Gua

- Challenge yourself to see how many coins you can find in a week. Set up the expectation in your mind that you will start finding money in unexpected places. It can help to focus on finding one kind of coin, such as a dime or a quarter. Every time you find a coin, pick it up and say, "Thank you! I am a money magnet. I love finding more money every day!"
- Be alert to judgmental thoughts you may have about yourself, whether about money or other things. Note them in your Prosperity Journal, so you can start the process of re-programming how you think about yourself and your capabilities.
- Make a collage of images and words that represent what prosperity and abundance mean to you... a gorgeous house, new car, a boat, artwork, luxury travel, other activities that you may wish you had the time or money for: yoga classes, gardening, a ski or spa vacation, or a week at the beach with your kids. Place this across from your bed where you will see it first thing in the morning and last thing at night. (This is a "virtual" *li gua,* because it is in the *li* position relative to you when you are lying in bed). Take a few moments in the morning and at night to look at these images, then close your eyes and imagine that you are really doing/experiencing these things... Use all your senses, and remember to end with a few moments of heart-felt gratitude for all of these blessings.

Li gua reminds us to be alert to beliefs and assumptions that may distort our observations and interfere with an experience of abundance. In the next step on our journey to prosperity, we take a closer look at the details of our household finances, represented by *jen gua.*

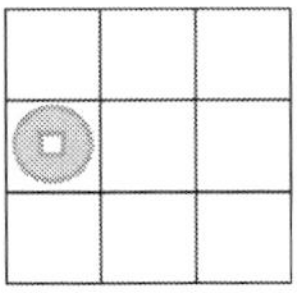

Jen Gua ~ Family

Step 7. BEGIN

Jen gua is the area associated with family life and, to a lesser degree, with health.* "Family" in this context includes your family of origin as well as the family unit created by yourself, your spouse, and your children. In a broader sense *jen gua* encompasses close friends, roommates, significant others, and your community. The *jen* area of your living room, family room, or dining room is a good place to display family photographs and cherished mementos from previous generations.

Jen gua governs those aspects of our lives that are most likely to drive our desire for prosperity, and where we spend the bulk of our income. We want to provide a nice home for our family, educate and indulge our children, care for our elders, and pamper our pets. And health care can be a significant source of debt and financial stress. Take a look again at your list of 108 Desires. Which of these are associated with the home and family qualities of *jen gua*?

Jen gua is where we confront the mundane, housekeeping aspects of our lives, such as getting our bills paid on time, and it is where we often find that our lives have slipped out of balance. For example, perhaps you are working two jobs in order to pay the bills, and no longer have much energy or quality time left to spend with your family. Medical bills or elder care could be adding to your stress level, causing increased irritability and impatience with your spouse or children and undermining your future health.

Compared to the "fortunate blessings" aspects of wealth that are associated with *hsun gua*, *jen gua* has a strong influence on household finances and the day-to-day tasks of earning a living and paying the

* Health is also governed by the *tai chi*.

bills. While we look to *hsun gua* to create an experience of abundance and prosperity, if your immediate challenge is to make ends meet and keep creditors from your door, *jen gua* deserves your attention. You may wish to go through the power spot steps on pages 15-17 again to identify the key *jen gua* areas of your home.

When we orient the *ba gua* to the compass directions, *jen gua* is in the east, associated with morning, springtime and new beginnings, whether of a major life cycle or a short-term project. *Jen gua* is associated with the WOOD element in its youthful form of young plants and trees. Its colors are the paler shades of green, and light blues are also used here. WATER imagery and colors (black and dark blues) are good accents for *jen gua*, as they nourish WOOD. METAL, FIRE, and EARTH influences should be minimized here.

Look for a place in *jen gua*—preferably in the living room, family room, dining room, or kitchen—where you can create a focal point with potted plants and/or a table-top water fountain. Place a large mirror on the wall behind the plants/fountain so that they are reflected in it. Use three or nine small houseplants grouped together for best effect; lucky bamboo and jade plants are especially auspicious here. Use the IVAG empowerment method with this cure to support regeneration of your cash flow or to attract new sources of income.

New Beginnings

On the inner level, *jen gua* has to do with caring appropriately for ourselves, our families, and our money. When highly successful people announce that they're giving it all up to spend more time with their family or attend to their health, they are heeding the call of *jen gua* to return to essentials and bring their lives back into balance. Mastering the inner aspects of *jen gua* involves exploring how you can initiate a new era in how you handle money, by drawing upon what you've learned in the previous six *guas* and taking action.

In the section on *kun gua*, we talked about the importance of nurturing and showing respect for your money. Wealthy people take good care of their money, and you should, too, no matter how little of it you have. In *jen gua* terms, that means paying attention to the details of household financial management: creating a budget or spending plan, tracking your expenses, having a plan in place for paying down your consumer debt and building up a savings account, and so on.

These simple but important tasks enable you to cultivate and grow your prosperity. Just like the young plants represented by *jen gua*, your finances require regular—even daily—attention, in order to thrive. What seeds of prosperity can you plant by developing the daily habits that will increase or solidify your fiscal responsibility and security?

Fear Drives Procrastination

The core aspect of *jen gua* most relevant to mastering the inner path to prosperity is this idea of initiating new money habits. Understanding the practical value of having (and sticking to) a spending plan, saving wisely, and getting out of debt, for example, does you little good if you don't take action on it.

Most often, when we know what we should do, state our intention to start doing it, and continue with our old habits anyway despite our knowledge and good intentions, what stops us is some form of fear. When your financial situation is precarious, taking a good look at the details can be very scary—no wonder so many people procrastinate on this important task.

If you are carrying a lot of consumer debt split among multiple credit cards, for example, you may put off adding up your total debt because you don't want to face that number. If you know that impulsive shopping is your downfall, you may resist tracking what you spend because that would force you to confront this irresponsible habit.

These kinds of feelings are understandable—and very common—but in the long run they disempower you. You can't gain control over your finances if you don't know what the size, scope, and nature of the problem really is.

When you avoid facing the details of your money situation, that vagueness tends to permeate all aspects of your financial life. People who don't manage the details of their money are more likely to be late paying their bills, to radically underestimate what they really owe, to overspend without awareness, and to convince themselves that everything is (or will be) okay. In reality, the situation is slipping further and further out of control.

Facing the Details

Open your Prosperity Journal, or get a pad of paper, and answer the following questions:

- What money-management tasks do you most often put off until later or ignore completely? (*making or sticking to a budget, tracking expenses, paying bills, balancing your checkbook, saving regularly, etc.*)
- What reasons do you give for doing this? (*lack of time; I'm too tired; it's not important; I'll do it this weekend; I'll start next month*)
- What are the *real* reasons you procrastinate on or ignore these takes? Ask yourself, "Why do I really put off taking care of my money?" Observe your thoughts and any physical sensations that come up. You may notice that you feel scared, threatened, rebellious, impatient, or sleepy if these or similar issues are true for you:
    - ~ *I'm afraid I'll never get out of debt.*
    - ~ *If I know how much I really owe, the stress will be overwhelming.*
    - ~ *I'm ashamed of how little I earn.*
    - ~ *I feel embarrassed that I'm not more successful.*
    - ~ *I feel guilty that I've handled my money so badly.*

  Recognize that sleepiness, shortness of breath, stomach tension or a sudden headache are signals that there are powerful emotional issues involved in your financial life. When you find the courage to acknowledge these issues, instead of avoiding them, handling your money well will become much easier.
- In what ways, if any, are family issues involved in your financial procrastination? (*not wanting your spouse or parents to know how much debt you are carrying, for example*)
- If you are carrying consumer debt (credit and store accounts), do you know how much the total amount you owe is, for all your accounts? If you don't know, make a guess (without looking at your latest statements), and write that number down.

Now get out your credit and store account statements (or check them online), make a list of all of the amounts you owe, and total them up. Was this total higher or lower than your guess?

- If you are carrying consumer debt, don't know within a hundred dollars how much you owe, but didn't complete the previous question, what stopped you? What are you feeling right now?
- Are you secretly hoping that by reading this book your financial situation will magically change for the better, and you will be able to prosper without facing your debt, changing your spending habits, or taking responsibility for your financial future into your own hands?

  I'm sure you are not alone if this is true, but it is my task to remind you that you can't keep doing things the same old way and expect to see a lasting improvement in your situation. The most effective feng shui in the world might bring you lots more money, but that is no guarantee that you will be able to manage it well or prosper from it in the long run if ineffective money-management or spending habits have not been corrected.

These questions, whether or not you've taken the time to answer them, may lead to some insights. Be sure to note them in your Prosperity Journal, and don't be in too much of a rush to put them behind you. Working through and releasing money issues is a lot like peeling off the layers of an onion: the same stuff keeps on coming up over and over again, and it takes a while to get to the center.

Experiencing the Inner Aspects of Jen Gua

The Heart Calming method with which you are now familiar is a good way to release the discomfort or stress that may have come up as a result of the preceeding questions.

If you did not notice a specific physical sensation in answering the journaling questions, take a moment to return your attention to your most-dreaded financial-management task. See if you can identify a place in your body where your desire to avoid that task becomes a physical sensation. If you can't pick up any physical clues, that's okay, too, just focus on your entire body as you do the following exercise.

RELEASING

Sit comfortably with your hands in the Heart Calming *mudra* (palms up, left hand on top of right, the thumbs touching). Inhale white light either into the place where you feel blocked or to fill your entire body, and exhale your tension or fear. Remember to take long, slow inhales through the mouth, and to exhale in eight short puffs followed by a final long ninth puff until your lungs are completely empty. Repeat for a total of nine breaths.

VISUALIZATION: "PERFECT SPENDING PLAN"

Imagine that you are out of debt, your family is well-cared for, you live in a comfortable home, and you have $1,000 of extra money available to spend on anything you want each month. ("Spend" here includes saving or investing, if that's a priority for you.) Using the *ba gua* template on the next page as your guide, think about all the different ways you might like to spend that money. Try to think of at least one thing for each area of the *ba gua*, although it's likely that you will have many more entries for some areas than for others.

Write your answers in the grid on the next page or in your Prosperity Journal. Don't worry about how much each item will cost, or whether they all add up to less or more than $1,000. This is a list of *potential* indulgences, and some of them can wait until next month. If you feel stuck, look at your list of "108 Desires" for ideas. When you've got at least one entry for each *gua*, find the three items that you think will bring you the most satisfaction, and list them in your Journal.

Use the scripting and visualization methods that you've learned in earlier chapters to develop a multi-sensory, detailed scene for each of your top three items. For example:

- If you put "weekend getaway with my wife" in *kun gua*, write a paragraph or more describing where you would stay, the romantic dinner you'd like to have, and so on.

- If you put "take a qigong class" in *ken gua*, describe what you'd like to experience during your first class, what the instructor and other students are like, and how you expect feel while doing the exercises and after the class.

Remember to include details that evoke all of the senses. The more specific your scene is, the better. If you've chosen to write a scene, also read it aloud when you are done, and take a few minutes to close your eyes and visualize it as well. When you close your eyes and imagine the details of your scene, it should make you feel very happy. If your scene doesn't make you smile, try to identify what's off or missing, and either revise or add to it before focusing on it again.

These scenes—and the other items on your 108 Desires list—can help you stay motivated to make the lifestyle and/or financial habit changes that will help you reach your prosperity goals.

Hsun ~ Wealth	Li ~ Fame	Kun ~ Partnership
Jen ~ Family	Tai Chi ~ Health & Life Balance	Dui ~ Creativity & Children
Ken ~ Knowledge & Spirituality	Kan ~ Career	Chien ~ Helpful Friends & Travel

Action Steps for Jen Gua

- *Jen gua* reminds us that "someday" is not an eighth day of the week, and that the best time to start practicing good money habits is right now. If you've been lax in tracking your expenses, making (or sticking to) a budget, or keeping up with your bills, it's time to make a fresh start. Challenge yourself to tackle one neglected money task and to stay on top of it for an entire month. Next month, add another one. Use your Prosperity Journal to record any issues and insights that may come up for you.
- Tithe to Yourself. If you are not yet setting some money aside on a regular basis, start tithing to yourself with your next paycheck. Choose an amount from 1%-10% of your net income to set aside. Personal finance advisors recommend having an emergency fund equal to at least six months of basic living expenses. If you don't have any savings yet, that can seem like an impossible amount. Don't let that stop you from getting started. Just do what you can, one day at a time.
- If you are in debt, make a commitment to figure out how you are going to climb back out. Without a specific plan, you are less likely to succeed in paying off your debts. This may be as simple as making some adjustments to your spending plan so you can set a little more aside for debt reduction every month, or you may need professional debt counseling. Some excellent books and resources are included in the Resources section at the back of the book.

Making a fresh start to practice new money habits is just that, a start. Your success will also depend on sticking with these tasks until they are done, represented by the final step in our prosperity journey, *dui gua*.

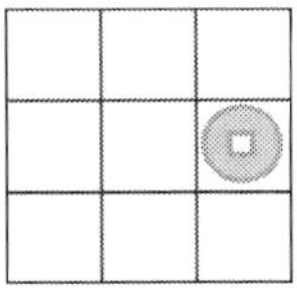

Dui Gua ~ Creativity & Children

Step 8. COMPLETE

Dui gua is associated with "creativity" and "children." Any creative endeavor is a form of giving birth—to an idea, a novel, a new recipe for coconut cake—and bringing a baby into the world is the most purely creative thing anyone can do. Because it is in the west according to the compass orientation of the *ba gua*, *dui gua* is associated with afternoon, autumn, and bringing things to completion, such as when a crop that was planted in the spring (*jen gua*) matures and is ready for harvest.

The element for *dui gua* is METAL, represented not only by metallic objects and colors, but also by white and by round and oval shapes. Six white votive candles in *dui gua* can bring light to your creative process, but in general it is wise not to add FIRE energy to *dui*, as fire destroys (melts) metal. WATER and WOOD will also deplete *dui gua*, but EARTH will support it, so all kinds of earth colors and ceramics are good here.

Coins are a natural choice for enhancing *dui gua* to support greater prosperity through creative work, and all kinds of natural and man-made crystals can be used here as well. Hang a faceted crystal ball in *dui gua*, or over your head as you work at a desk in a *dui gua* office, to enhance creativity. A mobile featuring white, yellow, or metallic colors will stir up new ideas here.

Taking Care of Unfinished Business

On an inner level, mastering *dui gua* has to do with taking care of unfinished business. Think of any kind of unfinished business as a cosmic glue trap that keeps you stuck in the past energetically, so it becomes harder to adopt new habits and make other important changes in your life. This is as true of that pile of clean laundry you've not yet folded and put away as it is of overdue bills and un-filed tax returns. Unfinished business leads to feelings of guilt, shame, or embarrassment. These low-energy states undermine your self-esteem and make it even harder to get the things on your "to do" list done.

You can gain a sense of how unfinished business is affecting you by doing a quick survey, room by room. Go through each room, including closets and under the bed or wherever you tend to stash things "temporarily" and then forget about them, and make a list of all the unfinished projects you find. This includes creative projects, like that baby-sweater you began to knit when your sister was pregnant (for a niece who is now 12) or the stripped-but-never-repainted dresser in the garage. Include tasks that you began with the best of intentions but dropped before they were done: cleaning out the fridge, weeding the garden, getting new curtains for the dining room, mending that rip in your jacket pocket, and so on. Unfinished business includes anything awaiting your attention, such as action step items from previous *guas* that you have not yet taken action on, unreturned phone calls, backlogged emails, and that pile of magazines you've been meaning to read someday.

As you go on your unfinished business hunt, you may be amazed—possibly even appalled—by how long your list grows. Lessening your burden of unfinished business will free up more of your energy for pursuing prosperity and adopting new habits.

If you have many items on your "unfinished" list, it's a good idea to prioritize by sorting them into these categories:

- *Who am I kidding?* — Things you have postponed for so long that there's no longer any point to them (last year's unsent holiday cards, for example, or plans for a garden project for last season). You might as well just cross these off your list.

- *What was I thinking?* — Projects that you no longer have any interest in pursuing (a half-finished needlepoint pillow for which you still have yarn and instructions, for example, or those scrapbooking supplies you are never going to use). Toss these, give them to a friend, or donate them to a thrift store.

- *Hey, I remember this!* — Things you put away some time ago and may have forgotten about, but that you would still like to get done. You may want to further sort this category by how long it will take to complete the project (less than 30 minutes; a couple of hours; a month's worth of free time if you ever have any, etc.).
- *I've been meaning to get to that* — Household chores that you've fallen behind on (cleaning out the freezer, sweeping the patio, doing the ironing). Again, sort out the stuff that will take less than an hour from the more time-consuming chores.
- *Unfinished financial business* — These are the tasks mentioned throughout this section of the book, such as creating a livable budget, balancing your checkbook, and setting up (and using) a system for tracking expenses. All of your debts are also in this category, including what is sometimes called "good debt" (your mortgage, for example, or student loans) as well as consumer debt (credit cards, store accounts), and any other monies you may owe.

Unfinished financial business, of course, deserves regular attention until you've caught up. If you haven't been doing anything in this category yet, give yourself a couple of weeks to figure out what tasks will most help you get a grip on the details, decide how you're going to tackle them, and get your system into place.

Create Moments of Appreciation

One good way to approach a money-related task that you usually dread (such as paying bills) is to change the inner and outer environments in which you usually tackle that chore.

Changing the inner environment means adjusting how you think and talk about that task. For example, at the end of the previous paragraph, I used the phrase "tackle that chore" to describe whatever it is you need to get done. In our discussion of *kan gua*, you learned how important it is to be conscious of the language and self-talk you use about money. So, instead of thinking of paying your bills as "tackling a chore," choose to see it as a gesture of appreciation for the goods and services you have received.

For example, when you are paying your cable bill, take a moment to think about the benefits you've received from having cable service this past month, such as entertainment or the convenience of a high-speed internet connection. Write "Thank you!" on the check or on the payment stub. As you place your check in the envelope (or click to complete an online payment), consciously focus on having completed that transaction, even if it is only a partial payment of what you owe.

You might like to invest in a self-inking "PAID" stamp—available at any office supply store—and stamp your receipts as you pay each bill. If you doubt that using a "PAID" stamp will give you much of a thrill, you might be in for a surprise—especially if your bill-paying procrastination is driven by a rebellious inner child. Give any two-year-old an ink pad and something to stamp with and watch how much fun is had. Why deny yourself that pleasure? Stamping your bills "PAID" is satisfying in a very tactile way, more so than any click of a computer mouse could be.

Improve the outer environment for money management tasks by creating a pleasant space in which to do them. Arrange for a little peace and quiet, put on some relaxing music, and pour yourself a glass of wine or a cup of your favorite herbal tea. Instead of rushing to get it done as quickly as possible, make this a special moment of appreciation for all that you do have, regardless of how much you might owe.

JOURNAL QUESTIONS

Prosperity coach Joan Sotkin points out that taking care of our money means that we have to grow up, and that on some level many people, no matter how old they are, don't want to do that. She blames this "rebellious Inner Child" for hard-to-change behaviors and beliefs that may be keeping you in debt or earning less than you deserve.

- In what ways might your own financial habits be driven by a rebellious Inner Child?
- What new behaviors or habits will put your inner Responsible Adult back in control of your money?
- What are three things you are doing now that you will need to do less of in order to take better care of your money?

- What are three things you will need to start doing that you aren't doing yet?
- Review your list of unfinished financial business: What three items on that list cause you the most stress, guilt, or embarrassment? Why?

Experiencing the Inner Aspects of Dui Gua

Mastering the challenge of *dui gua* to take care of unfinished business requires willpower that is stronger than your urge to procrastinate. The emotions that interfere with the *jen gua* task of getting started in the first place (guilt, fear, shame, and embarrassment) also keep you from getting things done... which leads to more guilt, fear, and shame in the long run.

To get a sense of how these emotions may be affecting you, sit in a comfortable chair (your back should be straight), and relax by taking several slow, deep breaths. Now think of a time when you felt guilt, shame, or embarrassment about money. Allow yourself to experience this emotion until it becomes a physical sensation in your body. Most likely this will be a contraction or feeling of congestion in the solar plexus at the middle front of your torso just beneath the center of the ribs. Your shoulders may slump forward, curving your torso to protect this area.

This is the *chakra* or energy center associated with willpower. When your will and determination are strong, this area will feel light and open—the opposite of how it feels when you are experiencing guilt, fear, shame, or embarrassment.

You can use the by-now-familiar Heart Calming method to help release tension and congestion from your will center.

Hold the Heart Calming *mudra*, and remember to take long, slow inbreaths through the mouth, and exhale in eight short breaths plus one long one. As you inhale, imagine your solar plexus bathed in bright yellow light, and imagine that it is absorbing all negativity in that area.

As you exhale, visualize all guilt, shame, fear, or embarrassment about money evaporating. After nine breaths, check to see if you feel more relaxed in the solar plexus area. You may notice that your posture has improved, and that you no longer hunch over.

The key issue of *dui gua*, getting unfinished things done, requires you to step into action. Instead of a visualization or scripting exercise for this *gua*, jump right into the recommended Action Steps, below.

Action Steps for Dui Gua

- For one week, pay for all of your daily expenses with cash. Electronic transactions such as debit or credit card purchases and online bill-paying make it easy to lose touch with how much we really spend. Paying for everything with cash for a week can help put you back in touch with your money and how much of it you are spending.

  Start by estimating how much money you need to get through the next seven days, paying for all of your daily expenses—coffee, train tickets, picking up the dry-cleaning, meals, movies, groceries, and so on—with cash. Withdraw that amount from your bank account, and use it for all your purchases this week, paying attention to how it feels to spend cash instead of using a credit or debit card.

  Each time you pay for something with cash, notice that this transaction has been completed. There's no debit card receipt to save, nothing to record in your checkbook, no new charge to appear on your next credit card bill. Just hand over the cash and you're done. How simple!

  And guess what: your next checking account and credit card statements will be simpler as well. In our rush to embrace the convenience of paying with plastic, we've lost touch of the very simple pleasure of paying for the things we need with cash.

  If you run out of cash before the end of the week, was it due to an unexpected expense, or did you underestimate your normal expenses? If you have not been tracking your expenses, you'll probably be surprised at how much money you spend, and at how quickly smaller purchases add up.

- Commit half an hour a day to tackling your Unfinished Business list until you've caught up. You may find that many tasks are things you could finish while watching TV (sewing on a loose button, for example, or catching up with the ironing). Each time you finish something, take a moment to congratulate yourself on completing that task before moving on to whatever you are going to do next.

- Instead of a "to do" list, create a daily "what I got done" list. If doing this makes you feel like you aren't accomplishing as much as you thought, perhaps you are not claiming credit for enough small things, like getting a load of wash into the machine, or remembering to call a friend who's been ill to see how he or she is doing. Or it could be a sign that too many time-wasters are nibbling away at your day, whether that's unnecessary meetings or computer solitaire. Take another look at your schedule with an eye to freeing up a few more productive minutes every day—at least until your Unfinished Business is under control.

- Rank all of your debts according to how much you owe, from smallest to largest. Make minimum payments on the larger amounts and focus on paying off the smaller amounts first. Some financial advisors say to pay off your highest-interest-rate debts first, to minimize your total finance charges. My feng shui take on this is to encourage you to pay off your smallest debts first so you can feed your soul by being able to say, "I'm done with that one." Transferring the bulk of your higher-interest-rate balances to lower-rate accounts, so your smallest-balance accounts are also the highest-rate ones, allows you to enjoy the benefits of both approaches.

As you complete more and more of your unfinished tasks, you will discover how reliably this provides you with a feeling of satisfaction and control. Each small unfinished task that you complete frees up a little more of your psychic energy for getting on with the unfinished business of fulfilling your destiny. As you master this inner work of *dui gua*, you will start to feel lighter, happier, and less pressured—all characteristics of that state of mind we call "abundance."

I often describe the *ba gua* as a map of the energetic qualities of a space. This section has shown you the *ba gua* as a map of your own interior world, as you have explored the conscious and unconscious beliefs and behaviors that support (or distract) you on your path to prosperity. You've discovered why and how to allow money to flow not just into but through your life, to surrender control to a higher power, to recognize and appreciate the abundance that is all around you, and to overcome procrastination in order to take—and complete—appropriate action.

These are the steps that enable you to embrace your own power, discover what it means to live at your highest potential, and explore the nuances of what a life of abundance means to you. And they help to make the cash flow cures that you'll learn in Part III infinitely more effective.

Part Three

Cash Flow Rituals

Cash Flow Rituals

This section provides detailed instructions for conducting six different feng shui rituals to help increase your cash flow:

- COLLECTING COINS (page 126)
- COLLECTING WATER (page 131)
- WEALTH VASE (page 134)
- MONEY TREE (page 139)
- SEED MONEY (page 141)
- MONEY SPIRAL (page 144)

The Collecting Coins and Collecting Water rituals are based on BTB* methods; you will find variations of these cures in other sources. The Wealth Vase method is also widely used, with many variations. The Money Tree and Seed Money rituals are contemporary methods used by Western practitioners, and the Money Spiral is a new method that I created especially for this book.

The key factors in each ritual are your commitment to following through on a daily basis for the required period of time (nine or more consecutive days) and your strong intention to attract more prosperity into your life. Which ritual you choose is less important than is your consistent, daily, attentive repetition of the prescribed steps. Skipping or rushing through the empowerment process for each ritual would be like washing your hair without shampoo: you emerge from the shower feeling refreshed, but without having made a significant improvement.

---

* Black Sect Tibetan Buddhist feng shui

General Guidelines for Cash Flow Rituals

KEEP IT SIMPLE

I do not recommend that you try to do more than one of these methods at a time. Each ritual requires daily focus and attention; trying to do more than one at a time will divide your attention and weaken the process.

Cash flow cures can be very powerful, but that does not always translate into instantaneous results. Be patient as you are waiting for results, and don't assume that nothing is happening. Often the energy shifts start to happen invisibly long before there is any noticeable change in your circumstances.

Allow at least a month or more before trying another method (if you wish to do so). Rushing to start a new method as soon as one is completed implies that you don't trust the first one to work. And if you don't trust it to work, it probably won't. Six different methods are provided here so that you have a good variety of techniques to choose from; that doesn't mean you need to do them all.

TIMING

Good times to begin a cash flow ritual include:

- On the day of or shortly after the new moon
- Timed so the ritual will end on the day of a full moon
- Chinese New Year (solar or lunar)
- Your birthday or business anniversary
- Any other auspicious day as determined by either Chinese or Western astrology, if you follow either of those systems.

Do not do these rituals when Mercury or Mars is retrograde, as these influences tend to make a positive outcome less likely. (Astrological information is widely available on the Internet, or you can pick up a pocket guide for the year at most bookstores.)

ATTITUDE

As in all other feng shui methods, your attitude of confidence in a positive outcome is essential to the success of these cures. Be alert to thoughts or feelings of doubt or discouragements, and use the Heart Calming method and the visualization and scripting techniques that you learned in Part II to maintain your enthusiasm and detailed focus.

SPONTANEITY

Taking your ritual seriously doesn't mean you can't have fun with it. Doing a cash flow cure provides you with a daily opportunity to get into that state of mind and heart where you feel very positive about your future. Allow yourself to be guided by your intuition. If you feel moved to add something new in the middle of the ritual, or to adapt it to your specific needs or goals in some way, feel free to do so.

COMMITMENT & CONSISTENCY

Each of these rituals requires specific daily actions to be performed every day for a certain number of days. If you miss a day, you will need to start over again from the beginning, with fresh supplies. (You may want to wait until a new moon cycle before starting again.)

Missing a day means that you lost your focus. This could be due to external demands or situations that have distracted you, or from some inner resistance, doubt, or hesitation about manifesting a dramatic change in your financial circumstances.

If it's late at night and you are almost asleep when you realize you didn't complete the day's ritual yet, are you going to get back out of bed and do the ritual (with attention and focus, not just going through the motions so you can go to sleep!), or are you going to not bother with it because you are too tired? Perhaps you are simply not yet ready to fully commit to seeing the ritual through. That's okay. If you discover that you are not as ready to stick with it as you thought you would be, recognize that that's where you are at right now. Forcing yourself to continue when your heart is not in it is unlikely to lead to good results.

Collecting Coins

This is a slightly more detailed version of the BTB-inspired cash flow cure that I described in my first *Fast Feng Shui* book. Both versions are effective, as are other variations you may come across from other sources. With any ritual, the prescribed actions serve to focus your attention and intention on your desired outcome, and simple rituals can be just as effective as complex ones.

The Collecting Coins method requires making cash transactions daily. When we use debit and credit cards to pay for most things, the act of spending becomes rather vague and insubstantial. Instead of counting out and handing over cash, all you do is sign your name, or punch a few buttons on a keypad—actions that we often take in other contexts, such as signing a letter or making a phone call. I've updated the original ritual in ways that will help you pay a little more attention to cash and to your spending habits, and get you back in touch with the act of spending—and appreciating— your money.

Materials

- A new "piggy bank" or other container, preferably one that evokes wealth or prosperity in some way. This container must be new and purchased specifically to be used in this ritual. It should be large enough to hold a good quantity of coins.
- A 6" or 9" circle of red felt, velvet, or other fuzzy fabric (the nap helps money *chi* stick).
- A round mirror, slightly larger than the base of your bank or other container, 6" is usually a good size.
- A new red envelope, small enough to fit inside your container (it's okay to fold it, if necessary).

- A new pen with red, green, or purple ink, purchased specifically for this ritual.
- A recent photograph of you, small enough to fit inside the red envelope (it's okay to trim the photo to fit); "recent" means it was taken within the past 60 days. A casual snapshot is fine. If possible, choose a picture that shows you smiling and happy!

Preparation

- Place the mirror on top of the fabric and the bank or container on top of the mirror.
- Take the pen, inhale deeply and, while holding your breath, write on back of the photo: "Abundant prosperity comes to me now!" Add your signature (still holding your breath!) and slip the photo into the red envelope. Once the photo is in the envelope you may breathe normally again.
- Put the red envelope into the container.
- Place the fabric-mirror-box set in *hsun gua* of your prosperity altar, in *hsun gua* of your bedroom, or under your bed in the *hsun gua* position (the *hsun-li-kun* side of the *ba gua* is at the pillow end of the bed; *ken-kan-chien* is at the foot). If you share a bed, place the box where it will be under the base of your spine while you sleep (most people move around a little while sleeping, so this will be an approximate position).

Daily Procedure

Every day, for the next 27 days, you must *pay cash for all your normal daily transactions*. Do not use a credit or debit card to pay for: lunch, parking, movie tickets, groceries, haircuts, dry-cleaning, dinner, things from the hardware store, etc.

This "cash-only" policy does *not* apply to paying regular monthly bills: rent or mortgage, phone, utilities, making payments on your credit accounts, etc. It does apply to all other expenses, including impulse purchases. If you stop at an antique store during your weekend getaway to a friend's country home, and see an adorable console table for the bargain price of just $1700, pay in cash or don't buy it! (Following this rule will also force you to pay more attention to time. If you need to stop for gas on your way to work, you'll need to allow a few extra minutes to pay in cash, rather than using plastic at the pump.)

In addition to paying for your daily purchases with cash, you must also *save all the coins you receive in change for your purchases*. Do not spend any coins that you receive in change from a cash transaction. (Paper money received can go back in your wallet.) It's a good idea to carry some kind of change purse to collect these coins in every day.

Every night, for the duration of this ritual, you will add the day's coin harvest to your "piggy bank" or box. This must be done *before midnight*. Try to make at least one cash transaction every day, so you will have something to put in your bank/box. If you are unable to gather any coins on a particular day (such as if you are home with the flu), that's okay. Just do the IVAG empowerment process anyway:

Intention

As you place each day's coins in the container, focus on your intention to experience an increase in your cash flow.

Visualization

Take a moment to visualize your income steadily increasing, just like the quantity of coins accumulating in your box/bank.

Affirmation

Say: "My cash flow is increasing steadily every day," or a similar statement that affirms prosperity to you.

Gratitude

Focus on feeling appreciation for all of the transactions that you were able to make today, using the money that has already come to you. Give thanks in advance for all the future prosperity that is on its way to you.

These four steps, including gratitude for the blessings you expect to receive, are a very powerful process and an essential part of the ritual. Do not skip or rush through them.

After the 27th day, count up your coins, and make a donation to a charity of that exact amount (you can write a check, but don't use a credit card unless you pay your balance in full every month). By giving away what you've saved, you create a flow of money that continues to pull more in after you've finished the ritual. If you have done this ritual diligently, you could have a fairly sizable pile of cash by the time you are done. Go ahead and give it all away. You can use the IVAG method as you write and mail your donation check, to reinforce your intention that what you give comes back to you multiplied.

Leave your ritual container in *hsun gua* with nine or 27 coins in it (you can recirculate the other coins), and empower it to continue to attract a substantial flow of money into your life.

SUMMARY OF STEPS

1. Set up your container as described on page 127, and place it in your selected *hsun gua* location.
2. Every day, for 27 days, pay cash for all your daily transactions.
3. Collect the coins you receive in change; do not spend them!
4. Each night, before midnight, add the day's coins to your container and use the IVAG empowerment method.
5. After the 27 days are completed, give the money away to charity (it's okay to write a check), with the intention that even more will continue to flow in.
6. Keep the container in a place of honor in a *hsun gua* power spot.

Notes

- You can do the set-up steps in the evening, and start Day 1 on the following day. It's a good idea to mark Day 27 on your calendar so you will know when to stop.

- After set-up is complete, you can use the pen for any other purpose... except for doing this ritual again, in which case you will need a brand new pen.
- Be very clear and specific with your intention! The first time I did this cure, I just focused on more money coming in. It worked like a charm, and over the next few months my income increased by over 70%. The problem was that the new income came from a huge increase in my workload, so I was exhausted and stressed all the time. If there are limits to the hours you are willing to work, the number of clients you want to attract, and so on, be sure to include in your IVAG empowerment that the money comes to you with ease and in perfect ways.
- The original BTB method on which this variation is based instructs that at the end of the ritual the coins you collected must never be spent. I feel strongly that this creates a vibration of hoarding, which (as you know from Part II) can dry up your prosperity faster than anything. Also, in my view, money that you can't use is literally useless, so what should be a source of power instead becomes merely clutter—another feng shui no-no. Giving the money away at the end of the ritual is energetically far more powerful.
- You can make this ritual even more powerful by adding a 27-day follow-up period immediately after it. For 27 days (*i.e.*, days 28-54), give away some amount of money anonymously every day. If you choose to do this, you can give away the same coins that you collected, a few a day over 27 days, rather than giving one lump sum away.
- I believe this particular ritual becomes much more powerful if you keep it secret. I don't mean you can never tell anyone about it, ever, but do refrain from talking about it until you have completed it.
- Remember, *if you miss a day, you have to start all over again,* with new supplies (bank, pen, red envelope, etc.)!

Collecting Water

In this ritual you bring water—symbolizing money—from prosperous businesses into your home every day for nine consecutive days.

Materials

- A new small bottle with a tight-fitting cap, 2- to 4-ounce capacity, purchased specifically for this cure. You will carry this bottle with you for nine days, so it should not be too large, heavy, or fragile.
- A vase with a narrow neck, large enough to hold 8-12 ounces of water. This vase also should be new, purchased for this ritual. Green, dark blue, or purple are the best colors.
- A 6" or 9" circle of purple fabric.
- A 2" or 3" square of green or gold (metallic, not yellow) fabric.
- A piece of purple or red satin ribbon: 9" or 18" length, enough to wrap around the neck of the vase and tie a knot or bow.

Preparation

The vase represents your financial resources: income, investments, and bank accounts. The purple circle, with the green fabric square centered on top of it, goes underneath the vase. A square within a circle is the shape of a Chinese coin, and adds additional money energy to the cure.

Set up the vase in *hsun gua* in your living room or home office. I have seen a variation of this ritual that says to place the vase in the kitchen next to the stove. I do not recommend this because the stove represents FIRE element. FIRE and WATER are enemies, and you do not want your experience of prosperity to include conflict or arguments.

Daily Procedure

Each day, for nine consecutive days, go to a successful business location and collect an ounce or so of water, using the bottle you purchased for this ritual. When you get home at the end of the day, pour the water into the vase, following the IVAG steps:

INTENTION

As you pour the water into the vase, focus on allowing a strong flow of money into your life.

VISUALIZATION

Take a moment to visualize your financial resources steadily increasing, just like the water level rising in the vase.

AFFIRMATION

Say: "My financial resources are increasing steadily every day," or a similar statement that affirms prosperity to you.

GRATITUDE

Imagine that an abundant flow of money is already enriching your life in very specific ways. Experience a feeling of gratitude for all of the blessings that you are about to receive, even though they have not manifested yet.

On Day 9, after adding the day's water to the vase, tie the ribbon around the neck of the vase with the intention that it seals the money *chi* in the vase. This is so the vase will retain its symbolic power even after the water has evaporated.

Notes

The success of this method is in the details. Here are some important considerations:

- A small about of water is enough; more water does not equal more money. Pay attention to the capacity of your vase, and don't collect so much water that the vase fills up before the ninth day.

- Transfer the water from your collection bottle to the vase as soon as possible after you return home.
- It's a good idea to collect water from several different types of businesses, unless you are a business owner, in which case you may target businesses in your industry
- Banks, hotels, restaurants and stores are all appropriate places from which to collect water, as are successful small businesses such as yoga studios, beauty salons, etc.
- Do not collect water from bathrooms, religious institutions, hospitals or doctor's offices (unless you are a physician).
- Try not to attract attention as you collect the water.
- You may not *purchase* the water. Remember, your intention is to *attract* money, not spend it. If the waiter in a restaurant pours you a glass of water without being asked, you may use that water for this cure. If you have to *ask* for the water, it counts as a purchase.
- Drinking fountains are an easy source of water. Unfortunately, they are often located near bathrooms, which is less than ideal.
- Keep in mind that while the appearance of prosperity is a good clue, it can sometimes be misleading. Use your local knowledge to target businesses that you know are doing well.
- If you hear that a business from which you collected water within the past six months has gone out of business or filed for bankruptcy protection, it would be a good idea to toss out any water remaining in your vase and do the ritual again. Use a new bottle, vase, colored cloths, and ribbon if you repeat the ritual.

As you can see, this simple ritual is not so simple to do well. Plan to scout out potential water sources before starting the ritual, and be sure to locate one or two back-up locations, too. Careful planning, attention to detail and a certain degree of flexibility are all necessary, not only for this cure but for long-term financial success as well.

Wealth Vase

Many cultures have a tradition of keeping a wealth vase in the home to encourage financial abundance. Whether you create your own wealth vase or use one of the many kits available, a wealth vase is easy to assemble. While a kit of course offers great convenience, I believe that going to the extra effort to seek out, select, and purchase the individual components yourself creates the opportunity to imbue all of these elements with your own energy and intention.

Materials

Wealth vase kits come with all the materials (and instructions) included. The items included in the kit, as well as the instructions, are likely to vary somewhat from the information here. There is no one correct method, as multiple variations have evolved over the many centuries that wealth vases have been in use. As with all other feng shui cures and rituals, your own focused, dedicated intention is the key factor to success.

If you choose to create your own wealth vase without using a kit, you will need to acquire the materials listed on the next page, or similar items that have strong personal meaning of wealth and success for you. You do not have to use all of the items listed here, but you should include both real and symbolic money, a lucky figurine of some kind, real or symbolic gemstones, and several kinds of grains. Another option would be to purchase a kit and customize it with additional items that have personal significance for you.

That said, here's a list of power items that you could include in the ultimate wealth vase. If you don't have a local source for these items, visit the product pages at www.fastfengshui.com, where we have links to a variety of online vendors of feng shui supplies and accessories.

- A ceramic vase, preferably with a design that includes good luck symbols of some kind. (Many wealth vase kits include a blue and white vase with the Chinese double happiness symbol, but you can use a different design if you like, so long as the vase is attractive to you. Don't use a vase you don't like!) Some Asian vases come with a domed lid, but this is not required. Your vase should be at least 9″ tall, in order to hold all the other ingredients of the cure, without being completely filled up (space in the vase allows room for your money to grow). Do purchase a new vase to use just for this cure.
- A small handful of soil from the garden of a wealthy friend (kits won't include this, but if you can get some, use it). Exact amount doesn't matter.
- Money: some loose coins in your local currency, plus some foreign currency (to represent money coming to you from many places).
- A piece of yellow or gold fabric—preferably something elegant and rich-looking such as a brocade—a little larger than the width of the vase (9″ or 12″ square should be big enough, unless you are using a very large vase).
- Small figurine of a Chinese Wealth God, Laughing Buddha, Ganesh, Lakshmi, or other lucky deity of your choice.
- Chinese "gold" ingots: most often 1 large one and 6 smaller ones; 3, 6, or 9 small ones can also be used.
- Chinese coins (round, with a square hole in the middle and Chinese characters on one side; reproductions of ancient coins are widely available and acceptable to use here): 3, 6, 9, or 27 loose ones
- A few faux gemstones or crystals, or a piece of costume jewelry (such as a faux diamond bracelet), or a piece of quality jewelry (such as a gemstone ring) that you don't wear and are willing to donate to the cause.

- A set of three Chinese coins, tied with a red or gold ribbon, placed in a red envelope.
- A small globe (crystal is best, but not required).
- At least three different kinds of grains (five or six is better), such as rice, barley, millet, amaranth, dahl (split yellow mung beans), lentils, quinoa. A large spoonful of each is enough.
- Sandalwood incense (6 small cones is best, or break a stick of incense into 3 pieces), or sandalwood chips or dust.
- Semi-precious stone nuggets in colors that represent each of the five elements: (dark blue or black, green, red, yellow, and white). See page 173 for suggestions.
- A *ba gua* (or *pa kua*) coin: this has the same pattern of eight trigrams as the *ba gua* mirror shown on page 32. A Chinese zodiac coin can also be used; this includes the trigrams as well as representations of the 12 Chinese zodiac animals.
- 6-inch (or 18cm) squares of fabric, one each of the five element colors: (dark blue or black, green, red, yellow, and white). These should all be the same size, and large enough to cover the top of the vase and be tied around the vase neck.
- Narrow ribbon or heavy thread in the colors representing all five of the elements (dark blue or black, green, red, yellow, and white); length must be long enough to tie around the neck of the vase (preferably in a multiple of 9 inches or centimeters).

Assembly

1. Clean your vase inside and out with a damp cloth. If you can, place the vase in direct sunlight for a few minutes between 11AM and 1PM to symbolically purify and energize it.
2. Chant *om mani padme hum* into the vase 9 times.
3. Place the soil (if you are using it) in the bottom of the vase, and add your local and foreign currency.

4. Cover the soil and money with the larger piece of yellow/gold fabric.
5. On top of the fabric, place the other ingredients that you have chosen to use, in the order listed above—except for the set of five squares of colored fabric and the five-color thread or ribbon—ending with the *ba gua* or zodiac coin.
6. Chant *om mani padme hum* into the vase 9 more times.
7. If your vase has a lid, put it on.
8. Place the five pieces of colored cloth over the top of the vase, in this order: dark blue or black first, followed by green, red, yellow, and ending with white on top.
9. Tie the five colors of thread or ribbon around the neck of the vase, while chanting *om mani padme hum* 9 times. Fasten securely by knotting or braiding the ends together.

Placement

The wealth vase is a precious treasure, and should be kept in a place where visitors to the home will not see it, such as inside a cupboard or armoire. The best place for your vase is in *hsun gua* of the living room, to bring prosperity to your entire family. If that is not possible, choose a *hsun gua* power spot in the back half of the house. Do not keep your wealth vase near the front door.

Empowerment

Intention

As you position your wealth vase in its special spot, focus on your intention to experience a life filled with abundance.

Visualization

Visualize the wealth vase radiating prosperity *chi* to fill your entire home, with the result that you always have more than enough money to support and nurture yourself and your family. Think of specific details of what this will mean in terms of your daily experiences.

AFFIRMATION

Say: "I always have more than enough money to meet my needs," or a similar statement that affirms prosperity to you.

GRATITUDE

Stay with your imagined prosperity for a few more moments, focusing on feeling gratitude and appreciation for the new level of abundance the Wealth Vase will bring to you... even if it has not manifested yet.

Repeat this empowerment method every day for a total of nine days, to complete the ritual.

Maintenance

Once you have assembled your wealth vase, it should never again be opened! Take it out once a year on the Chinese New Year to dust or clean the outside, then return it to its place (unopened!). Re-empower it with the IVAG method.

Money Tree

If you don't have the time or attention to perform one of the more complex cash flow cures, here's a simpler method. *Hsun gua,* as you know is associated with "mature wood" as well as with money, so a money tree is an excellent addition to your *hsun gua* power spot.

Materials

- An indoor tree, such as a ficus, real or good quality artificial. Get the largest one you can afford. It should be in an attractive basket or pot, preferably black, dark blue, green, or purple. Avoid red, brown, yellow, or white.
- If you wish to improve active income from your work or business, a living tree is best. An artificial tree can be effective if you wish to encourage passive income (such as from investments).
- 27, 36, or 108 pieces of new paper money, in the denomination(s) of your choice. $1 is fine. The money does not have to be all of the same value.
- Lots of red string or narrow red ribbon: 9 inches for each day (27 or 108) that you plan to do this cure. You may cut all the pieces before you begin, or cut a new piece each day.

Procedure

1. Place the tree in *hsun gua* of your living room or office. Make sure that it is not exposed to any secret arrows (see pages 30-33). If a good *hsun gua* location is not possible, place the tree where it will be reflected in a mirror in *hsun gua.* (The mirror should be large enough to reflect all of the tree's branches.)

2. Every day, for 27 days, roll up one of the dollar bills (or whatever money you are using), tie it with a 9" length of red string or ribbon, and hang it from a branch of the tree.

3. Use the IVAG empowerment process daily:

   INTENTION

   As you hang money on the tree, intend that your prosperity will grow and multiply, like the branches of a tree.

   VISUALIZATION

   Take a moment to visualize a specific scene of financial abundance, in as much detail as you can.

   AFFIRMATION

   Say: "All of my efforts now bear the fruit of abundance," or a similar statement that affirms prosperity to you.

   GRATITUDE

   Imagine that an abundant flow of money is already enriching your life in very specific ways. Experience a feeling of gratitude for all of the blessings that you are about to receive, even though they have not manifested yet.

Maintenance

- If you use a living tree, make sure it gets the water and sunlight that it needs. If your tree does not stay healthy, your cure will be affected. If you use a living tree and it sickens or dies, use some kind of space clearing method in that area (pages 29-30) and start again with a larger tree or switch to an artificial one.
- If you use an artificial tree, dust it from time to time.
- If any of your money falls off, replace it will a new bill, using a new piece of ribbon, rather than rehanging the old one.

Seed Money

This cure is more powerful than you might expect, given its simplicity. I like this one because it so strongly incorporates an attitude of appreciation and gratitude, which is one of the most essential aspects for living a life of abundance.

Materials

- 36 small red envelopes (these must be new, purchased especially for this cure)
- 36 pieces of money (coins or paper, in your local currency, any denomination)
- 36 sheets of paper, and a pen; any kind of paper will do, but why not use something a little special?
- Uncooked rice or birdseed (a half cup or so)
- A new houseplant, attractive artificial plant, or a plant to go in the ground. (This is for day 36, so if you are planning to use a living plant wait until close to that time to purchase it.)

Procedure

1. Every day, for 36 consecutive days, make a list of 9 things that you would like to have or receive. Write this list by hand on a piece of paper. Do not use your Prosperity Journal for this (unless you want to tear the pages out), and don't type it on the computer; it should be hand-written.

1. Turn the paper over and on the other side list 9 things that you are grateful for having or experiencing.

2. Put the list in a red envelope.

3. Add a coin or piece of paper money to the envelope; the amount does not matter.

4. Place the envelope in a *hsun gua* power spot. You may wish to use a bag or box to collect the total of 36 envelopes. Take a moment to imagine that you have received the items on your wish list, focusing on specific details and with a feeling of appreciation and gratitude.

5. At the end of the 36 days, collect all your red envelopes and take out the notes and money. Set the money aside, and read through your lists. If you received anything that was on one of your lists, cross it out and write "thank you!" beside it.

6. Tear the lists and the red envelopes (not the money!) into very small pieces. If this is physically difficult for you, you may use scissors, or run them through a shredder (be sure to catch all the pieces), but it is best to do this by hand if you can.

7. Mix the torn bits of the envelope and lists with the rice or birdseed, and bury this mixture in *hsun gua* of your back yard. Either plant a living plant on top of the paper/seed, or place a potted living or artificial plant over it.

8. Use the IVAG empowerment method:

   INTENTION

   As you plant your money seeds, have the strong intention to experience all of the things that you wish to receive.

   VISUALIZATION

   Take a moment to imagine that the things you desire have already manifested for you. Focus on specific details that will make it seem real to you.

AFFIRMATION

Say: "The money seeds that I have planted bring me a bountiful harvest of financial abundance," or a similar statement that affirms prosperity to you.

GRATITUDE

Focus for a few moments on the gratitude you feel for blessings that you have already received, and for those that you are about to receive.

9. Give all the money away anonymously within three days.

Notes

- You do not have to come up with all new items for your lists every day, but if you think of new things be sure to include them.
- Your daily lists do not have to include everything you want or are grateful for, but they must each have nine entries.
- If you live in an apartment, put the paper shreds/birdseed mixture into the bottom of a potted plant (living or artificial) in *hsun gua* of your apartment or living room.

Money Spiral

Three pieces of paper money and a length of satin ribbon create a Money Spiral to attract an ever-increasing flow of prosperity into your life.

Preparation

For this ritual, you will be using three pieces of paper money of three different values, such as: $1, $5, $10; $5, $10, $20; or $1, $10, $100 (or appropriate sets of your local currency). The last option is the most powerful, because each increment multiplies by 10. This implies fast growth for the next numbers in the sequence.

Choose amounts that will be a bit of a stretch for you. For example, if you often carry $20 bills in your wallet, but only rarely have $50s or $100s, choose one of those larger amounts as your highest number.

You will be acquiring this money during the first three days of the ritual; do not use money that you already have. On Day 1, you will acquire one piece of your smallest amount of currency. This can be through payment received, change from a cash transaction, cashing a check, ATM withdrawal, etc. On Day 2, you will acquire the middle value of currency, and on Day 3, the third value. Plan in advance what amounts you are going to use and how you will obtain them.

The only other item you will need for this ritual is a 27″ piece of purple or red satin ribbon; 1" is a good width.

Procedure

DAY 1

During the day be sure to collect one piece of paper currency in the smallest amount you have planned to use.

In the evening, lay the ribbon out on a table with one end in front of you (if your ribbon has only one satin/smooth side, place it with that side down). Place the money the long way on top of the ribbon at one end. Roll up the money so the extra ribbon wraps up around it. Tuck the end of the ribbon under so it won't unroll, leaving a little tail an inch or so long hanging loose.

Use the IVAG empowerment method to focus on your intention to attract ever-increasing amounts of money into your life:

Intention

Hold the rolled-up money in your hands for a moment and focus on the extra ribbon acting like a symbolic "red carpet" welcoming a steady flow of prosperity into your life.

Affirmation

Say aloud: "Ever-increasing abundance comes to me now!"

Visualization

Imagine in as much detail as possible what it will be like to have more money coming in.

Gratitude

Once you have shifted to a feeling of "this is so great, this feels so good!," take a few more moments to express or just be with your gratitude for having received this abundance as though it has already come to you.

These four steps, including gratitude for the blessings you expect to receive, are a very powerful process and an essential part of the ritual. Do not skip or rush through them. When you are done, place the rolled-up money on your prosperity altar or in a power spot overnight.

DAY 2

Take the rolled-up money with you in your purse or pocket as you go about your business for the day. If you work at home, place it in *hsun gua* of your desk while you are working, and take it with you if you leave the house.

During the day you will need to collect one piece of the middle value of currency you have chosen to use. In the evening, unroll the ribbon and place today's money next to the first bill with the edges touching or overlapping slightly. Now roll up both bills and tuck the end of the ribbon under with a little bit hanging out just as you did on Day 1.

Repeat the IVAG empowerment steps from the previous page, then place the rolled-up money on your home altar, or in a prosperity power spot overnight.

DAY 3

Take the rolled-up money with you in your purse or pocket as you go about your business. During the day you will collect one piece of the highest value of currency you have chosen to use. In the evening, unroll the ribbon and add the money that you acquired today, placing it next to the second bill with the edges touching or overlapping.

Roll up all three bills and tuck the loose end of the ribbon under with a little bit hanging out. You now have a spiral of money, getting larger and larger from the inside out. The extra length of ribbon provides space for even greater amounts of money to manifest for you. (You won't literally be adding to the spiral; this is a symbolic space!)

Repeat the IVAG empowerment steps, then place the rolled-up money on your home altar, or in a prosperity power spot overnight.

DAYS 4-12

Each morning, take a moment to hold the strong intention that the Money Spiral will attract money to you during the day. Carry it with you throughout the day. When you get home at night, place the Money Spiral on your altar or on a prosperity power spot. Do the IVAG empowerment in whatever way feels good to you. You can use the same mental imagery and affirmation every day, or vary them as inspiration guides you. If some financial good fortune came to you during the day, be sure to include that specific incident in your gratitude focus.

After Day 12, you can continue to carry the Money Spiral with you during the day if you desire, or place it in a position of honor in a *hsun gua* power spot. You can also repeat the IVAG empowerment for a few minutes each day for as long as you want.

Other Considerations

- If you have to travel during these twelve days, or spend a night away from home, leave the Money Spiral in your pocket or purse at night. Do take a few moments at the end of the day to visualize that you attract more and more money everywhere you go, and to do the empowerment process.
- If you miss a day, unroll the spiral and spend the money. Burn or discard the ribbon, and start over.
- If you lose the Money Spiral or it is stolen from you, something about your energy, beliefs, or expectations is not in alignment with attracting money. Take some time for inner work if necessary before beginning the ritual again.

Closing Words

Whether this is your first venture into the exciting world of feng shui, or you are an experienced veteran, I hope this book has opened up new ways of understanding your inner and outer realities and the effects they both have on your life experience.

Approaching feng shui as a path to self-discovery and transformation has enabled me to transform my own life experience in ways that ten years ago I could barely have imagined. I hope that in some way this book will do the same for you, and that your feng shui adventures will be as extraordinary, delightful, and empowering as mine have been.

There is only so much that an author can fit into a book, and you may have questions about feng shui that were not answered here. I recommend a visit to the FAQs pages at FastFengShui.com. While there, you can subscribe to my newsletter and receive twice-monthly feng shui information by email. We are also expanding our product pages to include a great collection of feng shui products and accessories that I have personally selected from many separate vendor websites, so you can access them all from one convenient source. If you're looking for that special cure, just visit www.FastFengShui.com and click on the Products link on the menu bar.

One of the things I like best about the Western style of feng shui is the flexibility it provides for using creative and personal cures and empowerments. If you have come up with your own quirky ritual or a fun way to activate a prosperity power spot, let me know. If you have an idea for a unique activation or cure, but aren't sure if it's a good one, I'd be happy to offer my opinion. And if you'd just like to share with me what you thought of the book, I want to hear that, too.

You may contact me by email at Stephanie@FastFengShui.com. (I often receive more email than I can answer promptly, so do please be patient as you wait for a reply.)

Your Feng Shui Toolbox

APPENDICES

A. The Ba Gua

B. The Five Elements

C. Lucky Numbers

D. Wealth Symbols

E. More Feng Shui Cures
& Accessories

Appendix A.
The Ba Gua

The *ba gua* (*ba*: eight; *gua*: area) is a map of the energetic influences in your space. It is traditionally shown as an octagon with eight sections surrounding a central area called the *tai chi*.

For practical use, we extend the corners of the *ba gua* to form a square, then divide it into nine equal sections:

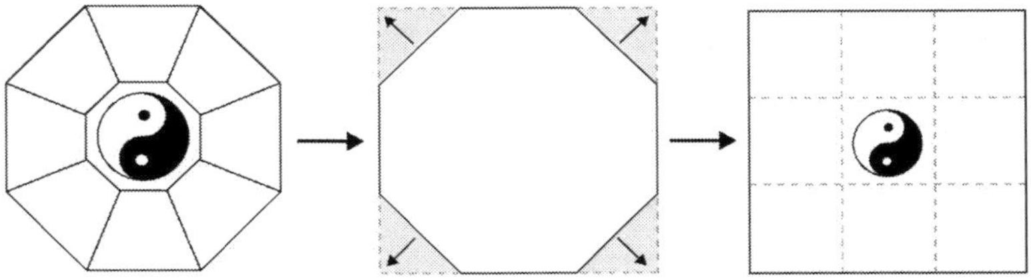

The *ba gua* divides any space into these nine areas, each of which corresponds to a different aspect of your life (see diagram next page). Whatever is going on energetically—good or bad—in each section of your space will affect the related area of your life.

Every space has a *ba gua*. There is a *ba gua* for your plot of land, a *ba gua* for your house or apartment, and a *ba gua* for each room within your home. You can even apply the *ba gua* to your desk, bed, or stove.

Meanings of the Ba Gua

The *ba gua* is rich with meanings and associations. The primary meanings of the *guas* are shown in the chart on the next page. You do not need to memorize the Chinese names, but they are a good reminder that each *gua* has many meanings. For example, many people think of *hsun gua* as just the "wealth corner." The more appropriate name for this *gua* is "Fortunate Blessings," which implies that prosperity and abundance are about more than money. Anything that you consider to be a blessing is related to this area. *Hsun gua* also has to do with your ability to receive and enjoy those things that come into your life.

When we apply feng shui to increasing our prosperity, *hsun gua* gets a lot of attention. However, all of the *guas* are important, and each has a role in helping you attract and appreciate prosperity, as is explored in detail in Part II of this book.

WEALTH **(*hsun*)** **Abundance** **Fortunate blessings** **Ability to receive**	FAME (*li*) Your reputation What you are famous (or infamous) for	RELATIONSHIPS (*kun*) Marriage Partnerships Everything feminine Your mother
FAMILY (*jen*) New beginnings Your ability to initiate Health Community	HEALTH (*tai chi*) Life balance (whatever happens here affects all *guas*)	CREATIVITY (*dui*) Your children Your ability to complete things
SELF- UNDERSTANDING (*ken*) Knowledge & learning Your spiritual life Self-awareness	CAREER (*kan*) Your life path Communication Social connections Wisdom	HELPFUL FRIENDS (*chien*) Benefactors/mentors Support systems Travel Your father

THE BA GUA AND COMPASS DIRECTIONS

Sometimes you will see the *ba gua* labeled with compass directions, with north at *kan* (career), and south at *li* (fame). In the Chinese system north is at the bottom, and south at the top, which is the opposite of how most of us in the West are accustomed to seeing maps.

This makes sense when you understand that north is associated with winter, darkness, stillness, cold, and midnight, and that south is associated with summer, brightness, movement, heat, and midday. When energy is cold and still, it settles; warm, active energy rises. East is at the left side of the *ba gua*, associated with springtime, increasing light, warmth, growth, and morning. West, on the right, is associated with autumn, lessening light, cooling, decay, and twilight. Thus the *ba gua* describes the ever-changing, never-ending cycle of birth, growth, decay, death, and rebirth.

In traditional Chinese feng shui, the *ba gua* is aligned according to the compass directions:

COMPASS	GUA	MEANING
North	*kan*	career, social connections
Northeast	*ken*	self-understanding, spirituality
East	*jen*	family, community, health
Southeast	*hsun*	wealth, fortunate blessings
South	*li*	fame, reputation
Southwest	*kun*	relationships, romance
West	*dui*	creativity, children
Northwest	*chien*	helpful friends, travel

This is a source of confusion, because in Western feng shui we align the *ba gua* with the main entry, not to the compass.* When you use the compass to place the *ba gua*, *hsun gua* might be in the front of one room, the back of another, and off to the right (or left) in a different space.

Fast Feng Shui follows the modern practice of placing the *ba gua* according to the doorway, because our physio-emotional experience of a space is determined by how we enter and move through that space, not by the compass directions. With this method, every time you step into a space you will know exactly where *hsun gua* is: the far left corner relative to the doorway.

If you have used the compass placement of the *ba gua* in the past, I suggest that you give the contemporary method a try to see what additional insights you may gain about your space. Think of the compass

* How to place the *ba gua* using the doorway method is explained in detail on the following pages.

directions as adding a second layer of understanding to your *ba gua*. For example, if your *hsun gua*—determined by the doorway—happens to be in the western corner of the room, that's a great place for feng shui enhancements to support prosperity through creative work.

Placement of the Ba Gua

YOUR PROPERTY BA GUA

The *ba gua* for your property is aligned so the bottom edge is along the street side of your yard, because your driveway is the entry or "doorway" to your property. The street end of your driveway will be in the self-understanding (*ken*), career (*kan*), or helpful friends (*chien*) area.

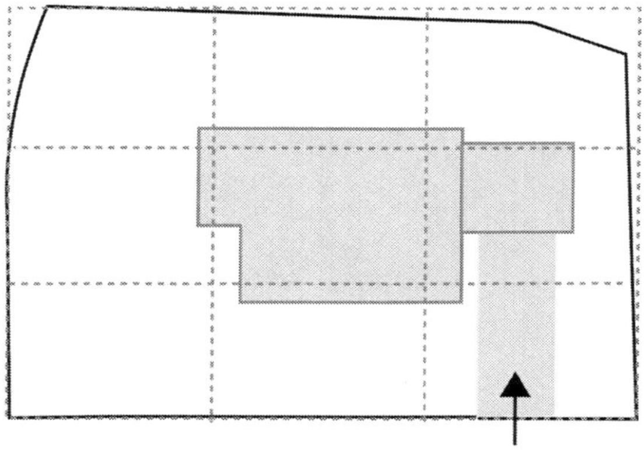

Stretch the *ba gua* sideways and lengthwise to cover the entire property. It's likely that parts of your property will not match the edges of the *ba gua* neatly. That's okay; aim for the closest match you can, and we'll address what to do about the untidy bits a few pages further on.

YOUR HOUSE OR APARTMENT BA GUA

To apply the *ba gua* to your home, align the bottom edge with the front door. Even if you usually enter your home through the garage or a back or side door, always align the *ba gua* to the front door. Now, stretch (or shrink) the *ba gua* to cover your entire space.

An attached garage which has a direct entry into the house is included in the house *ba gua*:

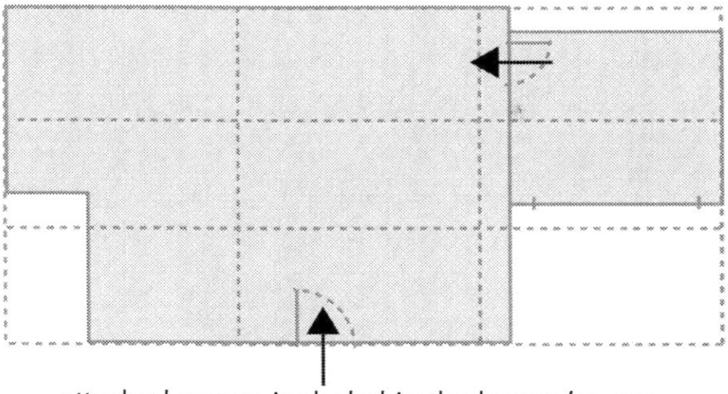

attached garage included in the house *ba gua*

If your garage is detached or it if does not provide direct access into the house, it is considered a separate structure (even if it shares a wall with the house) and is not included in the house *ba gua*:

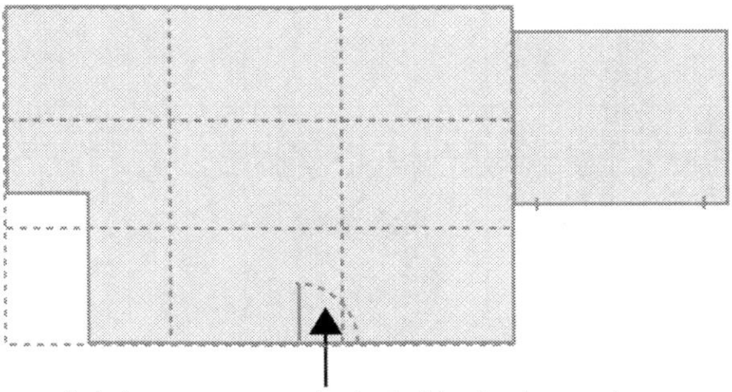

adjoining garage not included in the house *ba gua*

RECESSED ENTRY

Where there is a recessed entry, parts of the structure stick out in front of the doorway. These areas are extensions of *ken* (self understanding), *kan* (career), and/ or *chien* (helpful friends) *guas*.

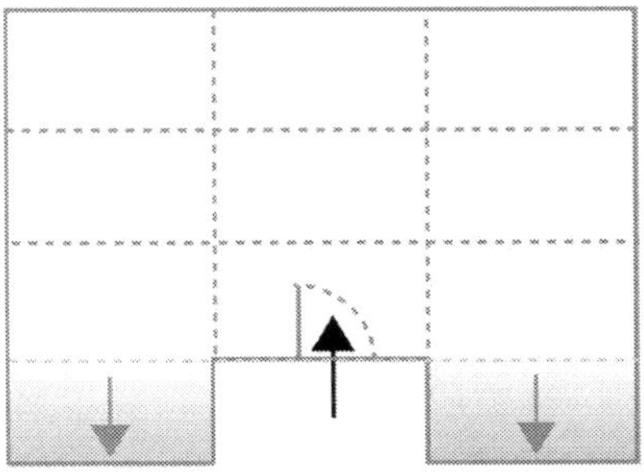

PROTRUDING ENTRY

Sometimes the entry itself sticks out from the main structure. If seems "tacked on" to the house (such as a small mud room on the side of a two-story house), place the *ba gua* over the main body of the house, with the entry as an extension (diagram A).

More common in apartments is a front hallway that leads to the rest of the unit. In this case, the door marks the point where you step from the common areas of the building into your unit, and the *ba gua* should start at the door. This creates a gap along rest of the front of the *ba gua* (diagram B), which should be treated as a "missing area."

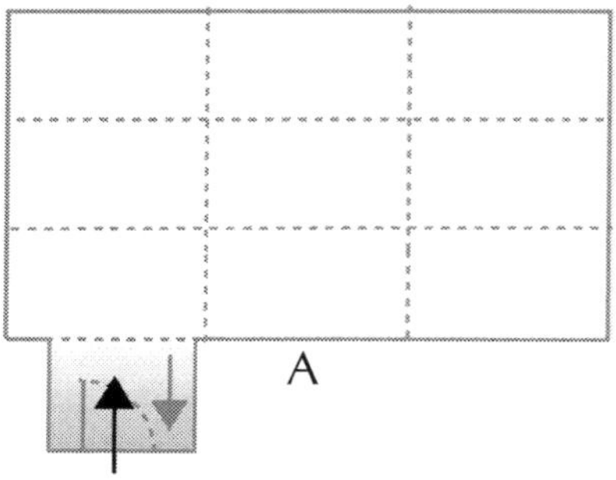
A

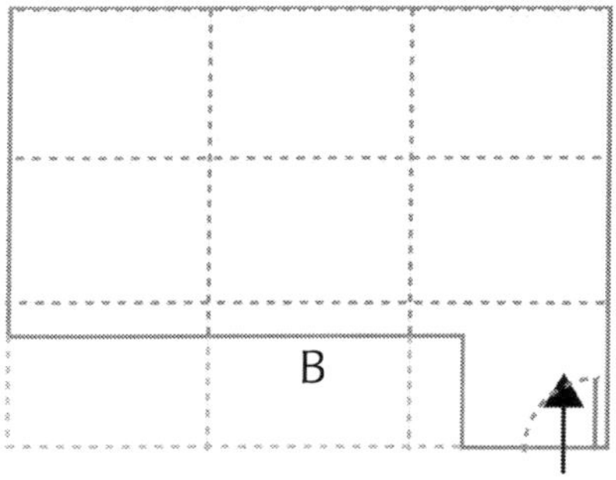
B

EXTENSIONS & MISSING AREAS

An extension is a part of the home that sticks out from the rest of the structure. The part that sticks out must be less than one-half the total length or width of that side of the house or room to be considered an extension.

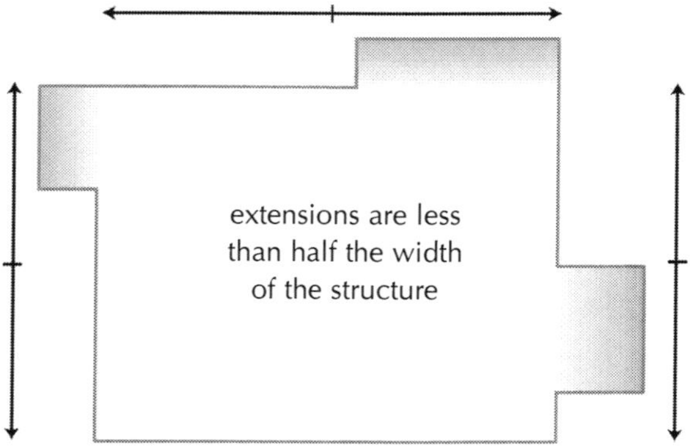
extensions are less
than half the width
of the structure

An extension increases the energy of that *gua*. An extension in *hsun gua* is a good place for feng shui enhancements.

A missing area is a place where there is a "bite" out of the floor plan of your home. This gap must be less than one-half the total length or width of that side of the house or room to be considered missing.

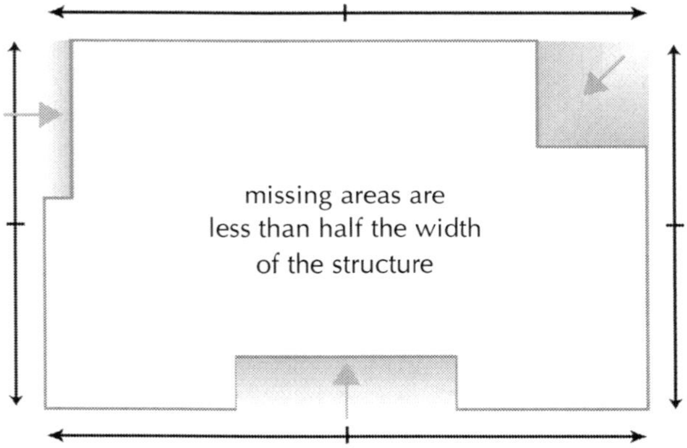
missing areas are
less than half the width
of the structure

A missing area weakens the energy of the affected *gua(s)*. If your home is missing part of *hsun gua*, your finances are likely to be adversely affected.

Although the space created by a protruding entry may not technically qualify as a missing area, you should treat it as one anyway, and take some kind of corrective measures, as described on the next page.

IRREGULARLY SHAPED HOMES

If your home's shape is irregular, it may be difficult or impossible to tell whether you've got missing areas, extentions or both. Very irregularly shaped homes always have unbalanced *ba guas*, so if a particular area of your life seems unsupported (such as your prosperity), it's a good idea to work with the *ba guas* for the major rooms in the home—the kitchen, living room, bedroom, and home office. Look for ways to strengthen and enhance *hsun gua* of those areas (see Principle 7, pages 42-48 for suggestions).

Exterior Cures for a Missing Area

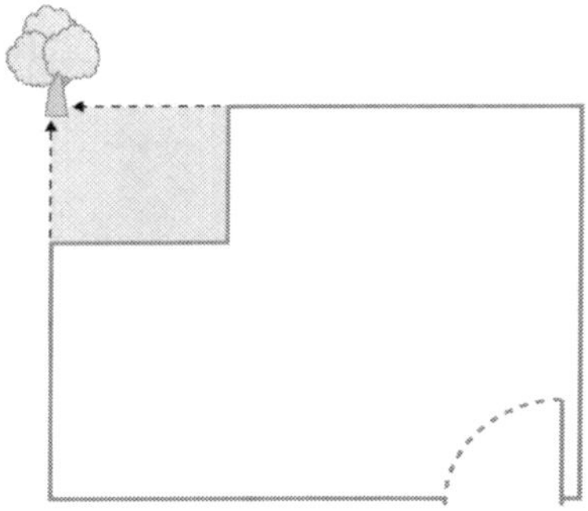

You can correct a missing area by placing a light, flag pole, bird bath, large stone, statue, or tree in the exact spot where the corner of the building would be if the area were complete. You can also use a floral border, hedge, or fence to complete the area. For a missing area in *hsun gua*, a tree, hedge, floral border, flag pole, or water feature will be most effective.*

Your placement must be very accurate for the cure to be effective. A few inches out of alignment will make a difference! If a porch, deck, or patio fills the missing space, use lights or plants to define the outside edges of the space.

Interior Cures for a Missing Area

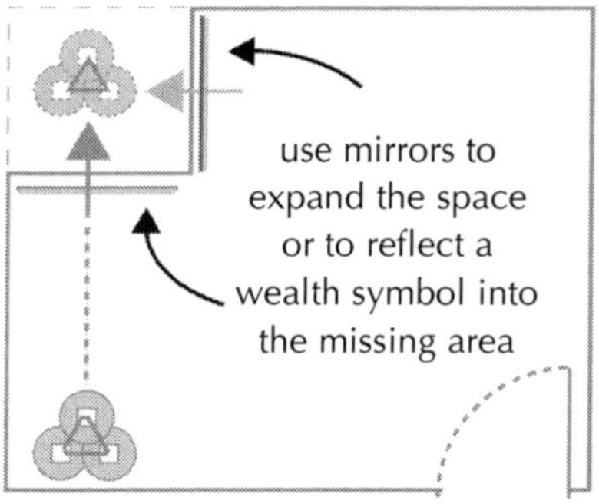
use mirrors to
expand the space
or to reflect a
wealth symbol into
the missing area

Where using an exterior cure is not possible, you can correct a missing area from inside the home by using mirrors to virtually expand the interior space into the missing area.

For even better effect, place symbolic imagery related to your goals—such as a wealth symbol from Appendix D—where it will be reflected in the mirror.

* These are WOOD- and WATER-type cures that will support the WOOD energy of *hsun gua*. For more information on the element energies used in feng shui, see Appendix B.

Another good way to balance a missing *hsun gua* is to place wealth imagery or objects (see Appendix D for ideas) in *hsun gua* of each major room within the house.

THE BA GUA FOR A ROOM

To apply the *ba gua* to a room, place the bottom edge at the doorway wall, and adjust the size to fit the space. As you stand in the doorway facing into the space, *hsun gua* is always to the far left. If there is more than one way to enter a space, orient the *ba gua* to the most prominent entryway architecturally. If the entries are equal, choose the one that is used more frequently. If you still aren't sure, use the doorway that opens into the more active area of the home.

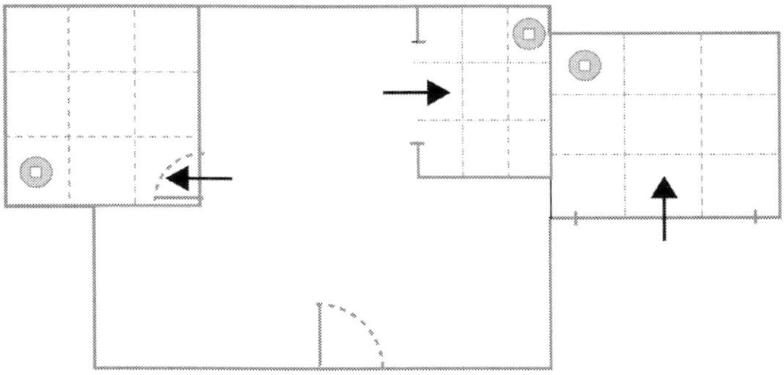

= *hsun gua* of the room

Sometimes you will find an extension or a missing area when you look at the *ba gua* of a particular room. This will strengthen or weaken the affected *gua(s)* within that room, but does not affect the entire house.

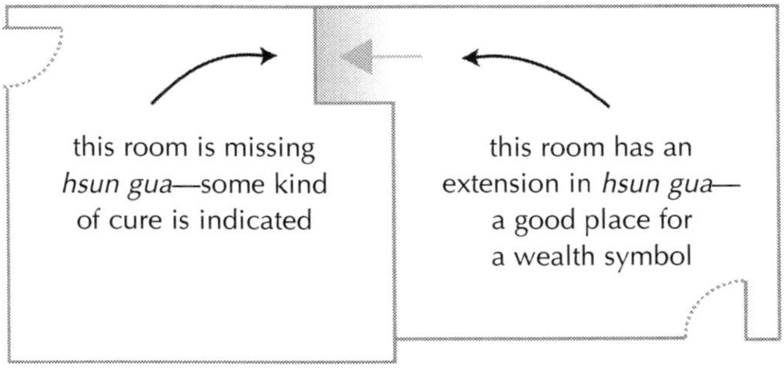
this room is missing
hsun gua—some kind
of cure is indicated
this room has an
extension in hsun gua—
a good place for
a wealth symbol

Appendix B.
The Five Elements

The five elements describe five essential qualities of *chi*, which you can use to enhance, control, or balance a space, depending on your needs:

- Wood—the quality of upward growth, easy progress; too much can make you aggressive or impatient, lacking in compassion
- Fire—the quality of excitement, expansion, quickness; too much can leave you stressed out and anxious
- Earth—the quality of settling down, being receptive; too much leads to depression, sluggishness, feeling stuck or weighed down
- Metal—the quality of contraction, sharpness, focus; when too strong, can make you sharp-tongued and critical
- Water—the quality of flowing, making connections; too much can make you "wishy-washy" and indecisive

Each element can help shift your energy and the energy of your space, and you can use this when you address prosperity issues:

- Metal helps you concentrate and get things done; its inward focus helps you reassess matters when you need to move on from a situation that is no longer working for you.
- Water is helpful when things have been stuck for a while (think of ice melting), and for improving communication, so it's helpful for networking and creating opportunities.
- Wood energy is associated with new beginnings, and it can help you make smooth progress with a new job, project, or career.
- Fire creates heat and action, and is the energy to use when you want to increase excitement and intensity.

- EARTH energy is good when you need more stability in work situations or business relationships, or are dealing with issues of commitment and integrity.

Element Shapes and Colors

Each element is associated with specific shapes, colors, and materials. For example, green colors, tall shapes, and house plants all add the "easy growth" energy of WOOD to a prosperity power spot.

- WOOD—greens and light blues; tall narrow shapes; plants and flowers
- FIRE—reds, purples, bright oranges; triangles, flame shapes and other pointed or angular shapes; candles and lights
- EARTH—browns, yellows, beige; low, square shapes; ceramics
- METAL—white, gold, silver, grey; round and oval shapes, arches; coins and metallic objects
- WATER—black, dark blue; curvy, irregular, and wave-like shapes; water features, fountains, and fish tanks

Sometimes determining which element(s) an item represents is not as obvious as you might think. For example, a mahogany dining table is made out of WOOD, but it is square, flat, and brown in color. In energetic terms, then, it has more EARTH energy than WOOD energy, because the wood is no longer vital and growing, and the table's shape and color are associated with EARTH. A candle is a good example of the FIRE element, but a tall green candle also has a WOOD shape and color.

Many items have a combination of qualities, so you will need to use your own judgment about how much of what kind of influence it will have on your space. Try not to go nuts puzzling over what element something represents. If it's not clear right away, then chances are good it combines several different qualities and will not have as strong an impact on your space.

Keep in mind that function, placement, and your own intention are important, too. If you worry so much about choosing the right elements that you no longer enjoy your possessions, you're trying too hard! Feng shui should be easy, graceful, and fun. If you love something, it has good *chi* for you.

Element Cycles: How the Energies Interact

The five elements interact with each other in very specific ways, as described below and on the following pages.

THE CREATIVE CYCLE

Each of the elements is nourished, supported, or "fed" by one of the other elements. This forms a sequence called the Creative (or Productive) cycle, as shown in the diagram below. Use the Creative cycle when you want to increase the effect of an element in a particular space. Here's how it works:

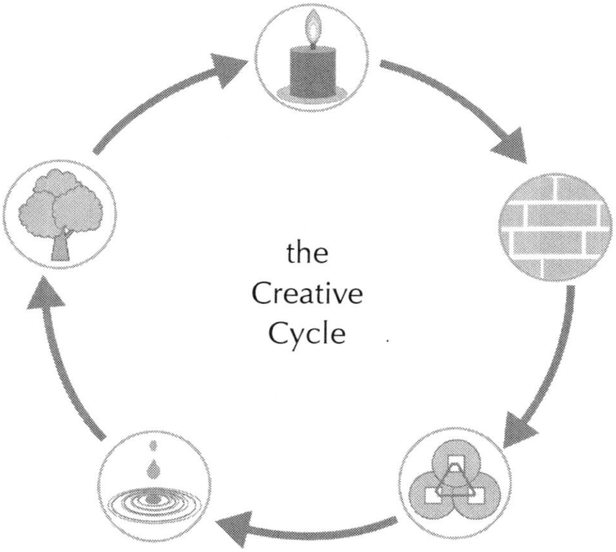

- Wood feeds FIRE (without fuel, fire cannot burn)
- Fire creates EARTH (as the fire burns, it produces a pile of ashes; think of a volcano creating a mountain)
- Earth produces METAL (metal is extracted from the earth)
- Metal produces WATER (think of moisture condensing on a cold can of soda on a hot day)
- Water nourishes WOOD (without water, wood will die)

THE REDUCING CYCLE

As each element feeds or nourishes the next in the Creative cycle, its own energy is reduced by the effort. For example, you can counteract the strong WATER energy in a bathroom by adding WOOD energy to the space (green towels, for example). This gives the WATER something to do (feeding WOOD), reduces its strength, and helps bring things back into balance. Here's how the Reducing cycle works:

- WOOD reduces WATER
- WATER reduces METAL
- METAL reduces EARTH
- EARTH reduces FIRE
- FIRE reduces WOOD

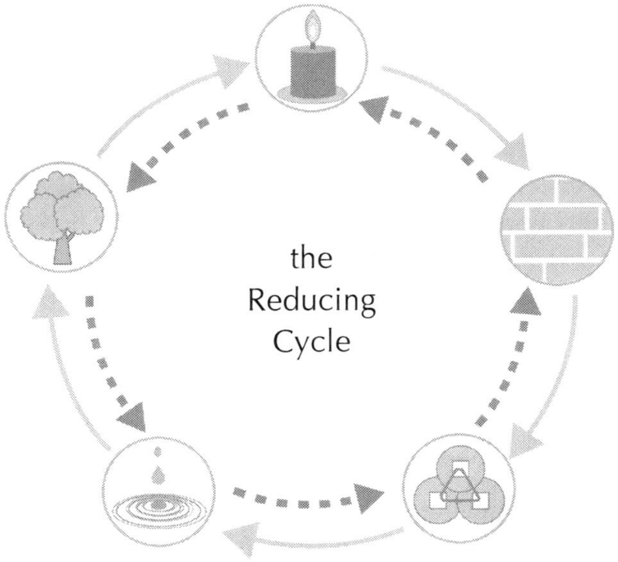

Use the Reducing cycle when you want a gentle way to bring a situation into better balance. It's easy to remember the Reducing cycle if you know the Creative cycle; just keep in mind that when one element nourishes another one, its own energy is reduced by the effort.

The Elements and the Ba Gua

Each *gua* is associated with one of the elements, as shown below. There are three EARTH *guas* (including the *tai chi*), two WOOD and two METAL *guas*, and one *gua* each for WATER and FIRE. The element of each *gua* determines the color or colors associated with it.

The colors for *hsun gua* are green and purple, green is for wood and purple is symbolic of great success and wealth. *Jen gua* (family) is associated with lighter shades of green. *Kun gua*, the relationship area, is red, pink, and white, because it is located between *li gua* (fame; red) and *dui gua* (creativity; white), and because pink is the color of romance. *Chien gua*, (helpful friends; metal) is grey, because it is located between white *dui gua* and black *kan gua* (career). Browns and other earth tones are appropriate for *ken gua* (self-understanding). Because of its postion between *kan* (black) and *jen* (green), blues are also appropriate here.

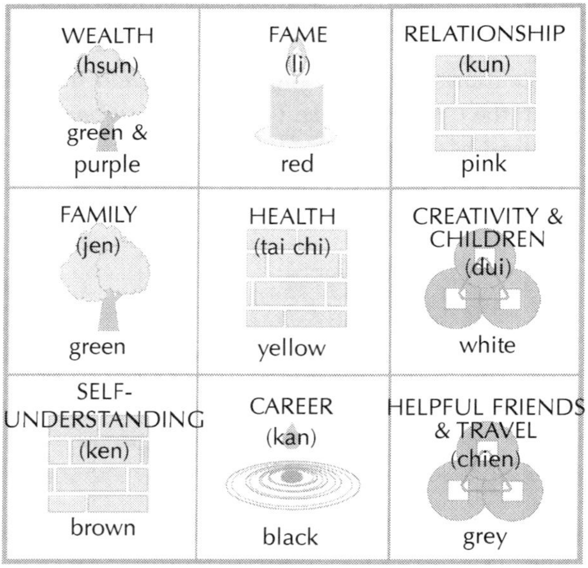

WEALTH
(hsun)
green &
purple
FAME
(li)
red
RELATIONSHIP
(kun)
pink
FAMILY
(jen)
green
HEALTH
(tai chi)
yellow
CREATIVITY &
CHILDREN
(dui)
white
SELF-
UNDERSTANDING
(ken)
brown
CAREER
(kan)
black
HELPFUL FRIENDS
& TRAVEL
(chien)
grey

Each element is naturally strong in some *guas* and weak in others, information that you can use to fine-tune your feng shui adjustments. See the Five Elements Reference Chart on the next page for details.

FIVE ELEMENTS REFERENCE CHART

	WOOD	FIRE	EARTH	METAL	WATER
QUALITIES	uplifting growing initiating	active radiating empowering	settling grounding stabilizing	focused internal analyzing	flowing connecting communicating
COLORS	greens, light blues	red purples hot oranges	browns yellows beiges	silver, gold, metallic white, grey	black dark blues
SHAPES	tall narrow upright striped	triangular pointed sharp jagged	square rectangular flat hollow	round oval curved arcs	wavy irregular sinuous
STRONG IN	jen hsun kan	li jen hsun	ken kun tai chi li	dui chien ken kun	kan dui chien
WEAK IN	dui chien li	kan ken kun	jen hsun dui chien	li kan	ken kun jen hsun
CREATES	fire	earth	metal	water	wood
REDUCES	water	wood	fire	earth	metal
CONTROLS	earth	metal	water	wood	fire
CONTROLLED BY	metal	water	wood	fire	earth

Appendix C.
Lucky Numbers

As you may have noticed, feng shui cures and rituals very often use three, nine, or multiples of nine for quantities, measurements, or repetitions. Incorporating these lucky numbers into your feng shui cures and rituals helps increase their power and ensure their effectiveness.

3 The number three has special meaning in virtually every culture, symbolizing transcendence of the division of unity (one) into duality (two). Three is the number of trinity in all its forms: heaven, earth, and man; mother, father, child; mind, body, spirit; as well as the sacred trinity of Christianity's Father, Son, and Holy Spirit, to name a few.

9 Nine symbolizes completion and achievement. It is the highest single-digit number, as well as deriving special power as the result of 3x3. Nine is the most-commonly used number in feng shui for repetitions of mantras and other empowerment methods. All multiples of nine are considered powerful numbers for feng shui purposes, as the individual digits making up these numbers also add up to nine:
18 (1+8 = 9); 27 (2+7 = 9); 36 (3+6 = 9); etc.

27 Twenty-seven is even more powerful than nine because it multiplies the power numbers of 3 and 9 together. Feng shui rituals are often performed for a total of 27 days to ensure the best effect.

108 One hundred and eight is a number of great spiritual power. Malas and other prayer beads usually have 108 beads, often divided into four groups of 27. Repeating a mantra or ritual 108 times demonstrates your commitment to transformation.

Appendix D.
Wealth Symbols

This section is an alphabetical guide to a variety of wealth symbols from both Asian and Western cultures, along with suggestions for how to use them for best effect. In fact, any object or image that represents prosperity, abundance, ease, or success to you can be a powerful wealth symbol for your home or office.

Whatever wealth symbols you choose to use should be aesthetically and energetically appealing to you. If your dream is to own a sleek black Jaguar sedan, place a photograph of this car in *hsun gua* to inspire you. However, if you have no interest in luxury automobiles, this image would not have much power for you.

The more prominently your wealth symbols are displayed, the more important it is that you are satisfied with how they look in your space. If you like an eclectic decorating style, then adding Asian cures will not be a problem, so long as you have some understanding of what the image represents. If you wish to use a traditional cure but don't like how it looks with your decor, one option is to use a smaller size that can be placed inconspicuously on a shelf or inside a drawer.

Always be guided first by your intuition when choosing feng shui cures. If you are strongly attracted to a particular image, then it will be a powerful addition to your home regardless of the style of your décor. For example, if you live in a classic center-hall colonial home with very traditional furnishings, a lucky money frog could look quite out of place at your front door and you may want to choose something else instead. However, if a lucky money frog strongly appeals to you in spite of your home's décor, then go ahead and use it. It may be a sign that the traditional style of your home doesn't truly reflect who you are, and that you've been too firmly guided by convention in your life choices until now. Sometimes what you need is to try something really different, rather than doing things the same old way.

Acorns

The tiny acorn, from which a huge oak tree grows, is a symbol of great potential. Real acorns have strong natural energy, or you could purchase wooden ones from a craft store and paint them gold for money luck. Place three or nine acorns in a small bowl in *hsun gua* of your office to represent a long future of steady growth for your business.

Boats

The image of a ship under full sail on calm seas can be used to symbolize prosperity and "easy sailing" through life. Fishing boats hauling in full nets are another good wealth image. Avoid images of boats in stormy seas, engaged in naval battles, or with empty nets.

Coins & Currency

Money in any form is a great addition to *hsun gua*, which makes this a good place to keep your checkbook and account statements. When you receive a check, place it in *hsun gua* overnight before depositing it in the bank. Keep your loose change in a bowl or jar in *hsun gua*.

Chinese coins, especially when tied with red string, are a popular feng shui cure. Oversized versions of a Chinese coin can be used alone in *hsun gua* as a wealth enhancer. Cures made of multiple Chinese coins come in many styles and designs, from simple to ornate.

- A set of three coins tied together can be carried with you wherever you go in your pocket, purse, or wallet.
- A string of ten coins, representing the emperors of the ten dynasties, is a particularly powerful cure for *hsun gua*.
- A small bell can be added to a three-coin cure and hung on the outside the main door to symbolize that good fortune and prosperity will come knocking.

Dragons

The dragon is an important symbol of power, success, and prosperity to the Chinese. A golden dragon holding a pearl is a popular symbol of prosperity. Placed near a door or window in *hsun* or *kan gua*, it represents financial wealth as well as wisdom and happiness. Dragons carved from green jade are a good luck cure for the east sector of the home.

Dragon-Headed Money Turtle

This Chinese symbol is thought to enhance both wealth and longevity and to bring wisdom into the home. Display the dragon-headed turtle in your front hall or in *hsun gua* for long-lasting money luck.

Eggs

Eggs, like acorns, represent future potential. The term "nest egg" is often used to refer to a savings account that provides future financial security. Three, six, or nine eggs (real or decorative) in a bowl in *hsun gua* can be used to represent future prosperity. The Easter season is a good time to shop for egg-shaped objects to use as feng shui cures. Or decorate wooden or plastic eggs with paper or paint in purple, green, and gold colors. Chefs, here's a way to use your feng shui knowledge in the kitchen: many recipes require eggs to be at room temperature before use. Place them in a green or purple bowl in *hsun gua* of the kitchen (or on the rear left burner of your stove if it is not in use) while they warm up.

Fish

Fish are symbols of abundance and prosperity in many cultures. Fish images and figurines are displayed in the home at Chinese New Year to attract abundance throughout the coming year.

Carp

Carp are a Chinese symbol of great achievement and success. In Chinese legend, carp meet each year at a gateway called the Dragon Gate. Any carp that can jump over the Dragon Gate will become a dragon and live in luxury and honor in Heaven. The carp that fail to clear the gate will try again year after year until finally succeeding. Place a carp image in *hsun gua* to encourage long-term success and prosperity.

Fish Tanks

The motion of fish swimming in an aquarium is thought to activate money and luck *chi*. The best place for a fish tank is in *hsun gua*. For best effect, add nine coins to the tank, and have eight orange goldfish and one black one. If any of your fish die, this is thought to indicate that they absorbed a great quantity of *sha chi* on your behalf. Thank them for their generous service, and replace them immediately with larger ones.

Fountains

Fountains are a powerful symbol of unending prosperity filling your life. Indoors or out, a fountain is a wonderful addition to *kan* or *hsun gua*. If you use a fountain in your front hall, make sure that it is placed so that the main direction of water flow is toward the center of the home, not aimed at the door. Toss nine coins into your fountain while focusing on your intention to attract abundant money luck.

Fruit & Grains

All kinds of bounty from the earth are potent symbols of abundance. The cornucopia, or "horn of plenty" is a conical basket overflowing with harvest wealth. Plump bunches of grapes and fat juicy pineapples are also specifically associated with prosperity, as are sheafs of wheat, rice, or other grains. Place harvest imagery in *dui gua* (associated with harvesting the fruits of your labors) of your dining room to help ensure that your family will always dine abundantly on the finest, most nurturing rewards of nature's bounty.

Gemstones

Gemstones are a powerful symbol of wealth. If you are fortunate enough to own diamond or other gemstone jewelry, keep it in a red or purple jewelry box in *hsun gua* of your bedroom.

Semi-precious stones and crystals can also be used as wealth cures, depending on their specific meanings. Some stones associated with prosperity are: citrine (once known as the "merchant's stone; place it in your cash box to increase income from your business); green aventurine; moonstone; pearls; peridot; opal; ruby; topaz; and turquoise. All of these stones have other qualities in addition to their association with money luck. Often one type of stone will have different meanings in different cultures. If this topic interests you, a Google search for "gemstone meaning" will lead to lots of sites with additional information.

Amethyst

Amethyst is a good stone for *hsun gua* because of its purple color. This stone is thought to enhance spirituality and the ability to connect with your Higher Self. I like to have some amethyst in *hsun gua* to ensure that my prosperity is achieved in alignment with my soul's purpose.

Gemstones for Wealth Bowl

For a Chinese wealth bowl (see "Pot of Gold" below) or wealth vase (see pages 134-138) you will need a set of five stones in the colors of the five elements. Note that these stones are recommended for the wealth bowl based on their color, not on any esoteric meaning:

- Wood: green jade, moss agate, green aventurine, malachite
- Fire: carnelian, jasper, red aventurine, garnet
- Earth: yellow agate, yellow jade, tiger-eye
- Metal: howlite, hematite
- Water: onyx, obsidian, sodalite, lapis lazuli

Gold Ingots

Boat-shaped gold ingots (*yuen bao*) are symbols of prosperity and ease. Replicas of this type of ancient money, widely available in feng shui shops, are a very auspicious wealth symbol. Placed in *hsun gua* of your home or office, they symbolize the accumulation of a great fortune.

Lakshmi

Lakshmi is the Hindu Goddess of wealth and beauty. She is shown seated or standing on a pink lotus blossom, dressed in opulent clothing and jewelry, and with a shower of coins and pearls falling from her hands. Place Lakshmi in *hsun gua* of your bedroom or living room, and add some fresh flowers or jewelry around her image to honor her.

Laughing Buddha

The laughing Buddha is a popular symbol of joyful affluence. He shows a broad smile, has a generous belly to indicate his wealth, and usually is either carrying or seated on a bag full of coins. Place this charming figure in *hsun gua* to enhance money luck and enjoy prosperity.

Lifestyle Imagery

Anything associated with a prosperous lifestyle can be a good symbol of financial success, so long as it represents something that you personally aspire to. Magazines are a great resource for images of large homes, vacation properties, luxury cars, boats, jewelry, spa vacations, luxury travel, etc. I make collages of images that represent my aspirations, not only for prosperity and lifestyle, but also for professional recognition and spirituality. I have had some remarkable experiences of collage imagery manifesting for me, sometimes in entirely unexpected ways.

Lucky Bamboo

Dracaena sanderana, although it is not a variety of bamboo, has become popular in recent years as a feng shui cure. "Lucky bamboo" is most often sold as multiple stalks bound together with red wire or ribbon and placed in gravel in a small porcelain pot. It grows well in water, and can tolerate low light conditions. Lucky bamboo is especially good for celebrating the grand opening of a new business or for other special occasions. Placed in *hsun gua* it can enhance your money luck. If your lucky bamboo dies, you should replace it immediately with a larger, more expensive plant in order to forestall financial misfortune.

Lucky Money Frog

The three-legged toad, perched on a pile of coins with another coin in its mouth, is one of the most popular Chinese symbols for attracting success and prosperity to a home or business. It is said to appear at the full moon near the homes of people who will receive good financial news the following day. In a place of business, put the lucky money frog near the cash register, by the front door, or on the owner's or manager's desk. At home, the lucky money frog can be placed inside the front door (facing into the space), or in *hsun gua* of the living room. Some feng shui practitioners say that you should remove the coin from the frog's mouth each night and return it every morning. Others suggest fixing the coin in place with a drop of glue so it won't fall out and be lost. Since you can't do both, I suspect that this doesn't really matter.

Money Trees

A money tree is a good enhancement for *hsun gu*a, which is associated with the WOOD element in its mature, full-grown aspect. Instructions for how to make a money tree are provided on pages139-140. Another kind of money tree is formed from twisted wire (trunk and branches) with leaves carved from jade or other semi-precious stones. Choose one with jade or amethyst leaves to evoke the energy of *hsun gua*, and display it in *hsun gua* of the living room or in your main entry.

Pearls

Pearls represent purity, virtue, and feminine beauty. Wearing pearls is said to attract the blessings of Lakshmi (see above) for both worldly and spiritual prosperity. Before cultivated pearls made these treasures more affordable, these gems from the sea were so highly prized that the famous Cartier building on Fifth Avenue in New York City was purchased for one strand of perfectly matched pearls! Even today a strand of top quality natural pearls can fetch hundreds of thousands of dollars. In feng shui terms, the pearl's white color and round shape evoke the qualities of *dui gua*, the seat of creativity. For those in creative professions, pearls in *dui gua* or in *hsun gua* of your office or studio will be a powerful feng shui cure for attracting financial and artistic success.

Pi Xui

The *pi xui* (say "bee-shay") is a mythical Chinese creature similar to the western Unicorn. While its primary symbolism is purity and protection, it is also used to bring luck to gamblers. Place a *pi xui* figurine in *hsun gua*, to bring luck to your lottery tickets.

Pot of Gold

A pot of gold is a common wealth image in both Western and Chinese cultures. The Chinese version can be a few gold ingots (see above) placed in a bowl, or a large vase or urn adorned with ingots, pearls, dragons, and other wealth symbols and inscriptions, with a laughing Buddha and his sack of gold perched on top.

Dragon Wealth Bowl

The Dragon Wealth Bowl is a Chinese cure consisting of a ceramic bowl decorated with a five-clawed dragon symbolizing power and success. Gold ingots and semi-precious stones in the colors of the five elements are placed in the bowl.

Pot of Gold

The Western version of a pot of gold is usually depicted as a cauldron-shaped pot filled with gold coins. I don't recommend the image of a pot of gold at the end of a rainbow for feng shui, as this is famously elusive. You want to receive and enjoy prosperity, not chase it forever.Your wealth pot image can be placed in *hsun gua* of your home or office, or prominently displayed in your foyer or on your coffee table or dining table to announce the prosperity of your business or family.

Wealth Vase

A wealth vase ensures that your family will never run out of money. See pages 134-138 for instructions on how to create a wealth vase.

Sacred Gourd

Hollow dried gourds were used by ancient travelers to carry water on their journeys. The gourd shape, symbolic of health and longevity, also brings luck and prosperity in business. Place a sacred gourd (*wu lou*) on you desk to help you achieve your goals.

Waterfalls

Waterfalls, like fountains, represent an abundant flow of financial blessings into your life. A painting or photograph of a waterfall is a powerful enhancement to your entryway or for *hsun gua*. An indoor water fountain can be used to represent a waterfall.

Wealth Gods

The image of the Chinese God of Wealth, *Tsai Shen Yeh*, is a popular symbol for increasing money luck. He is usually shown seated on a tiger, with a dragon image on his robes, and carrying a gold ingot and/or string of coins. Place this image in your main hallway or in *jen gua*, and make sure that it is facing the front door in order to attract money luck to your home. Any deity associated with prosperity, from any culture (see Lakshmi, above), can be used as a feng shui wealth symbol.

Appendix E.
More Feng Shui Cures & Accessories

Feng Shui Crystals

Faceted crystal balls are a popular feng shui cure. Their ability to refract a beam of light (and *chi*) and send it radiating in all directions makes it an ideal protection against *sha chi* (negative energy). Faceted crystal balls can also be used to empower and activate a space. They radiate blessings wherever they are placed, and are powerful magnifiers of your intention. Faceted crystals can be used anywhere you want to enhance *chi*. Good places to hang crystal balls include:

- In the center of a long, narrow hallway
- In front of a window through which too much *chi* is escaping
- Anywhere you'd like to activate *chi*

Crystals can be placed on a desk or table, but are most often hung from the ceiling, in a doorway or in windows. For added impact, hang your crystal ball from a red string or ribbon cut to a multiple of nine inches or centimeters. The ball can hang any distance from the ceiling; it's cutting the string into a nine-unit length that's important. Tie any extra string into a bow or knot. If you buy crystal balls from a feng shui supplier, they may come with red cord already attached.

You can wear a little crystal (20mm size) on a red ribbon around your neck to activate your personal *chi*, or hang one from the rear-view mirror of your car to enhance, bless, and protect you while you drive and to deflect any *sha chi* headed your way.

Wind Chimes

The sound waves created by a wind chime will slow down and help disperse *chi* that is moving too quickly. If the path from the street to your front door is long and straight, hang a wind chime by the door to slow the *chi* down so it enters your home gently.

Wind chimes are also good for lifting the energy of a space. If one corner of your yard is lower than the others, *chi* may settle there. Hanging a wind chime from a tree in that corner can stir the *chi* up and keep it moving.

Wind chimes come in many sizes, from tinkly little tiny ones to great big resonant ones. Match the size of the wind chime to the size of your space. A large brass wind chime might be overwhelming indoors, while a very small chime may not be strong enough to have much effect. Metal chimes have the most penetrating tone. The most important consideration is that the sound be pleasing to you, so pick the one whose tones you like the best.

Water Fountains

In feng shui terms, moving water brings prosperity and good luck to the home. The sound and motion of gurgling water activates *chi* and adds humidity to a dry room, helping to balance *chi*. Moving water gets things going when the *chi* has been stagnant for a while (think of ice melting in the spring). Use moving water cures anywhere you want to enhance WATER or WOOD energy. Water fountains come in many shapes and sizes; pick one that:

- Suits the style of your décor
- Is an appropriate size for the place you intend to use it
- Incorporates the materials, shapes, and/or colors of the element energies you want to add to that space

You can usually adjust the sound of a water fountain by changing the water level. Some fountains also come with an adjustable pump, so you can vary the speed with which the water flows. Experiment until you find a tone and volume that sounds right.

Place your fountain so that the water flows toward the center of your home, not toward the front door. (If your fountain flows around all sides, this is not an issue.) Add more water to your fountain as it evaporates, to avoid possible damage to the pump if the water level gets too low. Depending on your climate and the size of the fountain, this could be once a week or every day. If you will be away from home for several days, unplug the fountain while you are gone.

Some people find the sound of a water fountain distracting, and a fountain is generally not recommended for the bedroom unless you turn it off while you are sleeping. Be guided by your personal response, and choose another cure if a fountain isn't right for you.

Fish Tanks

An aquarium can be extremely effective at increasing wealth and luck. Both the water pump and the fish swimming around in it keep the water moving and the *chi* going strong. Be sure to keep your fish tank immaculately clean. Less-than-fresh water and algae-clogged filters won't do your fish any good, and will send yucky-water *chi* out into the room.

Mirrors

Mirrors have been called "the aspirin of feng shui" because they solve so many feng shui probems. By creating the visual experience of a larger, deeper, or wider space, mirrors energetically enhance and expand a room or *gua*. For this reason, they are the best way to correct a missing *gua* from inside the space.

Mirrors can also be placed to correct a narrow or blocked entryway and to help brighten up any space that is too dark. Mirrors are especially useful for providing you with a view of the doorway to a room when it is impossible to place a key piece of furniture—such as your bed, desk or stove—in the command position (see pages 34-35). You can also use a mirror to reflect something with good *chi* (such as a beautiful pond or a lush green tree outside a window) into an indoor area, to enhance that space.

If there is a bathroom in one of your power spots, hang a full-length mirror on the outside of the door and empower it to prevent *chi* from entering the bathroom, where it may be depleted by the draining effect of all that plumbing.

If you can hang a mirror on the wall above your stove so that it reflects the burners, this is thought to symbolically double your income and prosperity.

When you choose to hang a mirror in your home, always check to see what's reflected in it, to make sure it is doubling something with positive energy. Avoid hanging a mirror so that the top of your head is cut off in the reflection; this can cause self-image problems, and may give you a headache.

Small round mirrors (1″-6″ in diameter″) are also useful in feng shui. Place one under a personal power object to enhance its energy.

Light

Poorly lit rooms have dull, depressing *chi*. If your power spots are dim and dark, your feng shui cures will have to work harder to achieve the desired effect. To use light as a feng shui cure:

- Put a bright light anywhere you want to lift or activate *chi*.
- Drape a string of little lights over a large houseplant to support FIRE energy.
- Use a bright light anywhere you want to strengthen the FIRE or EARTH elements, or to control METAL.
- Place a bright light in a *li gua* (fame; illumination) power spot if one of your goals is to understand a situation better.
- Use a spotlight to emphasize the significant imagery you have chosen for a key position in a power spot.
- Use an uplight on the floor in a power spot with a slanted ceiling, or under an overhead beam.
- Use a timer to activate a light cure each night between 11 PM and 1 AM—so long as it will not disturb you or your neighbors.

Chi-Activators

Colorful flags fluttering in the breeze are a great way to stir up *chi*. Activate an exterior power spot with a flag, banner or whirly-gig. Flag poles, tree branches, eaves, and porch columns can all carry a flag or windsock. Choose shapes and colors based on the appropriate elements for added impact.

Mobiles and whirly-gigs can be used to enhance *chi* inside your home. Look for a mobile with imagery that supports your intentions; angels or stars are always good for blessing a space, for example. Check home and toy stores as well as feng shui suppliers for wind-powered *chi*-activators that appeal to you. If you use this type of cure in a place where there is not much air current, set it in motion manually from time to time as you walk by.

Plants and Flowers

You can enhance the *chi* of your garden by planting flowers that correspond to the different *guas*. For example, any flower with purple or red blossoms will enhance *hsun gua* in your garden or on your property. If you decide to use feng shui in your garden, be sure you select plants that are appropriate to your climate and landscape.

Garden feng shui is a complete topic of study all on its own. In addition to plant selection and garden layout, it includes:

- Creating a harmonious balance of sunshine and shadow
- Shape and placement of paths, trees, and flower beds
- Appropriate paving and ground-cover materials
- Selection and placement of water features such as streams, ponds, waterfalls or water fountains
- Selection and placement of garden accessories, such as bird baths, benches, trellises, and the like

Indoors, plants and flowers are among the most powerful of feng shui cures, because their living *chi* brings natural vitality into your home. Of course, they only bring good *chi* so long as the plants and flowers are healthy. Be sure to get rid of any failing plants or wilting flowers before they have an adverse effect on your space!

As you plan where to use plants and flowers in your home, look for ways to use them in multiples of three or nine:

- Place three or nine small plants or vases together in one spot
- Put three or nine blossoms in a vase
- Use three of the same kind of plant, and place one in each of three power spots

Remember that you can use life-like artificial plants anywhere there is insufficient light for a living plant. Avoid dried flowers, which no longer have any living energy.

Stones and Statues

Stones, boulders, and statues are all good for stabilizing fast-moving *chi*. Place a large boulder in your front yard if your house is very close to a busy street, to keep all that rushing *chi* from draining the vitality from your property. Indoors, a heavy statue or object placed near a window can serve the same function.

Bells

Bells are most often used in feng shui where there is a need for some kind of warning or protection. If you are unable to put your desk in the command position (pages 34-35), for example, you can hang a bell on your office door to alert you when someone enters. You can also hang a bell wherever you would like to energize or enhance the space.

Bells are rung to signal the beginning and end of ceremonies and meditation practices. The sound of the bell penetrates the space, and signals a shift in the energy. Bells are also a powerful tool used in space clearing rituals.

Bells come in all kinds of shapes and sizes, with or without handles and clappers. The type of bell you choose will depend on how and where you plan to use it. Again, be sure that the tone of the bell is pleasing to you—the quality of the sound is more important than the design. If you are hanging a bell on a string, use a red cord, string, or ribbon cut to a multiple of nine inches or centimeters..

Power Objects

Firecrackers, fu dogs, talismans, and images of saints or deities are just a few examples of power objects that can protect you from negative energy. In addition to the traditional feng shui power objects, any item or image that has strong protective energy for you can be used as a feng shui cure in your home. Be sure to use the IVAG empowerment method (page 8) when placing your power object cures.

Resources

Websites

FastFengShui.com

Our flagship feng shui website offers:

- Information about contemporary Western feng shui
- Extensive *Articles* and *FAQs* pages
- Detailed descriptions and excerpts for all *Fast Feng Shui* books
- Free e-booklets to download
- Feng shui products and accessories—water fountains, wind chimes, lighting, candles, air purifiers and environmental health products, Chinese feng shui cures and accessories and more
- Free twice-monthly newsletter
- Extensive *Links and Resources* pages providing access to the best of the Internet for feng shui and related topics.

FengShuiEbooks.com

Instant access to e-book editions of our popular *Fast Feng Shui* books, other digital products, and free e-booklet feng shui guides.

AllAboutProsperity.com

Resoures for personal and financial success, including audio programs, teleclasses, books, e-books, free articles and audio-library, and more. Learn from the hottest names in wealth building, achievement, and prosperity consciousness: Robert G. Allen, Robert Kiyosaki, Deepak Chopra, Dr. Wayne Dyer, Suze Orman, Dr. Jill Ammon-Wexler, Lee Pulos, and many more...

ClutterFreeForever.com

Liberate your home and reclaim your life with my *Clutter-Free Forever! Home Coaching Program*. Detailed ebook and weekly lessons help you declutter from the inside out. Exclusive online support group just for program participants.

Audio Programs & Teleclasses

(for details on any of these programs, please visit www.AllAboutProsperity.com)

Infinite Possibilities: The Art of Living Your Dreams ~ Mike Dooley

There is nothing you can't do, nothing you can't have, and nothing you can't be. Blood, sweat, and tears are not what it takes to live in abundance, health, and harmony. Discover how effortless the art of living your dreams can be.

The Prosperity Game ~ Jeanna Gabellini & Eva Gregory

Internationally-acclaimed 12-week teleclass that will blow the lid off what you think is possible for you and abundance. No longer must you believe the lie that says you have to work hard or fight to get the results you want. When you come up against old fears or limitations, you discover by simply changing your perspective, you can create new ideas and solutions.

Prosperity Partnership Program ~ Elyse Hope Killoran

Experience accelerated personal evolution while magnetizing worldly success. Integrates the spiritual and material paths to prosperity in a true "best of both worlds" approach. Learn the secrets to achieving success without fear, stress, struggle and overwork. A balanced system full of wisdom, discernment, and grace.

The Sedona Method ~ Hale Dwoskin

The scientifically proven Sedona Method® is an elegant, easy-to-learn system that will show you how to tap your natural ability to let go of any negative thought or feeling on the spot. Get immediate relief from the effects of negative thinking and break the patterns of thought and behavior that prevent you from having what you want—including financial security.

SynchroDestiny ~ Deepak Chopra

A mind-opening program that will change the way you perceive the world forever and enable you to manifest abundance in every area of your life. Much like a powerful magnet, you will begin to attract material wealth, emotional well-being, spiritual fulfillment, and a deep awareness of your life's true meaning and purpose.

Recommended Reading

(This is a short list of some of my favorite books about prosperity consciousness and wealth-building; for more information on these and other great titles, please visit www.AllAbout Prosperity.com)

Ask and It Is Given ~ Esther & Jerry Hicks

The Attractor Factor ~ Joe Vitale

The Courage to Be Rich: Creating a Life of Material and Spiritual Abundance ~ Suze Orman

The 11th Element: The Key to Unlocking Your Master Blueprint for Wealth and Success ~ Bob Scheinfeld

The Energy of Money: A Spiritual Guide to Financial and Personal Fulfillment ~ Maria Nemeth, Ph.D.

The Feel Good Guide to Prosperity ~ Eva Gregory

The Game of Life and How to Play It ~ Florence Scovel Shinn

The HeartMath Solution: The Institute of HeartMath's Revolutionary Program for Engaging the Power of the Heart's Intelligence ~ Doc Lew Childre and Howard Martin

How to Get Out of Debt, Stay Out of Debt and Live Prosperously ~ Jerrold Mundis

The Laws of Money, The Lessons of Life: Keep What You Have and Create What You Deserve ~ by Suze Orman

Lucky You! Proven Strategies You Can Use to Find Your Fortune ~ Randall Fitzgerald

The Millionaire Code: 16 Paths to Wealth Building ~ Paul B. Farrell

Multiple Streams of Income: How to Generate a Lifetime of Unlimited Wealth ~ Robert G. Allen

9 Steps to Financial Freedom: Practical and Spiritual Steps So You Can Stop Worrying ~ Suze Orman

The Power of Intention: Learning to Co-Create Your World Your Way ~ Dr. Wayne Dyer

Prosperity is an Inside Job: How to Release Personal Issues Blocking You From Your Success ~ Joan Sotkin

Rich Dad, Poor Dad: What the Rich Teach Their Kids About Money That the Poor and Middle Class Do Not ~ Robert Kiyosaki

Secrets of the Millionaire Mind: Mastering the Inner Game of Wealth ~ T. Harv Eker

The Secrets of Wealth: The Beginner's Guide to Financial Freedom ~ Fabio Marciano

The Sedona Method: Your Key to Lasting Happiness, Success, Peace and Emotional Well-Being ~ Hale Dwoskin

The Seven Stages of Money Maturity: Understanding the Spirit and Value of Money in Your Life ~ George Kinder

Smart Couples Finish Rich : 9 Steps to Creating a Rich Future for You and Your Partner ~ David Bach

The Spontaneous Fulfillment of Desire: Harnessing the Infinite Power of Coincidence ~ Deepak Chopra

Your Money or Your Life: Transforming Your Relationship With Money and Achieving Financial Independence ~ Joe Dominguez, Vicki Robin

Glossary

ba gua A map of the energetic qualities of a space. *Ba gua* means "eight areas"—eight *guas*, or sections, surround a central space, the *tai chi*. Each *gua* has a symbolic association with a specific life aspect or aspiration, such as wealth, career, or relationships, for example. Whatever is going on energetically in each *gua* of your home will affect the related aspect of your life.

Black Sect feng shui A very popular method of feng shui, especially in the U.S., introduced by Master Thomas Lin Yun. Also called "BTB" (Black Tibetan Buddist) feng shui, this approach aligns the *ba gua* with the entry, rather than to the compass. Black sect feng shui emphasizes the power of intention, and incorporates many "transcendental" cures and rituals.

chi The life force present in all things. The practice of feng shui is based on analysis and correction of the *chi* of a space.

chien The area of the *ba gua* associated with helpful friends and travel. See page 152 for the qualities and location of *chien gua*.

Compass school feng shui A traditional Chinese method of feng shui. Analysis and diagnosis of the feng shui of a building is based on compass orientation and year of construction. More complex and often more difficult to apply than Western feng shui.

Contemporary Western feng shui —feng shui as it is often practiced in America today, with the *ba gua* oriented to the main entry instead of to compass directions. Conscious intention is an important factor in this style of feng shui.

cure An adjustment made with the intention of removing or neutralizing a negative influence or *sha chi*, in order to improve the *chi* of a space. Sometimes also used to refer to feng shui enhancements made to enhance or activate a space, where there is no negative influence to be corrected.

dui The area of the *ba gua* associated with creativity and children. See page 152 for the qualities and location of *dui gua*.

earth One of the five elements used in feng shui. See the reference chart on page 167 for a summary of the qualities, shapes, and colors associated with the EARTH element.

empowerment The process of adding the power of your own intention to your feng shui cures and enhancements. Empowering your feng shui changes with the power of body, speech, and mind is thought to dramatically improve the outcome. The IVAG method (pages 7-8), unique to Fast Feng Shui, adds the emotional power of gratitude to the intention, visualization, and affirmation empowerment steps.

enhancement An adjustment made with the intention of improving and activating the *chi* of a space. Faceted crystal balls, water fountains and wind chimes are popular feng shui enhancements. Objects and images that have a strong, positive symbolic meaning for the individual are effective enhancements.

extension A part of a room or building that sticks outfrom the rest of the structure and adds strength to that room or *gua*. See page 190 for how to identify any extensions in your home.

Fast Feng Shuitm I created this term to describe my approach to Contemporary Western feng shui. My emphasis is on: recognizing and working with your feng shui style; targeting your efforts to your individual power spots for maximum results with minimum wasted effort; personalizing the affirmations and visualizations used to empower your changes; the importance of approaching feng shui as tool for change and personal growth.

feng shui The practice, originally from ancient China, of adjusting the *chi*, or life force, of a space so that the inhabitants experience greater happiness, success, prosperity, and vitality.

fire One of the five elements used in feng shui. See the reference chart on page 167 for a summary of the qualities, shapes, and colors associated with the FIRE element.

hsun The area of the *ba gua* associated with prosperity and fortunate blessings. See page 152 for the qualities and location of *hsun gua*.

jen The area of the *ba gua* associated with family and health. See page 152 for the qualities and location of *jen gua*.

kan The area of the *ba gua* associated with career. See page 152 for the qualities and location of *kan gua*.

karma The fate that you created for yourself in this life as the result of your actions in past lives; the effect that your current actions will have on your future existence.

ken The area of the *ba gua* associated with self-understanding and spirituality. See page 152 for the qualities and location of *ken gua*.

kun The area of the *ba gua* associated with marriage and relationships. See page 152 for the qualities and location of *kun gua*.

li The area of the *ba gua* associated with fame and reputation. See page 152 for the qualities and location of *li gua*.

mantra A sacred word or phrase used for meditation, prayer, and blessing.

metal One of the five elements used in feng shui. See the reference chart on page 167 for a summary of the qualities, shapes, and colors associated with the METAL element.

missing area A part of a room or building that is indented from the rest of the structure and weakens that room or *gua*. See page 157 for how to identify any missing areas in your home.

power spot A focal point for your feng shui efforts, determined by what life issues you want to address at this time and by the unique qualities and layout of your home. Feng shui becomes easier and more effective when you concentrate on your power spots first, before working on the rest of your home.

red envelopes Feng Shui practitioners of the BTB school follow the tradition of asking for payment to be presented in red envelopes. The red color empowers the client's wishes and provides protection for the practitioner. Red envelopes can also be used to empower a wish or blessing written on a slip of paper and placed in the envelope.

secret arrows *Sha* (negative) *chi* created by sharp objects and angles.

sha chi Harmful *chi* that can cause or aggravate stress, restlessness, and a variety of health problems.

space clearing Specific rituals and other practices designed to remove stale, old, or negative energy from a space.

tai chi The central area of any space, especially the center of your home. Anything going on in the *tai chi* of your home will affect all of the *guas*, so it is a very important area to keep free of clutter and other negative influences.

water One of the five elements used in feng shui. See the reference chart on page 167 for a summary of the qualities, shapes, and colors associated with the WATER element.

wood One of the five elements used in feng shui. See the reference chart on page 167 for a summary of the qualities, shapes, and colors associated with the WOOD element.

Index

It Was Only One Damn Night 2

A novel by Lady Lissa

Published by Unique Pen Publications, LLC

Final chapter from book one…

Marcus

Two weeks later…

I had taken the day off to take my wife to her doctor's appointment. The babies were growing because Melina was getting huge. I still couldn't believe that we would soon be the parents of twins. We were planning a baby shower in two weeks. By that time, my wife would be 30 weeks along. Dr. Lambert said sometimes the babies came early, but the longer Melina kept them inside the womb, the healthier they would be. Dr. Lambert said that once she got to 32 weeks, she would put her on bedrest to make sure she would make it to at least 36 weeks.

I just wanted my wife to have a healthy delivery and deliver some healthy babies. They were my main concern. My brother Kendrick and I had got the nursery together over the weekend and Melina and her sister, Sarah along with our mothers decorated it.

I watched my wife waddle her butt out of the bathroom and plop down on the bench at the foot of the bed. I grabbed her shoes and helped her put them on her feet. I sat down next to her and rubbed her belly.

"You okay?"

"Yea, just tired. I never knew carrying two babies would be this hard," she said as she leaned her head against my shoulder.

"It'll be over soon babe," I said as I held her.

"I love being pregnant and I wouldn't change it for anything in the world. I just wasn't expecting to be so big babe. I gained five pounds since the last visit," she complained.

"I know, but you're eating for three. The average pregnant woman eats for two. Can you imagine how these women who are pregnant with more than two feels at this point?"

"I don't even want to think about it because I don't know how they do it," she said.

"You wanna reschedule your doctor's appointment and stay in bed?"

"No, because Dr. Lambert is waiting for me. She also said that we need to go every two weeks so she can make sure the babies are okay. We also have to go to the hospital for another ultrasound, remember?"

"Damn! I forgot about that shit!"

"Yea, we have to do the ultrasound before we go to Dr. Lambert's office."

"Then we'd better get going."

I stood up and helped her up. Then I escorted her out to the car because climbing in the truck was too hard for Melina now. I drove her to the hospital where we got the ultrasound done. Seeing how big our little girls were getting was a beautiful thing. I couldn't believe I had almost thrown our family away not that long ago.

Erika printed the baby pics for us and sent us on our way. I held Melina's hand as I walked her to the passenger's side of the car. I helped her in then went around to the driver's side.

"I love you Marcus," she said once I started the car.

"I love you too baby. You and the babies mean everything to me. You guys are my whole world," I said as I leaned in and kissed her.

I put the car in drive and merged onto the highway to drive the short distance to Dr. Lambert's office. I stopped by the convenience store and grabbed a bottle of water for my wife and a Powerade for myself. Then I pulled into the parking lot of the doctor's office and parked.

I went around to help Melina out of the car. We walked hand in hand to the office and I held the door open for her. "You can have a seat. I'll go sign you in," I said.

I walked up to the counter and signed Melina's name on the sign- in sheet. "Hello, Mr. O'Connor, I'm gonna see if we can get you and your wife in and out as soon as possible," Rebecca said.

"It's okay. While I appreciate that, I'm off today so we aren't in any rush," I said with a smile.

"I'm just trying to keep the peace Mr. O'Connor. Give me two minutes and I'll have them call your wife back."

I didn't know what was going on with that girl. I guess she was worried about Melina's comfort in the office. I sat down next to her and massaged her shoulder.

"Rebecca said she was going to get us in and out. I guess she's worried about your level of comfort," I said.

"Well, I'm not mad at her. I'm ready to go home already," she said.

"Melina O'Connor!" one of the nurses called out. I helped my wife up from the seat and we headed to the back area.

After Denise weighed Melina and checked her vitals, she was sent to the restroom with a piss cup. A couple of minutes later, she emerged from the restroom and we were shown to an examination room. I helped

Melina up on the table and we waited for Dr. Lambert to come examine her.

Not long after, Dr. Lambert knocked on the door and walked in followed by another nurse. “Hey, you guys, how are you all feeling?” Dr. Lambert greeted.

“I am tired. My back hurts. I can’t see my feet...”

“All common when you’re carrying twins,” Dr. Lambert said with a smile. “Have you been eating and sleeping okay?”

“I eat any and everything my husband puts in my face,” Melina said with a smile.

“How about sleeping? Are you sleeping okay?”

“Not really.”

“She has a hard time getting comfortable at night, even with the body pillow,” I offered.

“Well, that’s to be expected. The further along in the pregnancy you’ll get, the more discomfort you’ll feel. You guys have to keep in mind that instead of one baby growing inside her, there are two and the space is extremely limited,” she explained.

“I know. I never thought it would be this hard. I’m excited though. I can’t wait to hold my little ones,” Melina said.

“Well, let’s listen for the heartbeats. Did you guys go for the ultrasound?”

“Yea, we went before we came here,” I stated.

"Okay. I'll check the file before you leave. Sometimes, it takes a little longer to get them."

She placed the gel on Melina's stomach and then the wand. We listened to the thumping of one of our babies' hearts before she moved it to the other side for us to hear the other baby's heart.

"Your babies' heartbeats sound really strong," Dr. Lambert remarked. "That's a really good sign. So, you're at 28 and a half weeks along. I'll see you in two weeks and from there you'll start coming every week."

"Okay."

Dr. Lambert cleaned her wand and Melina's belly before she checked her computer. She looked at the ultrasound pictures and the report.

"Your babies are both growing just fine and healthy. Keep doing what you're doing and get as much rest as you can. I will see you again in two weeks," Dr. Lambert said.

"Gotcha," I said as we thanked her and left the exam room.

We walked over to the front counter where I paid Melina's copay and got the appointment card from Rebecca. "Thank you for getting us in and out so quickly Rebecca," Melina said.

"No problem. See you guys in two weeks."

I opened the door that led to the lobby at the exact same time the entry door opened. Imagine my surprise when the chick, I think her name was Kalisha or Kail, anyway, when she walked in. After months of running from that one night, it finally caught up to me as she stood before me and my wife. My mouth literally hit the floor as she placed her hand on her swollen belly.

"Well, well, well," she said with a smile. "Look what the cat done dragged in. Hello Marcus!" She stood there speaking to me but casting her gaze from me to Melina with a wicked smile on her face. In that moment, I knew shit was about to hit the fan.

"Aw shit!" I heard Rebecca express from behind me.

"We were just leaving," I said as I grabbed Melina's hand and tried to go around the woman. However, she blocked our path and the front door.

"Uhm, I've been trying to reach you for months Marcus. I hope you don't just plan on walking out before I catch you up to speed about everything that's been going on," she said as she rubbed her belly again.

Melina looked up at me and then at her with furrowed eyebrows. I could feel her hand trembling in my own as she asked the question I was never prepared for.

"Babe do you know this woman?"

"I met her once," I responded with the truth.

"Who is she Marcus?"

"Yea, Marcus. Tell your wife who I am. Let her know just how well we do know each other," Kalisha said as she rubbed her protruding belly.

Now that shit right there wasn't the least bit funny because she and I both knew that I wasn't that kid's father. But the manner in which she kept rubbing her belly while staring at me implied that I was.

I didn't know what the fuck was going on or who thought this shit would be a good practical joke, but it definitely wasn't funny at all. As the sweat formed over my top lip and my forehead, I prayed some natural disaster would happen to help me out of this mess.

What the fuck was Kalisha doing here and why was she trying to stir up trouble between me and my wife? Granted she didn't know that I was married because that wasn't something that I hadn't discussed with her that night. My marriage was my business and no one else's.

I wanted to know who the hell had gotten her pregnant though because I knew darn well it wasn't me! What the fuck was really going on here? Was this why she had wanted me to call her? Surely, she couldn't be carrying my baby. It was only one damn night we had together. Just one!

Damn. I had so many fucking questions right now, but at the same time, all I wanted to do was run.

God if you're listening, I need you help ASAP! Get me out of here! You can even give me a heart attack as long as you don't let me die. Melina and the girls are going to need me. It doesn't matter what you do to me Lord, JUST GET ME THE HELL UP OUTTA HERE!!

Chapter one

Kalisha

I woke up this morning feeling like shit. I hadn't slept well last night because I was almost due to have my baby. The closer it got to his due date, the more uncomfortable I was. So, last night wasn't a good night. My back hurt, my pelvis felt as if a dirt bike had run through it and I felt so much pressure at the bottom, I just knew I was going to deliver this week. I slid out of the bed by the hardest and went straight to the toilet to relieve myself. As I sat on the toilet and peed, I wondered what it would feel like to have Marcus here to help me.

Seeing that his wife was pregnant and knowing that he was over there helping her had me feeling some kind of way. I hated that he was there for her and not me, even though I knew I didn't have a right to feel that way. I couldn't believe Marcus didn't tell me that he was married. Why would he keep something so important from me? Unless...

Unless he never planned on seeing me again. The more I thought about it, the more upset I became. He either knew before or after we slept together that he had no intentions on ever calling or seeing me again. Yet he still went through the motions of having sex with me and taking my number afterward.

I had been trying to reach him ever since I found out that I was pregnant by him. I didn't have his number. I didn't have his last name. I didn't know where he worked. And I most certainly didn't know where he lived. I had no way to contact that man at all to let him know what was going on with me. I got dressed this morning all with that shit heavy on my mind.

I grabbed my purse, phone and keys and left the apartment. I was excited about my doctor's appointment because I just had a feeling that she was going to send me straight to the hospital. My due date was two and a half weeks away, but I didn't think that my baby boy was going to wait that long before making his appearance. I arrived at my appointment ten minutes early and waddled my overweight pregnant ass into the office. I couldn't wait to sit down in the chair because my back was killing me.

As I was pulling the door open, I felt it being pushed towards me. Imagine my surprise when I came face to face with my baby daddy and his wife. I had no idea how this happened, but I had no one to thank but

God. I knew this was his doing and it meant everything to see the look on his face in that moment.

I wasn't trying to start no shit with him and his wife, but I wasn't about to be ignored any longer.

"Well, well, well," I said with a smile. I couldn't believe how my luck had changed. "Look what the cat done dragged in. Hello Marcus!" I rubbed my protruding belly as I glanced from Marcus to his wife.

She looked like she was about to pass out or something. I didn't know how far along she was, but she was huge. She must be due around the same time as I was. That was when I remembered that she was carrying twins. I wasn't trying to start any trouble with them, especially since I was sure she didn't know who the hell I was. But considering that we shared the same baby daddy and our kids were siblings, she deserved to know who I was. Judging from the look on Marcus' face, I could tell that he didn't agree.

It actually looked like he was praying for me to disappear. That wasn't about to happen though. I had been kept in the dark for way too long already.

"We were just leaving," Marcus said as he quickly grabbed his wife's hand and tried to scoot pass me. But I stood in front of the door because we had some shit to discuss. Granted this wasn't the time or place, but it would have to do.

"Uhm, are you just going to leave without speaking to me. I've been trying to reach you for months Marcus. I hope you don't just plan on walking out before I catch you up to speed about everything that's been going on."

His wife glanced at me with her eyebrows practically touching in the middle of her forehead. I almost felt sorry for her because no pregnant woman deserved to find out her husband had cheated on her like this.

"Babe do you know this woman?"

"I met her once," he said.

Well, technically he wasn't lying. But he knew what happened that one time we met, so he needed to stop acting like he didn't know me.

"Who is she Marcus?"

"Yea, Marcus. Tell your wife who I am. Let her know just how well we do know each other," I said.

"Melina let's go babe."

"Not until you tell me who she is," his wife stated as she jerked her hand back.

"She's just someone I met," he responded.

"Marcus are you gonna tell your wife the truth or do you want me to do it?" I asked, tired of this little dance he and I were doing.

"I'm sorry, what's your name?" he asked as he scrunched up his face.

"You know exactly what my name is!" I said through clenched teeth.

"Uh, no I don't. We only met one time and it wasn't all that!" he said as he held up one finger. "Just one damn time!"

"I know we only met once. You don't have to keep reminding me!"

"Right. So whatever game you're trying to play right here is not going to work!"

"Game? I'm playing games?" I asked as I touched my chest. "You've been hiding from me for months!"

"Hiding?" his wife asked.

"Who are you?" I asked his wife even though I knew exactly who she was.

"I'm his wife!" she said with an attitude as she thrust her big ass ring in my face. That shit really made me want to cry. He can buy his wife the Hope Diamond but won't give me the time of day pertaining to our son.

"His wife? Marcus, you didn't tell me that you were married," I said as I cast my gaze from her to him.

"That ain't none of your business! We only met one..."

"Yea, yea, yea, one DAMN TIME!!" I finished for him. "You don't have to keep saying that. I was there, remember?"

"Okay, Marcus what's going on with this woman? What is your connection to her?"

"Nothing is going on baby! And there ain't no connection between me and her!"

"No connection my ass!"

"This woman is clearly delusional! I don't know what the fuck she's trying to pull, but I'm not fixing to listen to her bullshit!" Marcus fumed as he grabbed his wife's hand. "Girl get out of my damn way!"

"Not until you give me your phone number and information on how I can reach you," I said.

"Reach me for what girl?! You know what? Forget I asked that because it ain't important. As you can see, I have a wife! I'm a happily married man expecting twins in a few weeks..."

"And a son in a couple of weeks! Now what?!" I asked as I looked at his wife's face for her reaction.

"What?" his wife asked as she looked up at Marcus with tears in her eyes.

"Look girl, I'm not trying to step on your toes or steal your man or nothing..."

"Don't listen to this chick babe! She obviously got the wrong dude!" Marcus said. "I'm telling you her ass is delusional!"

"Boy, quit playin' with my good nerves!" I said as I waved my hand at him. "Lady look, I ain't lying! Your husband had sex with me, and he is the father of my kid!"

"That's a damn lie! I never slept with that girl!" Marcus said in such dramatic fashion, I almost believed him.

"You better quit lying to my wife Marcus!" I said.

"You better get out my damn way and go find your real baby daddy cuz I ain't the one!" he bellowed.

"Oh my God! Are you really going to stand there and lie to your wife with a straight face like that, Marcus?" I asked, flabbergasted, but not surprised that he would deny sleeping with me. I mean, had it been just the two of us, he might have admitted it, but with her standing right there, I knew he wasn't going to tell the truth.

"Marcus you slept with this woman?"

"Hell naw!"

"Is she carrying your baby?" his wife asked.

"HELL NO!! Look girl, I don't know what kind of game you playin'..."

"GAME?!! OH, YOU THINK THIS SHIT IS A GAME?!!" I asked as I lifted my shirt so he could see my belly.

"PUT YOUR FUCKIN' SHIRT DOWN!! QUIT EMBARRASSING YOURSELF!!" Marcus said. "I AIN'T NEVER SLEPT WITCHU!! QUIT LYING!!"

The fact that he wouldn't admit we slept together wasn't surprising at all, especially with his wife standing right there. But how could he deny his own kid? I didn't know why he slept with me that night because it looked like he and his wife were pretty solid. I mean, apparently, they were having sex because she was carrying his babies.

But just because he had a wife, that didn't give him the right to disown my baby. I watched as he grabbed his wife's hand and pushed his way pass me. I couldn't believe that after I had been trying to find him for months, this was it. All I was going to get out of him was denial and lies. But I wasn't lying, and he knew that. He knew that he was the one standing there lying about that shit. If he thought I was just going to go away because he was denying that night, he'd better think again. As he and his wife walked outside, I followed them. No, I wasn't going to chase them in the parking lot like a fool.

He ushered his wife into the car and rushed to the driver's side. He looked at me with anger in his eyes before he opened the door and slid into the seat. I didn't panic. I waited until he started the car then pulled out my phone so I could take a picture of the license plate before he drove off. As I positioned my camera, a pain hit me that sent me to my fucking knees, making me drop my phone.

"Shit!" I fumed as I picked up the phone with shaky hands. By the time I had my phone positioned, Marcus and his wife were already gone from the parking lot.

I got back up by the hardest and slowly made my way inside the office. I was having cramps, so the last thing I needed to do was miss this appointment. But you best believe that as soon as I'd be done with the appointment, I was going to head over to Donya's office.

If anyone could help me solve this mystery now, it was her. Marcus had me fucked up if he thought I was going to just leave him alone now. We both were responsible for this baby that I was carrying, not just me. When I walked inside the doctor's office, all eyes were on me.

"What the hell y'all looking at?" I asked. "Y'all ain't never seen no baby mama drama before?"

I walked up to the counter and as I was signing my name on the list, Rebecca looked up at me. “Are you okay?” she asked.

I just knew she wasn’t asking me if I was okay out of concern. Especially not after what she had just witnessed. “Does it look like I’m okay Rebecca?” I asked as I mugged her ass.

“Not really. You seem to be in pain, which was why I asked if you were okay,” she said with a smirk.

I just waved her off and went to take a seat. As I inhaled deeply and exhaled while rubbing my belly, I could feel my baby calming down. A couple of minutes later, my name was called to the back. After taking my vital signs, the nurse gave me a urine cup to pee in. I left the pee in the bathroom, exited and followed her to exam room three. While I sat and waited for the doctor, I started having cramps. I took deep breaths in an effort to calm myself and to help relax my nerves.

I wasn’t expecting that run in with Marcus and his wife, even though I had prayed that day would come before I had my baby. Dr. Lambert knocked on the door before walking in with her nurse. “Hello Kalisha,” she greeted.

“Hi doc,” I greeted back as I sucked in some more air.

"Are you feeling alright?" she asked, concern on her face.

"Yea, just a few cramps is all."

"How long have you been having cramps?"

"They just started a couple of minutes ago," I explained.

She grabbed her little fetal monitor and squirted gel on my stomach. She rolled the monitor over my belly until the sounds of my baby's heartbeat filled the room. It always made me happy when I heard those sounds. She removed the monitor, gave me a towel to clean off with and wiped the gel off the little wand.

"How are you feeling now?" she asked.

"Well, I'm not in any more pain. It was probably from all the excitement..."

She looked at me sideways with a straight line on her face. "I do believe it's because of all the "excitement" as you put it. Your blood pressure is a little elevated. Most likely from all the "excitement" you participated in while waiting to be seen," she said as she side eyed me again.

"I'm really sorry about that Dr. Lambert. I really didn't mean to bring any drama or my personal business to your office. It's just that I have been looking for that man for months now."

"Why were you looking for my patient's husband, if you don't mine me asking..."

"No, I don't mind. Frankly, I don't care who asks about this situation. I've been looking for him since the day I found out that I was pregnant because he's my baby's daddy," I said as I sat up straight on the exam table giving both the doctor and nurse 'that look'. You know that look that said if they said something slick about it, it was gone be on and poppin' up in here.

"Oh my!" Dr. Lambert said.

"Right. So, now I hope you understand why I had to say something to him. I didn't mean to turn it into what it was, but when he denied that we slept together..." I paused and took a deep breath before blowing it out. "Whew, chile! I just wasn't prepared to see him and his pregnant wife. I really feel sorry for her because unfortunately, she got caught up in her husband's bullshit."

"Well, it isn't my place to get involved in my patient's business, so I'm going to have to ask you that if you two happen to run into each other again here, to keep it to a minimum. Not just because the other patients don't need to know what's going on in you all's personal lives, but for you and your baby's sakes. High blood pressure is very stressful on your unborn baby. You're almost at the finish line so the last thing you need is complications with your pregnancy or delivery," she said.

"I will and again, I'm sorry."

"So, how's the pain now? Are you still cramping?"

"No, it stopped."

"Okay, well, that's good. Even though your due date is still a couple of weeks, your baby could still come any day. Try to keep your stress to a minimum because of your blood pressure," Dr. Lambert advised.

"That's easier said than done Dr. Lambert. I just saw my baby daddy in your office with his pregnant wife. So, you can imagine how shocked I was to see him here today," I explained.

"I'm sure it was a shock, but you still need to keep your stress to a minimum. A spike in your blood pressure could be risky for you and your unborn son."

"I'll do better," I promised.

"Well, make an appointment with Rebecca to come in next week. If you should go in labor sooner, get to the hospital and have them give me a call," she said.

"I will Dr. Lambert. Thanks."

With her help, I slid off the table and made my way to the receptionist's counter. I couldn't wait to have this baby because it was getting harder and harder for me to get around these days.

"The doctor wants to see you back in a week," Rebecca said. Then she looked at me with a worried expression on her face. "Are you okay?"

"Yea, I'm good. I should be apologizing and thanking you..."

"Thanking me?" Rebecca asked in surprise. "For what?"

"For scheduling me and Marcus' wife's appointments at the same time..."

"Oh, there's no need to thank me. I had no intentions on the two, well three, of you seeing each other. Her appointment just ran a little longer and you came a bit earlier..."

"Then it must have been the work of the Lord," I said as I looked up at the ceiling.

"I guess so," Rebecca said as she handed me the appointment card. "Take care of yourself Kalisha. Try to keep your stress level down."

"That's a nice thought Rebecca, but did you not see what the hell I'm dealing with? My child's father won't even acknowledge that we had sex! That means he has no intentions on taking care of this baby, so please, enlighten me as to how I'm supposed to keep my stress level down!"

I knew Rebecca meant well, but she should just do her fucking job. I was willing to bet any amount of money that minding my business wasn't in her job description at all. I snatched the appointment card from her perfectly manicured hand and turned around to walk out the door. Before I could put my hand on the knob, a thought came to my head. I turned back around and went to the counter. Rebecca plastered a fake smile on her face.

"Forget something?" she asked.

"Yea, clearly from the conversation earlier you know that Marcus is my baby daddy..."

"I don't know that."

"Yes, you do. I mean, do you think I go around claiming random men are my baby's father?"

"I didn't say that. Anyway, what can I do for you Kalisha?" she asked as she linked her hands together and placed her chin on top of them.

"Well, if you could give me Marcus' phone number or address..."

Before I could finish, she was already shaking her head no. "I already told you that was against office policy," she said.

"Rebecca please, I have to get in touch with Marcus!"

"I'm sorry, but my hands are tied. I could lose my job giving you that information!" Rebecca insisted.

"C'mon, you know Dr. Lambert is not going to fire you..."

"No, she isn't because I'm not going to give her a reason to fire me!" Rebecca said. "You know it's very sad that you're going through this. But for you to try and put my job in jeopardy this way..." She paused and took a deep breath. "I'm sorry, but I can't help you!"

"Fine!" I said and turned toward the door. That shit was embarrassing to say the least.

Once I was out of the building, I took a couple of deep breaths. I was happy to be out and breathing some fresh air. I didn't realize how stifling Dr. Lambert's office was until just now.

"Ugh!" I admonished as I headed to my car.

I unlocked the door and slid in behind the wheel. I could kick myself for not being able to get the plate number on Marcus' car. All I could do when I got in the car was cry. I just felt so defeated at this point.

Chapter two

Melina

Marcus took me to my doctor's appointment as he had been doing every two weeks since I passed the 28-week mark of my pregnancy. I was now 32 weeks along and my babies were still growing and healthy. I thanked God every day for this wonderful man. I knew that Marcus was going to be just as great a father as he was a husband. Sure, we had some rough patches, but what married couple didn't go through those? I didn't think there was one out there who hadn't gone through some type of issue to strengthen their marriage.

That was part of the trials and tribulations we expected. I loved Marcus and he knew it. I also knew that he loved me because if he didn't, we wouldn't still be married. Marcus and I had found a way to put our marriage back on track, and I couldn't be more grateful. Once Dr. Lambert listened to the babies' heartbeats, she told me that for the next eight weeks, she wanted to see me every week to check and monitor my progress.

She explained that sometimes the babies ran out of room to grow, so this was around the time some pregnant mothers went into labor. I prayed that the twins stayed inside at least another four weeks. That would put me at 36 weeks and Dr. Lambert said that would give them more time for their little lungs to grow.

We were just leaving after having made our appointment for next week when a very pregnant young woman walked in. I didn't think nothing of it until she started speaking to my husband. I had no idea how she knew him or what the deal was... at first. I soon found out that she was claiming my husband to be the father of her child.

I couldn't believe that Marcus would do something like that. I mean, cheat on me, maybe. But to father someone else's child while we were still married.

As soon as we got in the car, I wanted to go off on him. But instead, I stayed quiet. I decided it was better to wait until we got back home. I was furious with my husband though.

"Babe, I hope you not believing that chick back there. I didn't do shit with her!" Marcus said as soon as we exited the parking lot.

I didn't say anything in response. I just sat there quietly while he continued to plead his case. "You hear me baby? I didn't sleep with that girl! I don't even know who she is!"

I continued to stay quiet while he continued to argue his point. He reached out for my hand, but I pulled it back from him. Tears streamed from my eyes at the thought of my husband in the arms of another woman. I wanted to give Marcus his firstborn child, but if that woman was right and he was her baby's father, then she would give birth to his firstborn instead of me. She would give him a son before I would. My heart was hurting so badly right now.

No matter how hard I prayed and how much I wanted what that woman said to not be true, I couldn't help but feel that it was. How did she know my husband's name was Marcus? He said he met her once, but where? How is it that she remembered his name, yet he couldn't remember hers? When did they supposedly have sex? Those were all questions I should have asked her when I was in her face, but I was too embarrassed.

There I was in my eighth month of pregnancy in the doctor's office being confronted by some woman who claimed to be having my husband's baby. I couldn't even look at those people in the faces during that time. I just wanted to be sucked down a manhole or something so I could disappear.

"Babe I know you don't believe that girl! How can you believe some stranger over your own husband?" he asked. "Seriously babe, I'm really hurt by the fact that you don't believe me."

I didn't respond as I brushed away my tears. A short time later, he pulled into the garage and shut the door. He hopped out of the driver's seat and rushed over to the passenger's side to help me out. I waddled my way inside the house with him following right behind me.

"Babe can we please talk about this?" he asked.

"Did you do it?" I asked as I finally looked him in the eyes.

"What?"

"You heard me Marcus. Did you sleep with that girl and get her pregnant?"

"HELL NO!" he yelled.

"You do know that what's done in the dark always has a way of coming to light, right? You do know that if you did sleep with that girl, I will eventually find out? I'm sure you also know how easy it will be to determine if you're that baby's father or not once its born."

"Babe, I'm telling you..."

I held my hand up for him to stop talking. "Please don't say nothing else. All I want to know is if you slept with her. The other part can be determined once the baby comes. For right now, all I want to know is if you cheated on me." Tears were streaming from my eyes, but I needed my husband to be honest with me. If he would just tell me the truth, we could go to counseling and fix things.

However, if he didn't come clean with me now and I found out later that he lied, I wasn't sure if our marriage would survive. All I needed was the truth.

"Babe..."

"Did you sleep with that woman Marcus? That's all I want to know. A simple yes or no is all I need to hear right now. I just want you to tell me the truth," I begged as I looked into his own watery eyes.

"Babe, I promise that I didn't sleep with that girl."

"So, there's no way that she could be carrying your baby, right?"

"Hell no! I never laid a finger on that damn girl. I only met her once!"

"Must've been one helluva meeting," I remarked.

"Actually, it was the night of the Super Bowl," he said. "I was with Kendrick, Gary, and Greg at Smitty's all night. I swear."

"So, you weren't alone with her anytime during the night?"

"No! I was with the boys until I got in my truck and went home! That's why I don't understand why she's accusing me," he said.

"How did you meet her?"

"Well, apparently, Gary invited her friend to chill with us. We didn't even know they were coming until they got there. Then Gary was like I invited her. I forgot her name," he explained.

"I just don't understand why that woman would single you out as the father. I mean, if you all were hanging together, why not choose one of the other guys?" I questioned. There was something about the story that was off, but I didn't know what it was.

"I don't know babe. All I know is that I never laid a finger on that chick!"

Looking into his eyes, he did seem to be telling me the truth. I just hoped my husband wasn't playing me for a damn fool. When he reached for me, I allowed him to hold me because I needed to feel his arms around me. He held me close, kissing my forehead and gently rubbing my back.

"I love you babe. I want you to know that I would never do anything to hurt you," he said as he lifted my face with his forefinger against my chin. "We're a family babe." He rubbed my belly with his other hand as he brought his lips to mine.

I prayed that my husband wasn't lying to me because the last thing I needed was for him and I to get divorced. That was exactly what would happen if I found out that he had lied to me. I just wouldn't be able to handle that.

My phone started to ring, so I checked it to see who was calling. It was my mom.

"Hey mom," I answered, trying to give her the most cheerful response.

"Hey baby. I was just calling to find out how your doctor's appointment went."

"It was good. Dr. Lambert wants to see me every week now until I go in labor," I said.

"That's good. So, the twins are okay?"

"Yea, they're both fine. I have to go for an ultrasound tomorrow."

"I'm gonna run out and get something for us to eat. You want anything in particular?" Marcus whispered in my ear.

"Not really. Whatever you bring is fine," I said.

"Tell Mama B I said hello." He kissed me on the cheek, grabbed his keys and headed out the door.

I made my way to the living room and sat down on the sofa. I wanted to tell my mom what happened at the doctor's office to get her take on the situation but decided against it. I didn't want her to feel some kind of way about Marcus, especially since he said he didn't do what the girl was accusing him of. I wanted so badly to believe my husband, so I just kept those thoughts to myself.

"Melina!"

"Huh?"

"Don't you hear me talking to you?" my mom asked.

"I'm sorry mom. I just got a lot on my mind," I said being truthful.

"A lot on your mind like what? Did you get some news you aren't telling me about?"

"No, not at all. The twins are fine. I'm fine. Everything is great!"

"So, if everything is so great, why don't you sound happy? You don't sound like yourself at all," she said.

"I'm sorry mom. I guess I'm just nervous about being a mom to twins. I always thought when I'd finally get pregnant that I'd have one baby. Never in my life did I expect to be told that I was having twins!"

"God saw the need to bless you with twins, baby."

"I wonder if that's because he thinks it'll be hard for me to conceive again," I pondered.

"You mustn't think like that Melina! God gives us trials and tribulations through life to test our strength. The fact that it took you a little while to get pregnant was a test on your marriage... and you passed!" my mom said.

"Yea, we did huh?"

"Y'all sure did, baby. Whatever happened to get you both to this point was God's will and you mustn't question it. Your marriage to Marcus was one of your greatest accomplishments, sweetheart. Together you two can do anything you put your minds to. You've already proven how hard you are willing to work to stay together. So, don't ever let anyone or anything come between you and your husband. Your grandmother used to tell me and your dad the same thing," she said.

Well damn! If I was thinking about divorcing Marcus, my mom sure killed that thought. I knew that there was no such thing as a perfect marriage. Hell, we proved that in the beginning when I couldn't get pregnant. However, I just wanted a marriage that we could both find happiness in.

"I know. I think Marcus and I are in a good place right now," I said.

"A good place? Y'all are in a great place. Melina, that man loves you baby, and I know that you love him. I don't know what it is I'm hearing in your voice, but it sounds like you've got some conflicted feelings. Please baby, just pray. Put whatever issues that you and Marcus are going through in the good Lord's hands. I promise that you two will be okay," she said. "Do you need me to come over there?"

"No mom, I'm fine. All of this is just a little overwhelming, that's all."

"Like I said, just pray my baby. Mommy is here if you need anything."

"I know. Thanks mom."

"Give my son a hug for me," she said.

"I will mom."

"I love you baby."

"I love you too mommy."

"I'll talk to you soon," she said.

"Okay."

We ended the call and I laid on the sofa to think about everything my mom had just told me. Before I knew it, my eyes had gotten droopy and I was falling asleep.

Chapter three

Marcus

I couldn't believe the shit that had just happened. To have Kalisha in the same doctor's office as me and Melina was ridiculous. For her to be pregnant and claiming that I was the father was retarded. When Ms. Belinda called, I saw that as an opportunity to head out and go get something for me and my wife to eat. As soon as I got in the truck, I called my brother Kendrick.

"What up bro? Y'all still at the doctor's..."

"Man look, you are never gonna believe what happened at that doctor's office!"

"What? Don't tell me Melina is in labor..."

"No, but she coulda been if it was up to that bitch!"

"Wait, wait, you lost me! What bitch?"

"That bitch from the night of the Super Bowl!"

"The one you drove home?" Kendrick asked, confusion in his voice.

"Yea, that one!"

"What happened with her?"

"So, apparently, she goes to the same doctor as Melina."

"So, she's pregnant too?"

"YEAAAAA! But get this bro, she says the kid is mine!"

"What the hell? Please tell me you didn't sleep with that girl," Kendrick said.

"Bro..."

"You did, didn't you?"

"Man, that shit was a mistake!"

"A mistake that could cost you your family! What do you think Melina will say when she finds out?"

"That's the thing... that bitch made a big ass scene in that doctor's office in front of my wife! She told Melina that kid was mine, but I know it ain't my kid!"

"How do you know that? Did you use protection?" Kendrick asked.

"No. I was so damn drunk, bro, I don't even remember where I nutted at!"

"Apparently, she does remember. Damn bro!"

"I know. Look, I need you to do me a favor," I said.

"What kind of favor?"

"If Melina calls and questions you about that night, I need you to tell her we were together the whole night..."

"So, in other words, you want me to lie to your wife."

"It's not a total lie. Technically, I was with y'all the whole night."

"Right, but then you left and gave ol' girl a ride," Kendrick said.

"NO! That shit never happened! Do you understand me?"

"Bro, this shit is going to backfire all up in your face," Kendrick advised. "Did you and Melina have a discussion about that shit?"

"Yea, and I told her the bitch was lying and that I was with you guys all night!"

"So, lemme ask you something."

"What Kendrick, man?!"

"Did you ever think about the possibility of that kid being yours?"

"NO! That ain't my fuckin' kid and that's that!"

"Denying the shit ain't gonna make that baby go away bro. What if she goes to court for a DNA test? What are you gonna do if that kid is yours?" Kendrick asked.

"Whose side are you on bro?" I asked.

"I'm on the right side. I love you to death bro, but if that chick is carrying your kid, that's my niece or nephew. I just think you should sit Melina down and tell her the truth."

"HELL NO!!" I yelled. "Is that your idea of helping me out?"

"Look, aren't the two of you still in counseling?"

"Yea, so what?"

"Well, come clean during one of your sessions. The counselor could help get you two back on track and get pass that issue."

"Hell no! I ain't bringing that shit to the counselor!"

"Bro, I'm trying to help you because you ain't thinking clearly right now. It's best to be honest with your wife now, rather than have her find out later. How you think she gon' feel if she finds out later on that you fathered a kid outside your marriage?" Kendrick asked.

I knew the shit sounded like the right thing to do, but I had already told Melina that I hadn't fucked that girl. How the hell did my brother expect me to go back to my wife and change my damn story? That wasn't about to happen. It was just going to have to be my word against Kalisha's.

"Bro, I'm sorry, but that's a chance I'm gonna have to take. I already lied to her and told her that I was with y'all all night. How the hell I'm supposed to go back and tell her that I slept with that bitch? That's why I called you so we could get our stories straight," I said.

"Aight. We gon' do things your way. I just hope she doesn't call me because I really don't want to lie to my sis like that. I really love Melina, so the last thing I want is for her to be mad at me for sticking to a lie that my brother told," Kendrick said.

"Bro, regardless of how you feel about this shit, you're my brother. Your loyalty should lie with me... period!"

"Yea, aight. Where you headed now?"

"I came to pick some food up for me and Melina at Mikki's."

"Aw, man! Don't tell me that shit bro! I'm hungry as fuck right now!" he said.

"I'd offer to bring you a plate, but I'm sure Melina is waiting to eat."

"It's cool, bro. Handle your business. I'ma get something to eat soon."

"Aight. I'm hit you up later," I said.

"Cool."

We ended the call and I got out of my car to go get the food. Thankfully, there were only four people ahead of me, so I didn't have long to wait. I ordered the pepper steak for myself and the stuffed turkey wings for Melina. Both orders came with rice and gravy, candied yams, and homemade macaroni and cheese. I even got Melina a slice of strawberry sheet cake with strawberry icing for her dessert. I paid my tab and headed back to my truck.

As I was backing out, I saw one of those chicks that was with Kalisha that night. Before she could see me, I backed out of the parking spot and zipped onto the highway. The last thing I needed was for her to tell her friend that she saw me. Man, it was crazy how I never saw none of those girls after Super Bowl at Smitty's, but now that Kalisha had told me I was her baby daddy, I ran into two of them.

"Jesus if you have any mercy on my soul, please let that chick be pregnant by someone else. The last thing I need in my life right now is chaos in my marriage. If you want me to say I'm sorry that I cheated on my wife, I'm so sorry. We just weren't in a good place at the time that shit happened. I shouldn't have slept with that chick, and I can admit that I was wrong. Please help me out Lord," I prayed as I drove back home. "If you help me out with this one, I promise to never be unfaithful to my wife and marriage again. All I want is for this shit to be a nightmare that I wake up from soon."

I didn't know what else to do. I took comfort in the fact that Kalisha didn't know my last name or where I lived. At least I was smart enough not to give her that information. I felt like a damn fool for fucking with that girl though.

"FUUUUUUUCK MAN!! I yelled as I banged my hand on the steering wheel.

Never in my life did I expect to be in this situation. My phone began to ring, and the screen lit up with Gary's name and number.

"Waddup G?" I answered.

"Aye man, I heard you had a run in with Kalisha today," he began.

"Aye man, fuck what you heard! I'm trying to put that night and today behind me!" I stressed.

"Uh, that might be easier said than done. Donya and Kalisha are here and they'd like to..."

CLICK!!

I didn't need to hear shit else Gary's ass had to say. I hung that phone up on that nigga so fast, I was sure he was still calling my name. He had me fucked all the way up with that shit! I couldn't believe he had the nerve to call me with that bullshit. He knew the shit that Melina and I had been through. He knew how hard we were working to get our marriage back on track. Why the hell would he call me with those two clowns in his presence? Yea, he was trippin' big time!

He called a couple more times, but I didn't answer. That last time, he left a voicemail, but I wasn't going to listen to it. I didn't want shit to do with Kalisha or Donya, so why would he call me with that mess? I was definitely going to tell him about himself the next time I spoke to him.

About 15 minutes later, I pulled into the garage and turned the truck off. I closed the garage door and grabbed the bag of food. I headed inside and was about to call out to Melina until I heard her softly snoring on the sofa. I went into the living room and gently nudged her awake.

She woke up with a sweet smile on her face. Shit, after what happened earlier, I had to wonder if that smile was meant for me or if she was waking up from a good dream. I helped her sit up on the sofa and she leaned her head against my shoulder. I draped my arm around her shoulder as we sat for a couple of minutes.

"You alright?" I asked.

"Yea, I'm fine. I spoke to mom earlier and she gave me some good advice," Melina informed me. She looked up into my eyes before she continued. "Babe I love you and I want us to continue down the path we've been going, so I just wanna forget about what happened earlier."

"Really?"

"Yea. Part of me wondered why that woman would choose you to point the finger at as the father of her baby, but after talking things out with you and hearing what my mom had to say..."

"You told your mom?" I asked in a panic.

"Of course not! I know how much you mean to her, so I wouldn't want to tarnish your relationship with her over something you said isn't true..."

"It's not!"

"That's all I need to hear. We never have to speak about this again," she said.

"Are you for real?" I asked, unable to believe what she was saying to me.

"Yea. We're about to be parents, so we need to focus our attention on our babies. We really don't have time to waste on other stuff that has nothing to do with us."

"Aw, babe! I love you so much!" I said as I kissed her.

Once the kiss broke up, she responded, "I love you too. Now, what'd you bring me to eat?"

"I knew you were hungry."

"I'm always hungry babe. I'm eating for three," she said with a smile.

I stood up from the sofa and helped her up. With my hand on the small of her back, I guided her to the kitchen where the food sat on the countertop. I handed her the plate of food I had purchased for her and I grabbed my plate. The two of us sat together at the kitchen counter on the barstools.

"Um turkey wings!" she marveled as she dove in.

We ate our food and when we were done, I put the leftovers in the fridge and joined my wife in the living room. I sat on the sofa and lifted her feet in my lap. I began to massage her feet as she moaned.

"That feels so good," she said.

This was what I enjoyed the most about our relationship. Melina always told me that it was the little things that counted the most... she was right. In that moment, this was the only thing that mattered. I just prayed that my one night out with the boys didn't come back to haunt me.

Chapter four

Donya

One week later...

Ever since Kalisha saw Marcus and his wife at the doctor's office last week, she had been stressing about trying to find him. As much as I wanted to help her, there wasn't anything more that I could do. The day she showed up at my office in tears, I didn't know what was wrong with her. Let me take you back to that day...

I was sitting in my office preparing for a case that was coming up when the receptionist buzzed me to let me know that Kalisha was there. I was shocked because usually she called before she just showed up at my office. I mean, I was an attorney, so I didn't just sit around twiddling my thumbs or daydreaming all day. I actually had a career that required for me to work every single day that I showed up at the office.

"Your friend Kalisha is here," Alexis informed me.

"Oh Lord!" I said out loud without meaning to. "Send her in."

"She's already on her way."

A couple of seconds later, Kalisha was in my office whining about some shit I couldn't understand. I grabbed the box of tissues and walked over to where she was standing. I handed her a tissue and led her to the chair across from my desk. She sat down and I sat in the other one next to her.

"Calm down and tell me what's going on," I urged.

She wiped her tears, blew her nose, then took a deep breath before she was able to speak. "I just saw Marcus and his wife at the doctor's office," she said.

"Oh shit! How did that go? You tell him about the baby?"

"He denied everything except meeting me!" she cried.

"Whaaatt?! Well, you did say his wife was with him, right?"

"Yea, but so what? Does that mean he has to deny our son?"

"Kalisha are you sure that is Marcus' baby?" I asked.

She had been adamant about the baby belonging to Marcus since she found out, but was she 100 percent sure? I mean, it wasn't like her ex- boyfriend wasn't still around. They had broken up not too long before she slept with Marcus.

"Really Donya? You're really doing this to me now?" she asked.

"I'm just saying that in order for you to go around accusing that man, you have to be absolutely positive that he

is your baby's father. Those are one of the first questions a judge will ask you, so I need you to be sure," I advised.

"Can you stop thinking like a lawyer and just be my friend, Donya?! I need your support right now more than anything! I felt like the two of them were ganging up on me or something!"

"I am being your friend, which is why I need you to explore all options."

"What options? Marcus is the father!"

"So, Carson..."

"HELL NO!! Me and Carson haven't slept together in months!" she proclaimed.

"It wasn't that long ago Kalisha," I said with a smirk as I side eyed her.

"It was long enough!"

"So, you don't remember telling me that you and Carson had sex not long before you slept with Marcus?" I asked.

"Okay, so we did have sex before Marcus..."

"Exactly what I'm saying..."

"TWO WEEKS BEFORE MARCUS!!" she shouted while waving two fingers in my face.

"Two weeks doesn't mean anything when it comes to paternity Kalisha. I know you want this baby to be Marcus'..."

"This is Marcus' baby Donya! Damn! Don't you think I know who baby I'm carrying?" she asked.

"Okay. So, what do you plan to do?"

"Well, I need to find him, and you have to help me."

"Help you how? I don't know that man any more than you do. So, what kind of help do you expect to get from me?" I asked.

"I need you to come with me talk to Gary. We have to convince him to give us Marcus' phone number!"

"I don't think that's a good idea," I said.

"Why not? Marcus is his best friend, so I know he knows how to get in touch with him."

"I just don't think it's fair to Gary to put him in the middle of y'all business like that," I tried to explain. However, those words fell on deaf ears with Kalisha.

"He's already in the middle and so are you!"

"Me? How am I in the middle?"

"Because I put you there. Once I find out where Marcus lives and works, I want you to represent me. I need child support and alimony..."

"Alimony is for the spouse. There is no way you're getting any alimony," I said as I busted out laughing.

"Well, whatever! It doesn't matter. Whatever Marcus owes me, and my child is what I want," Kalisha said.

"Gary can't help you," I said.

"Maybe not, but he will help you. I saw how sweet he was on you at the bar that night. You can't tell me that the two of you ain't been flirting and shit!"

"He has a girlfriend."

"So what? Marcus has a wife and that didn't stop him from giving me the business! Please Donya, do it for your godchild."

"My godchild?" I asked because that was the first time she mentioned it to me.

"Uh, who else did you think the godchild was gonna be? I don't trust no one like I trust you. You're my bestie for a reason," she said as she gave me the flutter eyes.

"Fine!" I said. I hated that she was able to get to me like that, but a child deserved both parents in his life. It wasn't fair that the mom always had to carry the entire burden.

The two of us left my office and made our way to Gary's office. Donya knocked on the door and just walked in without him even responding or inviting us in.

"Well damn! Y'all didn't even let me invite y'all in," Gary said in a snippy tone.

"I knew you would, so I just came in," Donya said with a smile.

"I'm almost afraid to ask the question, but what can I do for you ladies?" he asked as he side eyed us.

"Uhm, I need a favor," I started.

"What kind of favor?" Gary asked.

"The kind that will get Marcus on the phone," Kalisha said.

"Aw man, not that again," Gary said as he rolled his eyes.

"As you can see, I'm pregnant! My baby, Marcus' baby, is due in two weeks. I need Marcus to step up and be a father to my child, our child," Kalisha said.

"Well, I had a couple of conversations with Marcus and he said the two of you never slept together."

"Well, clearly, you can see that was a lie!" Kalisha said as she rubbed her belly. "You mind if I sit down? My back is killing me!"

"Nah, go ahead. Listen Kalisha, I see that you're pregnant and all, but whatever you and Marcus got going on ain't got nothing to do with me. I'd appreciate if y'all would keep me out of y'all's mess," Gary said as he looked over at me.

"Why are you looking at me? She wanted to come and talk to you, so I came with her. It seems we're both in the middle," I said as I shrugged my shoulders.

"I'm not in the middle of it because I have nothing to do with it," Gary insisted.

"Can you please just call Marcus for me? Let him know I'm trying to reach him," Kalisha asked.

"Man..."

"Please Gary. If you won't do it for me, do it for the sake of me and Marcus' baby," Kalisha said as she rubbed her huge belly.

"Man, I'ma do this for you one more time, but I'm not doing it again. Y'all gonna have to figure that out on y'all own," Gary said.

"Well, if you really don't wanna do get in the middle and call him, you can always just give me his number," Kalisha said as she grinned sideways.

"HA! You trying to get my ass caught up in some real shit! No thank you," Gary said as he picked up his cellphone.

I could see Kalisha cussing under her breath. She probably expected him to use the office phone to make the call. She would be able to get the numbers as he typed them in. Only he didn't use the office phone.

We couldn't hear what was being said on the other end of the line, but we heard Gary trying to get him to speak with Kalisha regarding their baby.

"Aye man, I heard you had a run in with Kalisha today," he began.

I wished he hadn't said anything about their meeting at the doctor's office. Marcus might still be hostile about that since it had only happened a couple of hours ago. Gary was quiet for a couple of seconds before he continued.

"Uh, that might be easier said than done. Donya and Kalisha are here and they'd like to..." Gary stopped talking for a minute then he spoke again. "Hello! Hello!" He pulled the phone from his ear and shrugged his shoulders. "He hung up on me."

"Dammit!" Kalisha said as tears sprang to her eyes. "Why won't he talk to me?"

"Cuz he's a coward! He was unfaithful to his wife and now that she's pregnant, he's the doting husband. I'm sorry Kalisha. We'll find another way to get to him," I said as I held my friend while she cried.

"Aye, I'm sorry that you're in this situation, but there ain't nothing that I can do. Marcus and Melina are happy in their marriage. They're expecting twins, so he ain't trying to have nothing interfere with that," Gary said.

"So, I'm just supposed to raise my baby by myself, without a father just so your boy can be happy with his wife and twins? I don't think so!" Kalisha said.

"I'm not saying that..."

"Good because it ain't gonna happen. If you won't give me the information I need to find him, we'll just hire a private investigator to do it!" Kalisha said.

"We?" Gary asked with raised eyebrows as he looked at me.

"Yea, we! As in me and Donya! She's going to represent me with my case for child support," Kalisha informed him.

"She can't do that!" Gary scoffed. "Child support cases belong in family court. Donya isn't a family court lawyer."

"I'm a lawyer, period!" I stated. "I've handle many cases before that were much tougher than child support."

"I repeat, child support cases are held in family court..."

"So what, Gary? That doesn't mean I can't represent her!" I repeated.

"If you say so. Just whatever y'all do, leave me out of it. Marcus is my friend and right now, he's pissed at me for calling him about y'all's mess!" Gary stated.

"I'm sorry I got you involved in "our mess" as you put it Gary. It isn't my fault that your friend slept with me and I got pregnant. Why is it that I feel like I'm being punished for a decision we both made?" Kalisha said sadly.

She went to stand up from the chair, so I helped her. "Give Marcus a message for me the next time you see him please. Let him know that I'm coming for him. It may take a little longer to find him, but eventually, I will find him," Kalisha said as she stared at Gary.

"That's between you and him. No disrespect Kalisha but keep me outta y'all's shit!"

The two of us walked out of his office and I walked Kalisha to the elevator. "Are you gonna be alright?" I asked.

"Yea, I'm just gonna pick up something to eat and head home. Thanks for everything Donya," she said as she hugged me.

"You're welcome. Whenever you're ready for me to start working on your case, let me know," I said.

"I'm ready now. What is it you need me to do?"

"If you don't mind coming back to my office, you'll need to sign some paperwork. It's just a formality to hire me as your attorney," I said.

"Let's do it!"

We returned to my office and went over the paperwork. She signed the necessary papers and then I walked her back out to the elevators. She gave me another hug and then she was on her way. I made my way back to Gary's office and barged right in.

"Uh, I thought I told y'all I was done!"

"Did you have to be so rude to my friend?"

"Look D, y'all keep coming to me with that shit even though it has nothing to do with me. What y'all finna do is fuck up my friendship with my best friend behind that shit. I ain't about to do that because Marcus and I have been friends for way too long!"

"I get that, but does that mean he doesn't have to face his responsibilities?"

"I don't know nothing about that!" he said. "Kalisha said he's the daddy. Marcus said he never fucked her!"

"Keep your voice down!" I said as I stepped into his personal space.

Gary was a really good- looking guy. He was a couple of inches taller than me at 5'11. He had a golden bronze complexion and some pretty eyes. His lips were full and plump and standing this close to him, inhaling his cologne and shit was doing something to me. I had to step back a little because what I wanted from him now had nothing to do with Kalisha, her baby or Marcus.

"I'm just saying that whatever y'all got going on doesn't involve me, so I don't want any parts of it. Please don't come to my office asking for favors like that again," he said as he licked his lips.

"I'm sorry. It's just that I don't want her baby to grow up without a father," I said. I really felt bad for Kalisha. Her son deserved to have his father in his life.

"Well, you can't force a man to step up if he doesn't want to. If that is Marcus' baby, eventually, the truth will come out and he will have to face the music. For right now, I'm done with this conversation."

He walked pass me and lightly brushed against me, sending chills up and down my spine. I had always had a crush on Gary, but things between us never took off. I wished he was single so we could see where things with us could go. Hell, I didn't even know if he wanted to try anything with me, but I was sure if he wasn't already involved, I'd be able to find out.

"Okay, cool. I'll do what I need to do to help her on my own," I said.

"You do that."

"I will," I countered as I walked toward the door on shaky legs.

"Good!"

Gary always had to have the last damn word. It was okay though because it gave me the opportunity to look back at him before walking off. I made sure to twist my hips just a little harder before I left. I didn't look back again, but I could feel his eyes on my ass. I made my way back to my office wondering how I could get Gary to be mine.

Now, here I was, a week later holding Kalisha's precious little boy. She had gone into labor at four this morning and called me. Not wanting her to go through labor and delivery alone, I slid out of bed and got myself together to go pick her up. I had to call out of work with my job because when it was time for me to get there, she was still in labor. Thankfully, around 11 this morning, she had given birth to a healthy seven- pound baby boy. He was perfect too, with all ten fingers and toes and a head full of straight, silky black hair.

My phone started ringing around 1:45 so I handed the baby to Kalisha and stepped out into the waiting room to answer. To my surprise it was Gary.

"Hey, why didn't you show up at work today?" he inquired.

"I'm sorry. I didn't think I had to clear my schedule with you first," I responded.

"HA! HA! I was just worried about you."

"Well, thanks, but I'm fine. I'm at the hospital..."

Before I could finish, he interrupted me.

"The hospital? I thought you said you were fine! What are you doing at the hospital if everything is okay?" He was asking so many questions that I had to ask him to stop and just chill for a minute.

"Kalisha went in labor this morning. She gave birth a couple of hours ago," I explained.

"Oh word! That's cool that you were with her," he said.

"She's my best friend. I had to be there. Did you miss or something?"

"I actually do. I was looking for you and wondered where you were."

I smiled at the thought of him missing me. "Well, I'm taking a couple of days off, but I'll be in Thursday."

"Aight. Take care of your friend."

"I will. Thanks for checking on me," I said.

"That's what friends do. Talk to you soon."

I ended the call with Gary and headed back to Kalisha's room. That man had just sent my heart racing just with his little bit of conversation. Lord only knew why I was lusting for Gary now. When I had the chance with him, I should've taken it. Now that he had someone, I didn't want to be known as a homewrecker.

Hopefully, things between them would end soon and I could be his shoulder to cry on.

Chapter five

Porsha

Things between me and Chandler had been so tense ever since that night we slept together. I wanted so badly for things between us to get back on track. I assumed after that night it would. I woke up the next morning and made him breakfast and everything. After he ate and took a shower, he said he'd holla at me later and walked out. I couldn't believe he just left me like that, without even giving me anymore dick.

I tried apologizing to him again for embarrassing him that day at the carwash. He didn't want to discuss it. I figured that meant we were good. I had been waiting to hear from Chandler since he left my apartment that day. The part that hurt me the worse was when I told him that I still loved him, and he shot me down.

"Didn't last night mean anything to you?" I asked as my voice cracked with tears.

"You were horny, I was horny, so I gave you what you wanted while relieving myself," he said.

"But I thought..."

"You thought what Porsha? That we were getting back together?"

"Well, yea."

"I don't know what made you think that. We ain't had shit to say to each other ever since that day at the carwash," he said.

"But you've still been coming with me to my doctor's appointments," I argued.

"You're carrying my kid! Did you think I wouldn't be there?"

"I just thought..."

"I know what you thought, and that might be my fault."

"But I still love you," I cried.

"I know. I have love for you too. You're the mother of my kid, but that's about as far as our relationship is gonna go. I already told you that I'm seeing someone," he said.

That brought me back to the conversation with that bitch last night. Before she hung the phone up, she made it very clear that she didn't want anything to do with Chandler. I was hoping that she meant that shit, and that if he contacted her, she hung up on him without letting him know why she no longer wanted to see him.

Before he left, he hit me with the hardest blow. "Look Porsha, I still care about you a lot, but I don't want you to be running around here with false hopes about where you stand.

We're better off if we just stay friends and co-parent our baby. To be honest, I'm much happier without you as a girlfriend. I have less drama in my life to the point where I even sleep better at night," he said.

My heart was crushed at that point. It seemed like no matter how I felt about Chandler, at that point, it didn't even matter. He had killed all hope for us having a future.

It had been a whole week since we last spoken, but we were going to see each other on Saturday. I was now six and a half months pregnant. My baby shower was this weekend, and I was hoping all my girls would be able to make it, but Kalisha went in labor earlier, so I knew she wouldn't be there. It was cool though because my party was co-ed, so it was going to be lit!!

Every day was a day of prayer for me. I was praying that Chandler wouldn't find out that I interfered with his relationship, even though I felt justified for doing it. That bitch had her claws in my man since the day I wanted to snatch her wig off. I knew what she was up to even then, only his ass couldn't see it. Now that she had decided to leave him alone, I couldn't be happier.

My ringing phone interrupted my thoughts. When I saw that it was my baby daddy calling, I couldn't answer fast enough. "Hey, you," I cooed into the phone.

"Hey, what you doing right now?" he asked.

"Nothing much. Just laying around. Why? What's up?"

"I'm coming by. I just wanted to make sure that you were home."

"Yea, I'm here."

"I'm on my way!"

"Oka..." Before I could finish speaking, he hung the phone up.

Well damn! I wondered who pissed in his corn flakes this morning. I wondered what he was coming by for. It didn't even matter that there was something strange in his tone. All I knew was that my boo was on his way to see yours truly. I dashed to the bathroom and hopped in the shower. I wanted to be fresh, fresh when he came through the door.

I wanted him to be able to smell me and my delicious coochie all the way to the front door, even though I was hundreds of feet away. When I was done in the shower, I dried myself off leaving my skin just a little moist to apply lotion. I had read that when you applied lotion to damp skin, the scent lasted longer or some shit like that. I had read so damn much that I might have read it wrong. All I knew was that I was supposed to apply my lotion to my body which was already damp.

After I passed lotion everywhere, even on top of my neatly shaved coochie, I sprayed myself with the same scented body mist, Beautiful Day from Bath and Body Works. It certainly was a beautiful day out and Chandler coming here was going to make it even more beautiful. By the time he knocked on the door, I was looking radiant and smelling good enough to eat.

I rushed to the door in the Gucci house slippers that Chandler bought me for my birthday. I had on some tight ass boy shorts and a bra top, exposing my booty and belly. I pulled the door back and my baby daddy's mouth literally hit the ground. He walked in and didn't even bother to say a single word to me. He took me in his arms and started kissing me as he backed me over to the sofa.

Yaaaaasss!! This shit is working out way better than I planned it!

He pulled my top and shorts off before he got naked and down to his knees. As I leaned back on the sofa, I watched as he parted my folds with his fingers and drove his tongue inside me. I gripped my boobs and squeezed my nipples as I watched him slurp, lick and suck all my juices out of my moistened kitty cat.

"Oh yes, baby! Suck my pussy!" I moaned.

A few minutes later, after I had saturated his tongue with my juices, he stood up. As his hardened shaft stared me dead in the face, I took it in my hands. I slid my tongue along the length of it before teasing his big mushroom headed tip.

"Shit!"

I finally placed his dick in my mouth and went to town, slurping and sucking like my life depended on it. My life may not have depended on it, but my family did. I needed Chandler in my life for us to be a family. I didn't want to be just a baby mama. I wanted to be a wife and I wanted Chandler to be my husband.

"Aw shit!" he said as he pulled his dick out of my mouth.

He pulled me up by the arm and turned me around. I placed my knees on the sofa and my elbows on the back of the sofa. Chandler positioned himself behind me and drove his dick so deep inside me that it caused me to gasp for air. I sucked in my breath and released it as he hit my G-spot over and over again. He held my ass cheeks open and plowed so deep I had to bite down on the sofa cushion.

"Oh my God!" I cried.

Chandler's phone started ringing but thank God he didn't check it. As my orgasm reached its peak, he continued to slam into me hard. I was delirious as my body shook to the core. His dick felt amazing inside my pregnant pussy. In that moment, I felt like his dick was made especially for my kitty.

About a half hour later, he succumbed to the pressures in his dick and squirted his nut all over our baby's head. He pulled out, grabbed his clothes and headed to the bathroom. I leaned against the back of the sofa inhaling and exhaling while trying to bring my breathing back to its normal pace. A few minutes later, Chandler emerged fully dressed with his phone and keys in his hand.

"Are you leaving?" I asked.

"Yea, I got some shit to handle."

"I thought you came by to see me," I pouted.

"I did. I saw that pussy, tore it up and now I gots ta go!" he stated.

"Wow! Really Chandler?"

"What's the problem now Porsha?" he asked.

"I feel like you used me, that's what the problem is!"

"I used you? Damn! You came to the door witcha ass all out! What did you think was gon' happen?"

"Well, I knew we would have sex..."

"And that's exactly what we did! Don't get mad at me cuz I got shit to do!"

"I just thought you'd spend the day with me," I said as I continued to pout.

"Nah, cuz we ain't together like that no mo', ya feel me? I ain't tryna confuse you about where you stand and shit!"

"So, you just gon' come in, fuck me, then bounce?"

"That actually wasn't my plan when I came here. I honestly came by to check up on you and chop it up a bit. But shiiiiddd, after you answered the door practically naked witcho pussy lips about to bust through the front of those shorts... well, a nigga had to handle his business!" Chandler said with a smirk.

"Fine! Just leave then!" I said angrily as I grabbed my clothes and headed to the bathroom.

I thought he'd come behind me to check on me, but he didn't. He actually left, which I realized when I heard the front door close. I wanted to cry because I couldn't believe that he was doing me that way. Now that he wasn't with that girl anymore, he could just be with me. Why didn't he want me?

I decided to take a shower, get dressed and go to the hospital to visit Kalisha and see her baby. I got in the shower and lathered my loofa with scented bodywash. When I was done, I applied lotion to my skin then got dressed. I made arrangements to be picked up by an Uber and waited for him on the stoop outside.

The driver pulled up about 15 minutes later and I was happy because I was ready to go. I practically ran to the car and jumped in the back seat. The whole ride there, I thought about what I wanted from Chandler. I loved him so much, but he couldn't seem to understand that. My phone rang a short time later and it was him.

"Hello."

"Yo, where you at?"

"I'm on my way to see Kalisha at the hospital," I said.

"Well damn! You coulda told me you were leaving," he said.

"What for? You were already gone when I decided to go visit her. Besides, you already said we aren't in a relationship, so I didn't need to keep tabs on you. So, uhm why do you feel the need to keep tabs on me?"

"Duh dumb ass! Cuz you my baby mama! As long as you carrying my fuckin' kid in your belly, I got a right to keep tabs on yo ass!" Chandler informed me.

I simply rolled my eyes thinking about how much of a double standard that was. For him to expect to keep tabs on me but didn't want me doing the same to him was preposterous.

"What can I do for you?" I asked, trying to avoid an argument with him.

"I want you to turn yo ass around and come back to yo crib," he stated.

"Ugh! Why?"

"Look, you coming or not?"

Dammit!

"I'm coming!"

"Don't keep me waiting too long either!"

"Well, you do know I'm on a ride with Uber."

"Hurry up!"

I ended the call and leaned towards the front. "I uh, I gotta go back home," I said.

"I'm sorry, but I have to take you to the destination on the map. If you need to go back to the place I picked you up from, you'll have to request on the app."

"Damn! For real?"

"Yes, that's how it works," the dude informed me.

I logged into my Uber app and proceeded to order another Uber to drive me back home. I had no idea what the hell was up with Chandler, but this shit had really pissed me off. If he was coming back to my place when he left, he should've said something. I had 10 minutes before I reached my destination and the app said the other driver would be pulling up in 11 minutes. That was really cutting it close.

"Can you drive a bit faster? If I'm not there by the time the other driver pulls up, he's going to leave," I expressed.

"I know, but we're obligated to follow all traffic signs including speed limits. I'm sorry, but I can't go faster than I'm already going," he said.

"Wooooow! Okay!" I huffed as I sat back in my seat.

That muthafucka was really trying me right about now. First, he couldn't take me back home. I had to order another damn driver. And now, he couldn't go a bit faster to help me reach the hospital in time. When we finally made it, I was getting out of the car when he turned to face me.

"Uh, I'd appreciate if you'd rate me a five. Thank you," he said.

"Yea, okay."

I got out the car and closed the door right before the other Uber driver drove inside the circle. I quickly jumped in the Nissan Altima and settled in the back seat.

"Looks like you got the weight of the world on your shoulders chile," the dude noted.

"Not really."

"If you wanna talk about it, go head and spill it," he said.

"I'm good homie. Just drive the car please."

"Well excuse me Miss Thang!" he said with a bit of an attitude.

I didn't care what kind of attitude he had though. All I wanted was to get home to find out what the hell Chandler was calling me back there for. I mean, he just left and didn't say shit to me about coming back. Now, he had made it back to my apartment and wanted to know where the hell I was. The guy pulled into the apartment complex half an hour later.

"So, uhm, a five- star review would definitely be appreciated. Thank you," he said with a smack of his lips.

What the hell was up with these drivers today? First, the other one practically begged for a five- star review even though he wouldn't drive me back to my place or speed to get me to the hospital in time. Now, this one was doing the same thing. They acted like they had done something so special for me. Like they deserved anything above a two.

I didn't even bother responding. I just opened the door and hopped out the car. I was on my way to unlock the door when Chandler stepped out of a burgundy Chevy Impala. I rolled my eyes upward. I couldn't believe he had purchased another car for himself while I was pregnant and still calling for an Uber. That shit was so selfish of him.

"Is this why you wanted me to come back here? So, you can show off your new ride?" I asked as I pointed to the car.

He smiled and rubbed his goatee. "Man, you always running yo mouth!"

"Because you be pissing me off!"

"How did I piss you off though?" he asked looking all innocent and shit.

"When you left here Chandler, you never said anything to me about coming back."

"I didn't think I had to tell you that. But aye, check this out." He smiled and walked closer to me. "Close your eyes."

"Boy bye! I am not fixin' to play games with you!"

"C'mon man! Close ya fuckin' eyes and quit acting childish!"

"Oh wow! I'm acting childish cuz I don't wanna close my eyes so you can probably put your dick in my hand," I said sarcastically.

He busted out laughing and I wondered what the hell was so funny.

"Girl, you really think I'ma pull my dick out in broad daylight? You've got to be kidding me! I ain't tryna have people thinking it's an eclipse around this muthafucka!" he clowned. "Just close yo eyes man! I ain't got all afternoon for this shit!"

I did as he asked seeing as how he seemed to be growing impatient. "Open yo hand."

My eyes popped open. "You see! I am not finna do..."

"C'mon bruh! Close yo eyes and open yo hand! Damn!"

"I swear if you put your dick in my hand..."

"Girl shut the fuck up!"

I closed my eyes and reluctantly opened my right hand. When I felt something hard in my hand, I didn't know what the hell it was. I opened my eyes and saw the key in my hand. "What's this?" I asked, afraid to believe what I wanted to.

"I bought you a car," he said with a smile as he rubbed his hands together.

"Boy quit playin'!"

"I'm serious. I can't have my baby mama catching rides like that. So, I went down to the dealership and copped you a whip!"

"You're serious?" I asked as a huge smile spread across my face. "You bought me a car?"

"Yea. Go check it out." He smiled as he headed around to the passenger's side.

I slid in the driver's seat and was in awe of this car. Chandler reached in the glove box and pulled out the paperwork. He handed it to me, and I opened the paperwork. The car was paid in full and was listed in my name only. I stared at my name with my mouth open for about 15 seconds.

"It's a push to start whip cuz it's a 2019. If you look at the dash, you gon' see that it has about 40 miles on it."

"You really bought me a brand- new car!" I said excitedly.

"Yea. So, to start the car, you gotta press the brake and the push to start button."

I did as he said, and the car purred to life. "I set all the radio stations I thought you would like on the way here. You got free oil changes for three years, so just take it to the dealership every five thousand miles and they'll change it for you. You have Wi-Fi, navigation, and OnStar. I tried to get you as many perks as I could."

"Oh my God! I can't believe you did this for me!" I said as I leaned over and kissed him.

It shocked me when he kissed me back, but the kiss didn't last long. "Look in the back seat," he said with a smile.

I turned toward the back seat and saw that he had already put the baby carrier in place. Tears sprang to my eyes as my emotions boiled over. Chandler said he didn't want to be with me anymore, but that might change soon. The fact that he did that for me meant he still cared about me. So, in my eyes, there was hope for us.

"Thank you so much babe. No one has ever done anything like this for me before. So, if you get mad at me, you can't take my car back, right?"

"Nah, it ain't my ride to take back. Even though I paid for it, it's in your name."

"I can't believe you did this," I said as I brushed away my tears.

"Well, now you can drive yourself to go visit Kalisha. I gotta get down to the carwash. I'ma holla atchu later," he said.

"Okay. Thanks again," I said.

He jumped out the car and walked over to his truck. I hadn't even noticed his truck sitting there until he went towards it. I was super excited about this car. I immediately connected my phone to the car and got on the road to go back to the hospital.

Chapter six

Chandler

I knew that the relationship that I had with my baby mama was confusing. That was most likely my fault. Even though I knew Porsha wasn't good for me because she was too damn immature, I couldn't seem to stay away from her. Fucking her pregnant pussy was different than any other pussy. I had never fucked a pregnant woman before, so having sex with Porsha these past couple of weeks felt good as fuck.

What I had noticed though was that I hadn't been hearing from Maya. Last time I spoke to her, we were on good terms. But ever since that night I went over to Porsha's place, I hadn't heard from her. I knew she didn't know what I had done. How could she? I just couldn't understand why she wasn't responding to my calls or text messages. I told myself that when I got a little bit of free time, I'd contact her. I mean, she was my financial advisor and marketing manager.

However, time hadn't really permitted for me to swing by her office. The carwash had gotten busier since that day of Porsha's blowup and I had been swamped.

Sure, I had people in place to manage my shop when I wasn't around, but I enjoyed being hands on in my own business. I was going to have to make it a point to go by Maya's office next week and find out what the hell was going on. But this weekend was our baby shower and I had to help Porsha get shit together.

I knew she would be surprised when I bought her the car, but to be honest, that was something I should've done a long time ago. As the mother of my child, she should have been had her own car. Since it was taking her longer to get it on her own, I felt it was my duty to get it for her. She was six months pregnant, so the last thing she needed was to be grabbing a ride with some nigga she didn't know. That was putting her and my son at risk and I couldn't allow that.

So, when I left her house earlier after I made the call, it was to pick up the car that I had specifically ordered just for her. The car was a rich burgundy color with a candy coat, so it sparkled. I knew that Porsha would have loved that. Her interior seats were a soft tan color but was smooth and leather. The look on her face when she saw that car was really for her was priceless.

I didn't know where things were going between Porsha and I, but I had to look out for her now that she was carrying my seed. After I surprised her with the car, I headed to the carwash. I had been spending a lot of time there, but I also had to be with Porsha when she had doctor's appointments.

I wasn't excited about having a baby when Porsha first told me. But once I saw my lil man on the monitor for her first ultrasound, I was super happy. Seeing his little heart beating on the screen let me know that I was really going to be a father. That meant that everything I did from this point on would reflect me as a parent. I didn't have my dad in my life. He died during a drive-by shooting when I was a kid.

Because I was only five when he was killed, I didn't have too many memories of him or us. Sure, my mom showed me pictures when I was growing up, and she let me know he was my dad, but I didn't remember him. I didn't want that for my little boy. I wanted him to know that I was his daddy and I loved him. If Porsha would grow the hell up and act her age, I wouldn't mind being with her while we raised our son.

I could admit that I had a lot to do with her insecurities. At one point and time in our relationship, I couldn't keep my dick to myself to save my life. But one thing was for sure, she could never say that I had given her an STD. I never fucked without a condom.

Well, except with Porsha and that was because we were in a relationship. When I decided to stop fucking over her, she couldn't let that distrust go. She continued to question me about my whereabouts and if I was gone without checking in with her for a couple of hours, she was blowing my fucking phone up. I just couldn't deal with the shit anymore.

I pulled into my spot at the carwash and greeted the workers outside. Then I went inside and greeted a couple of other employees, Pam on the register and Jacks in the lobby tending to the customers. I greeted those customers with handshakes and nods before going to the back office. Payroll was today so I had to make sure that everything was intact to pay these people.

I knocked on Patricia's, my human resources and payroll manager, door before walking in. "Good afternoon boss man," she greeted me while batting her long eyelashes. I swear if she didn't stop, one of those things would start flying on its own in a few.

"How you doing, Patricia?"

"I'm good. I'm glad you're here. The checks have all been printed, so all they need are your signatures. The employees are getting a little antsy because I had informed them you would be here since earlier."

"I know and that was my bad. I had some business that came up, so I had to handle that first. Give me the checks and I'll sign them and get them to you ASAP!" I said as I reached for the bundle of envelopes.

"Thanks boss," she said as she flashed her brightest smile, still flapping those eyelashes.

I took the stack of checks, which was about 15 or 20, and headed to my office. I forgot how many employees I had off the top of my head. As I sat down at my desk, I pulled each check out of the envelopes and got to signing. It didn't take me but ten minutes to complete the job. When I was done, I took them back to Patricia since they usually went to get the checks from her office. I went back to my office and logged into my computer. I needed to check my sales for today so far and for yesterday.

Sales were very good, and I was proud of myself.

KNOCK! KNOCK!

I looked up and there was my mom. I was shocked because my mom lived a couple of hours away from my shop. I wondered what brought her here today.

"Hey ma," I greeted as I stood up to hug her. "What are you doing here?"

"Well, aren't y'all having a baby shower this weekend?" she asked.

"Yep, sure are."

"Well, I came early in case y'all needed help setting things up."

"But ma, today is only Wednesday. The baby shower isn't until Saturday," I stated.

"I know that. I came because I wanted to spend some quality time with you and Porsha before Saturday."

"So, you're staying until the baby shower?"

"No," she said with a smile. "I'm staying until Monday."

Now, don't get me wrong, I loved my mom to death. She was the first woman I ever said I loved you to and meant it. However, having my mom at my place until Monday was definitely going to put a cramp in my style. She expected to spend time with me and Porsha. Damn! We didn't even live together no more because we broke up.

"Oh wow! I didn't know you had plans to stay that long," I said.

"I know. It was a surprise! SURPRISE!!" she yelled happily. "Me, you and that daughter in law of mine are going to have so much fun!"

"Uh, me and Porsha aren't married ma."

"Yea, I know, but it won't be long now, right? I mean, y'all done laid down and made a baby, so now y'all need to give that child what he deserves... a family!" she said in a matter of fact tone that let me know it wasn't up for discussion.

My mom really loved her some Porsha. Since the moment they met, they became best friends. That was the main reason why I hadn't told my mom that Porsha and I had broken up.

"Where's Porsha now? Is she at home resting?"

"No, she went to the hospital to visit one of her friends that had a baby today," I informed her.

"Damn! Must be something in the water that got everybody 'round here getting pregnant!" my mom said.

"Must be. Did Shawnie come with you?"

Shawnie was my sister. She was going to Spelman University on a full scholarship. I was so proud of her and couldn't wait to see her walk across that stage next year and collect her diploma.

"No, but she will be here on Friday evening though. Come show me around your spot! I can't believe my son is a business owner!" she said as she hugged me. "I am so proud of you baby!"

"Thanks ma!" I blushed.

"See, you're doing real good for yourself. The only thing left for you to do is make an honest woman out of Porsha and you will be batting a thousand!"

I could tell that she wasn't going to let this marriage thing between me and Porsha go until I told her that we weren't together anymore. I didn't know how I was going to be able to do that though. Lord have mercy! Talk about throwing a nigga a curve ball.

I took my mom around the carwash and introduced her to my employees. They all seemed to adore my mom and she seemed to like them too.

I completed the tour and we ended up near her car. "I'm going to call Porsha and see what time she's going to leave the hospital..."

"Don't do that ma. Let her visit her friend," I said.

"She can visit her friend. I ain't stopping her!"

"But you know as soon as she finds out you're here, she's gonna drop everything to come see you!"

"I know, and that's what I love about her! She always puts her family first," mom said. "I'm going to go by the grocery store and pick up a few things. If I know you, that refrigerator is probably bare."

"No, it's not ma. You don't have to go out shopping..."

"I want to. I need to get something to cook so when you get home, you have a hot meal waiting. I'm sure Porsha won't mind me being in y'all's kitchen. Maybe she could even help me."

All I could do was smile. I mean, what else was there to say? After I got my mom on her way, I pulled out my phone and called Porsha to give her a heads up.

"Hey," she answered.

"Hey, you still at the hospital?"

"Yea. Kalisha's baby boy is so adorable! If I wasn't already pregnant, I'd wanna get pregnant!" she said with a laugh.

"HA! Anyway, guess who's in town..."

"I don't know. Who?"

"My mom."

"Aw, Ms. Mary is here?! Where is she? How long is she gonna be here?" Porsha asked. I could tell that she was just as excited about my mom being here as I was.

"She went to the grocery store to get some stuff to cook tonight. But listen, she doesn't know we broke up..."

"What? You didn't tell her?"

"I couldn't! She was making all these plans for our future and shit. I could barely get a word in," I said in frustration.

"Our future? What do you mean by that?" Porsha asked.

"Never mind. Look, I just need you to come to the house when you're done at the hospital."

"For what?"

"Well, for one, so my mom can see you. For two, we're either gonna have to break the news to her that we're no longer a couple or we're going to have to put on this fucking façade and pretend we're still together," I said.

"I like the pretend part. Does that mean we get to sleep in the same bed?"

"Well, duh! It wouldn't make sense for you to come over if you're gonna sleep in the guest room."

"Shit say no mo'! I'll be there as soon as I can," she said happily.

"Yea, aight. See you then."

I hung the phone up and wondered how the hell I was going to last all weekend with those two. "Jesus if you can hear me bruh, I'ma need some serious help to get through this."

I ran my hand down the front of my face and headed back inside. I had to get out of here, so I needed to talk to my manager, Tommy and let him know that I was leaving. I needed a few drinks to get me through this first evening for sure.

Chapter seven

Marcus

These past three weeks had been very stressful for me. I had to consistently lie to my wife, go to counseling and pretend I didn't mind that my mother in law had moved in. If I could change anything in the past, it would be that one night with Kalisha. Well, at least that one hour at her place.

Convincing my wife that nothing happened between us was a bit harder than I thought it would be. But at the end of the day, thank God she was able to give me the benefit of the doubt and we were able to get past that bullshit Kalisha. I had no idea one night with that woman was going to cause this much trouble. For her to come and accuse me of being her baby daddy in front of my wife was definitely embarrassing. Since that happened, Melina and I had gone to see the therapist four times. All four times, I denied even knowing Kalisha on an intimate level. Was I wrong for doing that? Probably.

Was I scared that one day we'd run into Kalisha again? A little. Was I afraid that Kalisha would somehow find a way to hunt my ass down? Not in the least. She knew nothing about my ass. All she had was a first name and my description could match any nigga in this big ass city. She could kick rocks and find her real baby daddy because I was not him.

Melina and I had been seeing our marriage counselor through video chat, and she was real helpful. She helped Melina get pass her insecurities and now she believed me. I felt kind of bad for lying to my wife, but I wanted her to be happy

Melina had been taking it easy the past few weeks per Dr. Lambert's orders. She took her maternity leave from her job and was relaxing at home. I still had to go to work, but her mom had taken the liberty of moving in so she could keep an eye on my wife during the day. I loved my mother in law, but this living situation wasn't the best one. My wife had another five weeks or so to go before she delivered. Dr. Lambert said that if she were to go in labor now, the babies would survive but depending on how much their weighed at birth, they would most likely have to spend some time in the hospital. I prayed that wouldn't be the case because I knew my wife wouldn't want to leave the hospital without the babies, and neither would I.

I didn't know what I would've done without the help of our marriage counselor, I didn't know if the two of us would still be together. Melina was very upset that some woman was accusing me of being her baby's daddy. I had to swear so many times that I hadn't been with Kalisha and had only met her once. Technically, I had only met her once. I wasn't lying about that, but I'd be damn if I was going to admit to sleeping with her. As far as I was concerned, it was her word against mine.

"Mr. O'Connor, I have Mr. Batiste on the line for you," my secretary stated.

I rolled my eyes, not knowing why Gary was calling me this time. "Thank you. Put him through." A short time later, my phone began to ring. "Aye man, if you're calling because those two broads are in your office..."

"Nah, that ain't why. Look man, I owe you a huge apology. I was wrong for calling you like that, but the way they were coming at me... I'm sorry. I hope we can move past this shit," he said.

"We can move past it as long as you understand where I'm coming from," I said.

"I get where you're coming from, but I don't understand."

"What don't you understand Gary?"

"I don't understand how you cannot want to see or be a part of your son's life."

"I don't have a son, that's how. I have a family already Gary. I don't even know why that chick is coming at me instead of going after her real baby's father. I didn't even hit it!" I lied.

"Well, she seems pretty sure that you did," he countered.

"You gon' believe a drunk bitch over me?"

"She's not drunk!"

"She was that night!" I remarked.

"I guess. Look, are you sure that little boy ain't yours?"

"Nigga, you want me to hang up on yo ass again?" I asked, growing agitated.

"Nah, we cool. I won't mention it again," Gary said.

"Good!"

"I gotta go. I'll holla at you some other time."

With that being said, I ended the call. A couple of minutes later, my cellphone beeped, signaling a text message. It was from Gary, so I opened the message and almost dropped my damn phone. It was a picture of a newborn baby with a caption that read, "At first I didn't think this was your baby, but now that I've seen him, you gotta admit that he does look like you bro. I understand you wanting to keep your family together, but are you really going to just leave that little guy without a father? Think about it, bro."

I was so fucking mad at Gary right now. I had kept that shit off my mind for the past two weeks. I didn't think about Kalisha at all. The only thing I was focused on was my wife and our two daughters she was carrying. Now that I had seen this picture of Kalisha's son, I couldn't deny that her baby did have some of my features.

That was the last thing I wanted to see.

"Dammit!" I fussed as I brushed my hand over my head before swiping it down the front of my face. "Why the fuck did Gary have to send me that picture?"

All of a sudden, I felt a little warm. I had to get the hell up out of this office. I grabbed my jacket and briefcase and headed for the door. "See you tomorrow Lynette," I said.

"Are you leaving for the day?" she asked.

What kind of stupid question was that? Didn't I just say that I would see her ass tomorrow?

"Yes, that is precisely why I said I'd see you tomorrow. I suddenly don't feel very well, so if anyone asks where I am, let them know I went home," I said.

"Yes sir. I hope you feel better soon," she said.

"Yea, thanks."

I headed for the elevators and pressed the button that would take me down to the first floor. The car dinged and came to a stop before I hopped into it. I pressed the button to go down. I leaned against the wall and breathed deeply. I felt like I was having a heart attack, but I knew that wasn't the case. I just felt like my whole world as I knew it was about to be shattered. I closed my eyes and prayed harder than I had ever prayed before. The elevator came to a stop and I rushed outside, taking in huge bouts of air into my lungs.

Once I had calmed down, I headed to my truck and climbed in. Maybe I could go to Kalisha and offer her some money to stay out of my life. But what if that little guy was my son. Could I just walk away from him like that without any contact? I mean, he didn't ask to be here. He didn't have a choice in the matter. Now that he was born, he was depending on his parents to give him the best life possible.

Kalisha had mentioned that she worked as a barista as Starbucks. That couldn't bring in much money, so maybe if I offered her about ten G's she'd get out of my life. But man, how could I walk away from that little boy if he was my son? I didn't know if I'd be able to do that.

My phone started ringing and I saw that it was my mother in law. "Hello."

"Hey Marcus, I don't want to worry you, but I think Melina might be in labor."

"What? Is she in pain?" I asked as I hit the gas and cranked up the speed.

"Well, she said her back hurts and she feels pressure at the bottom. Usually, that means she's in labor, but maybe it's because she's carrying twins. I'm not sure, but I think we might need to get her to the hospital," her mom said.

"Okay. I'm already on my way home. I should be there within the next few minutes or so."

"Okay. Don't go catching no speeding ticket now!" she scolded.

"No ma'am, I won't."

We ended the call and I said a quick prayer for my wife and kids to be okay. I was glad Ms. Belinda was home with Melina. I knew she was probably scared right about now. I hoped she wasn't in labor yet because I knew she didn't want to leave the hospital without the twins. I pulled into the driveway about 20 minutes later. I parked the truck and rushed inside the house. My wife was sitting at the edge of the sofa practicing the breathing techniques we learned from YouTube videos. I had wanted to attend Lamaze classes with her, but with all the doctor's and ultrasound appointments, I couldn't do them.

"How are you feeling babe?" I asked as I sat beside her and rubbed her lower back.

"The pain seems to be subsiding. It's not as bad as it was before," she said as she sucked in air and breathed it out.

"Do you think you should go to the hospital?"

"Let's just wait and see what happens in the next half hour. I don't wanna rush over there for nothing," she said.

"Okay, but if you feel the need to go let me know. The last thing we need is for you to deliver in our living room," I said, trying to make her laugh.

It worked and she chuckled a little. "I don't want that either," she said with a smile. "How did you get here so fast?"

"I left the office early. I just had this feeling that you needed me, so I wanted to be here for you."

"Aw babe," she said as she leaned her head against my shoulder.

"Oh, hey Marcus," Ms. Belinda said.

She handed the glass of ice water that she was carrying to Melina. "Thanks mom."

"Hey Ms. Belinda. Thank you for calling me," I said.

"Well, of course. I mean, you are those girls' daddy, so you need to be there for my daughter whenever she delivers."

"I couldn't agree more," I said as I kissed Melina on the forehead.

"Owwww!" Melina cried as she grabbed her belly.

"Okay mama, I think it's time for us to get you to the hospital," I said.

I helped Melina to her feet and started walking her to the door. "Ms. Belinda, you mind getting her overnight bag and purse please?" I asked my mother in law.

"Sure," she said as she rushed to the bedroom.

I helped Melina to the truck and got her settled inside. She was still doing the breathing exercises she had learned. I ran back in the house to make sure that Ms. Belinda found the bag and purse. As I was going in, she was coming out.

"If you could put that in the truck, I'll lock up and be right out," I said.

She made her way to the truck and I locked the door. I headed back to the truck, hopped in the front seat behind the steering wheel and started the vehicle. Then I backed the truck out of the driveway, put the blinkers on and tried to get to the hospital as fast as I could.

"Are you okay babe?" I asked Melina as I held her hand.

She didn't respond... just kept breathing.

I pulled into the hospital parking lot about 10 minutes later. I rolled around to the emergency entrance and helped my wife inside. Her mom followed close behind. I walked up to the window.

"My wife is 35 weeks pregnant with twins. I believe she's in labor!" I said.

The woman stood up and rushed to get a wheelchair. Melina sat in the chair and before she was wheeled to the back, I let her know that I'd be right back.

"I just need to go park the truck," I said.

"Hurry back Marcus! I don't want to do this without you!" she cried.

"Give me two minutes babe... two minutes!"

I rushed outside to move my truck. I hopped in my truck and parked in the available parking spot before heading back inside. Once I made my way inside, the young woman at the desk told me that my wife had been wheeled to the labor and delivery floor. I ran to the elevators and pressed the button to go up. When the elevator stopped on the third floor, I stepped off when the doors opened.

I rushed to the nurse's station and told them who I was and asked for Melina. I was led to a room down the hall. Melina had changed into a hospital gown already and the nurse was putting the baby monitors on her belly. She needed two monitors since she was having twins. I pulled the chair next to the bed and held on to her hand.

"How are you feeling?" I asked.

"It hurts!" she said as she squeezed my hand.

"Just practice the breathing," I said as I breathed in and out with her.

"I need to check your cervix," the nurse said.

Melina placed her feet in the bed as the nurse checked her cervix. The nurse removed her fingers and looked at the two of us. "You're dilated at five centimeters already," Donna said.

"What does that mean?" I asked.

"It means your babies will be here very soon at the rate your wife is going."

"Can I get something for the pain?" Melina asked.

"I'll get in touch with your doctor. I'm sure she'll approve the epidural, so the anesthesiologist will be here soon."

"Wait, wait!" I said as I turned to my wife. "I thought we were gonna do a natural birth if possible."

"We?! Do you see a "we" lying on this bed Marcus?!" Melina asked as she stared me down angrily. Damn! I had heard that pregnant women spazzed out and shit, but I didn't see that happening to my wife. "I want that epidural!"

I didn't say shit after that.

"I contacted Dr. Lambert on the way here," I stated to Donna after a couple of seconds. My wife had definitely put me in my place just now. That shit was embarrassing to say the least.

"That's good. I'm sure she's on her way. I just need to contact her about the epidural," Donna said. "Just hang tight for a minute. I'll go make that phone call and be back shortly."

She scurried out of the room, leaving me and Ms. Belinda to comfort my wife. I went to the bathroom and grabbed a towel. I ran it under some cold water and returned to wipe the sweat from my wife's face. A short time later, another nurse walked in with an incubator. There was already one in the room, but we needed two.

About five minutes later, the nurse walked back in followed by another doctor. I was glad because Melina was about to break my fucking fingers. That was how much pain she was in.

"Hello, I'm Dr. Franklin, the anesthesiologist. Dr. Lambert should be here soon, but I'm here to give you an epidural," Dr. Franklin said.

"Thank God," Melina cried.

"I'm going to need the two of you to step out for a minute please..."

"Why does my husband and mom have to step out?" Melina asked in a panic as she squeezed my hand tighter. "I need him here with me!"

"I usually ask the significant other or family members to step out in an effort to keep the patient from any distractions. I promise it'll only be for a couple of minutes," Dr. Franklin said.

"Babe, it's okay. We'll be right outside," I said as I kissed her on the forehead.

Ms. Belinda and I walked out after she kissed her daughter's cheek. As we made our way to the waiting room, Ms. Belinda spoke to me before I could say anything.

"Don't take what Melina said in there too personal son. I'm sure it was the pain talking," she said with a smile.

"Yea, thanks Ms. Belinda. I'm trying not to," I said.

My mom rounded the corner a minute later. She rushed over to me and hugged me before giving Melina's mom a hug. "How is Melina?"

"She's in pain so the doctor is in there giving her an epidural," I said.

"I kind of figured she'd want that pain medicine," my mom said.

"Yes, she did," Ms. Belinda chuckled.

A couple of minutes later, the nurse walked into the waiting room and told us that we could go back in the room. I was a little upset with my wife for speaking to me in that manner, but Ms. Belinda was right. She was speaking from the pain that she was in and I shouldn't take what she said personally. With that in mind, I put on a brave face and returned to her bedside.

Upon walking back into the room, you would've never guessed that just a few minutes ago, my wife's soul had been snatched up by Poltergeist. Now she was laying in bed calm and cool like a cucumber.

"Mama Gail, you made it!" Melina said excitedly as she gave my mom a hug.

"Of course, I made it! I wouldn't miss this moment for anything," my mom expressed as she clapped her two hands together.

Melina turned her attention to me and reached for my hand. "I'm sorry I snapped at you earlier babe. I really didn't mean to. I was just in an extreme amount of pain," she said. "Can you forgive me?"

"Ain't nothing to forgive bae. It's already forgotten about," I responded.

"I love you."

"I love you too. How do you feel now?"

"Way better than a few minutes ago. I literally can't feel any pain, but I know I'm still contracting because I could see it on the monitor. Isn't that crazy?" she asked.

"It really is."

There was a slight knock on the door before Dr. Lambert walked in. "Well, good evening everyone!" she greeted. "I was told that your baby girls are ready to make their entrance into the world."

"I think so," Melina said.

"Well, let me check your cervix so we can get this show on the road," she said.

Dr. Lambert proceeded to check my wife's cervix and then looked up with a smile on her face. "You're almost at nine centimeters! You are doing awesome!" Dr. Lambert said. "I'm going to step out for a couple of minutes to check on another patient. I'll be back in a few minutes. By that time, you should be ready to start pushing those baby girls out!"

"I'm so excited and nervous at the same time," Melina said.

"Why baby?" Ms. Belinda asked. "You are going to be a great mommy!"

"Yes, Melina. You are one of the kindest, sweetest people I know. I couldn't have asked for a better wife for my son," my mom said.

Melina brushed tears away from her eyes. "Me and Marcus have been through so much to get to this point," she said as she looked at me.

"Yes, we have had our ups and downs, but I wouldn't change anything because everything we have gone through has made us stronger," I said as I smiled and kissed the back of her hand.

I loved the hell out of my wife right now. I wished I could take some of the mean things I said to her back, but I couldn't. All I could do was try my best to make up for them and not let do it again. There was another thing I wished I could take back... that one damn night with Kalisha. I tried to pretend like the shit wasn't bothering me, but in the back of my mind, there was this little voice that was screaming at me to step up and be a man.

I owed my wife a huge apology for that one indiscretion, but at this point in our marriage, I didn't want to go backwards. That run in with Kalisha happened weeks ago, and Melina had put it out of her mind. The only thing on her mind right now was giving birth to our twins so we could be a happy family.

I couldn't even imagine how she would act if she knew the truth about that night. I decided to put that shit out of my mind. Dr. Lambert and a team of nurses walked in soon after and it was time for Melina to push.

Thirty minutes later, both of our daughter had been weighed, washed and had their first meal. As both girls laid on my wife's chest for their skin to skin bonding experience, me, Ms. Belinda and my mom watched in awe. Both girls were gorgeous with their little tiny noses, heads full of sleek black hair and pretty brown eyes.

After several minutes, Melina looked at me and asked, "Do you want to hold them bae?"

"Them? As in both at the same time?" I asked.

"Yes, don't you remember the nurse said you need to do skin to skin with them too?" she asked.

"Yea, you're right. I just don't want to break them. They're so fragile," I stated.

"Yea, I know, but you won't break them. Take off your shirt," Melina said with a smile.

"You won't hurt those babies Marcus. They need to get used to you though," my mom said.

I removed my shirt, feeling weird being without a shirt in front of my mom and mother in law. But I wanted that connection with my daughters and the doctor said it was best to get that bonding time when they were just born. Melina handed one baby to me and I held her close as she held me the other twin. I sat down on the sofa with them and laid them on my chest.

I held them close for a good 20 minutes before the grandmothers started hounding me about holding them. I handed them each a baby then put my shirt back on. No sooner had I buttoned my shirt there was a knock on the door. I turned to see who it was, and it was my brother Kendrick, Greg and Melina's sister Patrice.

They hugged me and Melina and the grandmothers before turning their attention to the babies. We visited with everyone for about three hours or so. Then they bid us farewell so Melina could get some rest. Once everyone cleared the room, I sat with Melina and we talked about names for our beautiful girls.

"Are we going to get their names to rhyme?" I asked.

"I'd like it if we could get names that matched."

"What names were you thinking of?" I asked.

"I like the name Diamond..."

"Hell no, babe! We are not naming our baby after the stripper chick on *Player's Club*!" I said.

"Now you see, I had a totally different thought about that. I was thinking that diamonds are a girl's best friend, and since they're twins..."

"Uh uh," I said. I was adamant about our little girl not having that name.

"So, what names were you thinking of?"

"I don't know bae. What about Monica and Veronica?"

"Hell no! Those are some old ass names!" Melina shrieked.

"Well, how about Marina and Karina with a K," I suggested.

She smiled and said, "I love Marina because it's close to my name. How did you come up with those names?" she asked.

"I don't know. I just thought of your name and Marina popped up. Then Karina came in right behind it. I'm glad you like them."

"I love them!" she said happily with a huge smile on her face. "So, who's who?"

"I think you're holding Marina and this right here," I said as I kissed the top of my baby girl's head. "This is Karina."

"How are we going to tell these little girls apart?" Melina asked.

"Well, Karina has a little apple birthmark on her lower back. I noticed it when I was changing her earlier. Marina has a birthmark too, but it's on her belly."

"Wow! I hadn't even noticed."

"Uh, babe, you haven't changed their diapers yet," I pointed out.

"Oh, yeah!"

"I love being a daddy," I said with a huge smile.

"I knew you would. You're a natural," she said.

"So are you babe. Thank you."

"For what?"

"For giving me the family that I always wanted," I said to her as I winked.

"Right. I guess all we need now is a son," she said as she winked back.

Wow! She definitely knew how to pull the plug on my happiness. I was just feeling like I was on cloud nine from the birth of my daughters. However, once she mentioned a son, that high dissipated.

"What's wrong?" she asked.

"Huh?"

"Your face just spoke 1,000 words. Did I say something wrong?"

"No, not at all. I mean, we just had twins. Isn't it a little early to be thinking about another baby?" I asked.

"Well, I didn't mean let's run out and get pregnant now!" She laughed as she rubbed Marina's little back. "We can wait about six months or so."

"You trying to get right back on it huh?" I asked with a nervous laugh.

"I just want them to be able to grow up together, that's all."

"No matter when we decide to have another baby, they will grow up together. I can promise you that."

"I'm just so happy that we finally have kids!"

"So am I bae," I said. The twins started fussing so we knew it was feeding time.

As tiresome as the first 24 hours was, I wouldn't change it for the world. I looked forward to bringing my girls home and having them to myself.

Chapter eight

Porsha

To say that things between Chandler and I were going great would be an understatement. Since his mom had come by for a visit, things had been going so good. The baby shower two weeks ago had me feeling like we were married. By the time Ms. Beverly left Monday morning, I had moved in with Chandler. He told me that he hadn't explained to his mom that we had broken up, and since she had shown up early, he didn't want to break the news to her like that.

I didn't care why he hadn't told her. I was just excited that we were living under the same roof again. Me and Ms. Beverly were closer than me and my own mother were. My mom and I got along, but not like me and Chandler's mom. My mom was overbearing, judgmental, and bitter from her breakup with my dad. Ms. Beverly was always so supportive and cheerful.

No matter what me and Chandler went through, she always saw both sides. She let me know when I was wrong, but also let Chandler know when he was wrong too. My baby was due in less than two months. I had stopped working so that I could get ready for the baby. Since I had moved in Chandler's house, he and his boys had hooked up the baby furniture in the nursery.

Today, I was going to fix up the nursery. I was having a baby boy and Chandler was super excited about it. He couldn't wait for CJ to be born. This was the life I had always wanted for us. When he got dressed this morning, it surprised me because I thought we were going to spend the day together.

"Babe where are you going?"

"Uh, as much as I'd love to just lay in bed with you all day, I still have a business to run," he said as he gave me the side eyes.

"I know that, but I just thought you were gonna help me fix up the nursery," I said as I pouted.

"My part is done. We put together the crib, changing table, chest, rocker..."

"I know babe. You don't have to run down the list of things you did. I just thought..."

"Sorry bae. I have a meeting that I need to get to in an hour."

"A meeting? With who?" I asked.

"With my financial advisor."

"Oh, I didn't realize you had a new financial advisor?" I said.

I was happy to hear that Chandler had gotten a new financial advisor instead of that heffa Maya. She had been wanting my man since day one. So, a new advisor was exactly what he needed.

"A new advisor? Who said I got a new advisor?"

"Well, you said..."

"I said I had a meeting with my financial advisor in an hour. That's what I said. I didn't say anything about a new advisor," he said.

"I just thought..."

"Maya has been doing a great job! I don't see any reason to get rid of her," he said. "Now, if you'll excuse me." He bent to give me a kiss. "I'll see you later."

Before I could say anything else, he walked out the door. I wanted to call Donya, but she had a meeting. Joy was at work, so the only one left was Kalisha. I knew she was at home with her new baby, so she had nothing but time on her hands.

"Hello."

"Hey girl, you busy?"

"Not really. I just put my baby down. What's up?"

"I need you to tell me if I'm being unreasonable or not."

"About what?"

"Well, Chandler just left. He went to a meeting. Guess with who."

"Girl, I have no idea. Just tell me."

"Maya! Can you believe that shit?" I asked.

"Who's Maya?"

"The bitch he left me for! The one who was so say marketing his business!"

"Oooooooh! That one. I thought you said they weren't seeing each other anymore," Kalisha said.

"Well, they weren't. To be honest, I don't even know how when they started talking again. Last time I spoke to her, I told her that me and Chandler were back together, and she needed to stay the hell away from him!"

"Well, obviously, she didn't take heed to your warning."

"Apparently!"

"What's the big deal though? I mean, you and Chandler are living together now. You're happy, right?" Kalisha asked.

"As happy as we can be. I just don't need any outside interference from that bitch!" I said.

"What I wouldn't give to be living with my baby daddy," Kalisha said.

"Speaking of baby daddy. Have you heard from him?"

"Heard from him? That must be a trick question!" she said all loud and shit.

"I was just asking. You knew better than to ask anything about my triflin' ass baby daddy! I have left him several messages and he hasn't contacted me once. I need to get a DNA test to prove our son is his."

"Are you sure that Cameron is his?"

"Are you kidding me? We've had this discussion already! I AM 100 PERCENT SURE THAT CAMERON IS MARCUS' SON!!"

"Sorry, I didn't mean to hurt your feelings or make you mad. I just want you to be sure. The last thing you need is to get a DNA test and that baby isn't his."

"The baby is his! If I had even a shred of doubt, I'd be looking the other way," Kalisha said.

"You know Marcus has a wife, right? And that they're expecting twins," I said.

"Of course, I know he has a wife! Look Porsha, despite how I come off, I'm not trying to hurt him or his wife. All I'm trying to do is make sure my baby has his daddy in his life. We slept together that night and created a child. I hadn't planned on getting pregnant, but I did. We have a beautiful son, so he needs to step it up and be a father to Cameron. If he won't do it on his own, maybe the child support division can help."

"You think putting him on child support is gonna make him be a part of Cameron's life?"

"Not really, but it's a start."

"Putting a man on child support never works out in a good way Kalisha. If you do that, trust me when I say, that man won't want anything to do with you."

"So, are you saying that I shouldn't get my baby's daddy to help me financially support him? Is that what you're saying?" Kalisha asked with an attitude. I could picture her twisting her neck in hot ghetto fashion.

"I'm not saying that. What I'm saying is you can get more flies with honey that with salt," I said.

"I ain't trying to get no damn flies! I'm trying to get some cash to take care of my son! Do you know how much it costs to care for a baby? I've been out of work for the past three weeks and I don't get paid for sitting on my ass! If Marcus was any kind of man, he would've gotten in touch with me by now! This is our kid, not just mine! I shouldn't be the only one taking care of him!" I could hear the frustration in Kalisha's voice as she broke down. Thank God I didn't have those kinds of problems.

At least Chandler moved me in with him and took care of me. The fact that he couldn't wait until our baby was born let me know that he would be a great daddy.

"I'm sorry Kalisha. I didn't mean to sound insensitive."

Even though Kalisha and I hadn't always seen eye to eye, I hated that she was going through this. The two of us had gotten a lot closer during our pregnancies. She was done with hers, but I was still carrying my little one. I knew that she was jealous of my relationship with my baby daddy, but that wasn't my fault. I had to do a lot to get me and Chandler to where we were.

"I know you can't possibly understand what I'm going through since you and your baby daddy are working things out. But just because y'all are all happy and shit, doesn't mean you get to make me feel wrong for trying to look out for my baby the way you do yours!" she said sadly.

"I know, and I'm sorry. You're right, I don't understand what you're going through."

"I just wish I knew how to get in touch with Marcus. I have no phone number, no address, nothing. It's like I had sex with a ghost, even though I saw him not that long ago," she said. "He refuses to call me. Gary refuses to give me any of his information. Shit, I bet he's telling his wife he ain't been with me at all."

"I feel what you're saying. I'm sure it's pretty frustrating to have a baby daddy who ghosted you. Damn! I really wish your baby was for..."

"Don't even say his name!"

"Well, at least if your baby was his, he'd be around for him. I mean, you know how to reach him and stuff."

"Yea, but he isn't the daddy. I'm not going to accuse someone who I know isn't Cameron's father."

"I know. Anyway, what do you think I should do about Chandler?"

"What should you do about him? What is there to do?"

"I mean, should I tell him about my conversation with that girl? Should I confess to him that I answered his phone?" I asked.

"Hell no! Why the hell would you do that?" Kalisha asked. "I mean, if she ain't saying shit, why should you?"

"True. I'll just leave it alone. I just hope things work out for both of us," I said.

"Me too. Well, I gotta go check on my little one. Talk to you later girl," she said.

"Okay. Give Cameron a kiss for me."

"I will."

We ended the call and I went to the nursery to put some things away. My baby shower was a hit and I ended up with so much stuff. I prayed that things between me and Chandler would keep moving forward. He was my soulmate and I wanted to marry him, but if he didn't feel the same way, I didn't know where we'd go from there.

Chapter nine

Chandler

Things with Porsha had been going better than I expected. When my mom was visiting, she made me see how important it was for me to be in my son's life. I knew that I could be in my son's life without being with Porsha, but my mom was right when she said it was better for us to live together. I didn't want Porsha to have to wake up during the night by herself. I didn't want her to have to deal with colic and stuff by herself.

We both created CJ, so we were both responsible for him. I wanted Porsha to know that I was here for her and I would be here for my son. I was finally able to get Maya to see me. I didn't know why she had been ducking and dodging me for the past few weeks, but that shit wasn't cool. She always had her secretary relay messages to me pertaining to business materials and I was tired of that shit.

She was the one I had been dealing with from the start, so why all of a sudden, I was dealing with someone other than her. I knew it wasn't because me and Porsha were together because we didn't get together until she stopped fucking with me. It was like one day we were good, then the next day, she wouldn't answer my calls or text messages.

Today, I was finally going to get some answers from her, and I couldn't wait to hear why she had been avoiding me. Even if she was a little upset about me and Porsha, she still should've kept in touch with me. I mean, that was the professional thing to do. After all, she was my financial and marketing advisor.

I could tell that Porsha was upset about my meeting with Maya, but I couldn't worry about that right now. I was a businessman who had business to handle. I wasn't going to let my girl get in the way of me handling my shit.

I walked into Maya's office at 11:00 that morning.

"Hello, Ms. Renella, I have an appointment with Maya," I said.

"Good morning Mr. Watson. I will let Miss Avery know that you're here," responded Ms. Renella, Maya's secretary.

I took a seat and waited for Maya to come get me. I hoped she wouldn't stand me up because I'd be pissed. It was the end of April, so I needed to get the marketing for next month off the ground. A couple of minutes later, Ms. Renella looked at me and told me that Maya was ready to see me.

I stood up and walked to her office.

"Hey Maya!" I said when I saw her. I walked over to her and tried to give her a hug, but the attitude she was giving me let me know that she wasn't feeling it.

What the fuck happened to us?

"I think we should just concentrate on keeping our relationship on a business tip, if that's okay with you."

"That's fine Maya. I wasn't trying to do shit but give you a hug. If you don't want it, that's fine."

"Cool. Let's get down to business," she said.

We sat at the round table in her office and worked on coupons, marketing strategies and ways to bring more business to my carwash. Maya always had some great ideas. I was lucky to have her on my side because I knew my carwash would be a success. An hour later, I left her office and headed to the carwash.

I still had no clue as to what her problem was, but I wasn't gonna worry about it. I had way too much shit on my plate as it was. If Maya wanted to continue acting like a kid, fuck it!

I headed to the carwash and it didn't seem to be that busy. That was cool though since today was only Wednesday. I was sure that things would pick up by the weekend. What I wasn't expecting was to find two chicks fighting inside my lobby. I didn't know what the hell they were fighting for, but they were pretty heated.

I had never seen two women fight like that before. They looked like they were trying to kill each other. I jumped in to try and pull them apart. Travis helped me pry the two of them apart while Jake stood in the corner with his arms crossed over his chest. He had a smirk on his face which I couldn't understand.

The two women continued to argue like squawking hens. "AYE! AYE! IF Y'ALL DON'T GET THE FUCK UP OUT MY SHOP WITH THAT SHIT, I'MA CALL THE POLICE TO HAVE Y'ALL ASSES ARRESTED!!" I yelled angrily.

I was so pissed off and they knew it too.

"Don't let me catch yo ass again bitch!" one of the females yelled at the other one.

"Bitch bring it!" yelled the other one.

They both got in their cars and peeled out like their asses was on fire. I ran my hand down my face and looked at everybody.

"Can somebody tell me what the fuck was going on in here?" I asked.

They all pointed to Jake. I turned my attention to him and eyeballed him angrily.

"In my office NOW!" I said.

I headed to the back office and busted in the door like the police with Jake following behind me.

"What the fuck man?!"

"I didn't do shit boss man!"

"You had two chicks fighting in my spot!" I yelled.

"No, I didn't. They were fighting because they crazy!" He giggled.

"Nigga you think this shit is funny?! That shit ain't funny at all!"

"Sorry boss man, but you had to be here when they first started fighting. That shit was kinda funny," he said.

"None of that shit was funny! This is my business and your place of employment!"

"So, you ain't never had two chicks fighting over you?"

I knew exactly what he was referring to. He was talking about that day Porsha and Maya got into it. I couldn't even argue that the shit never happened because it did. However, the difference between my incident and his was that I didn't think that shit was funny. Not only that, but the women didn't exchange blows or punches. The fact that he thought that shit was funny let me know that he was just an immature kid.

"Regardless of whether I had women fighting over me or not has nothing to do with this shit at all! The fact that you thought that fight was funny makes me wonder... you know what man? You're fired!"

"What?"

"You're fired!"

"For what?!"

"For bringing that drama to my spot!!" I said angrily. "You are supposed to handle your personal business outside of this place!"

"So, you're firing me because two bitches couldn't control their fucking tempers?!"

"No, I'm firing you because that shit was unprofessional!"

"Wow! Ain't that about a bitch!" he said. "Man, I'm sorry about the shit with those bitches, but you know I'm on probation. I need this job!"

"Look man, while I sympathize and understand your need to be employed, I have been letting a lot of shit slide with you just so you can keep your job. Aside from the fight that happened a little while ago, you've been late quite a few times and you've also been on your phone more than you've been doing your job!" I said. "Enough is enough!"

"So, why didn't you fire me for that shit a long time ago?"

"Like I said, I thought you needed this job! I was trying to help yo ass!"

"I do need this job!"

"Apparently, not as bad as I thought you did for you to allow two women to fight over you in my establishment!"

"THAT WASN'T MY FUCKIN' FAULT!!"

"BUT YOU DIDN'T DO SHIT TO STOP IT!! As far as I'm concerned, you instigated that shit and just sat back and laughed about it! Tell me one fuckin' thing that was funny about that!" I was fuming mad at this lil nigga and he was acting like he didn't do shit wrong. Like he was entitled to

"You know what BOSS MAN?! I AIN'T ABOUT TO BEG YO ASS FOR NO DAMN JOB!! WHAT THE FUCK DO I LOOK LIKE BEGGING A NIGGA FROM THE HOOD FOR A JOB?!!" he asked. "LOOK HERE, YOU CAN TAKE YOUR FUCKIN' JOB AND SHOVE IT UP YOUR ASS!!" He took his work shirt off and tossed it on the floor. "You ain't gots ta fire me, homeboy! I QUIT!!"

With that, he turned his back and charged out of my office. He cussed and fussed the whole way out the door. I imagined he was going to head on over to one of those girl's houses, if not both, and kick their asses for him losing his job. A nigga like that always blamed everyone but themselves. That nigga had been slipping on the job for a long time. If he hadn't been on probation, I would've been fired his ass.

That was the only reason I had allowed him to keep his job as long as I had. But today's fight and his lack of interest to stop those girls from making fools of themselves was bullshit!

KNOCK! KNOCK! KNOCK!

"Come in!"

"You alright boss?" Patricia asked as she peeked in my office.

"Yea, I'm straight. I ain't allowing that lil nigga to knock me off my square," I replied.

"Okay. I just wanted to make sure you were good."

"I'm always good, but thanks for checking Patricia."

"You're welcome."

She left and went back to work. I leaned back in my chair and looked up at the ceiling. That nigga was lucky that I was in my place of business. Otherwise, he would've seen the hood side of me that he was referring to. I didn't play that disrespectful shit at all. One day, I'd run into his ass again. Of that I was sure.

Chapter ten

Melina

Two weeks later…

I was exhausted, to say the least. I adored my little angels, but they had officially worn me out. However, as exhausted as I was, I wouldn't change it for the world. Marina and Karina were my little miracles and they came at a time when I thought my marriage was over. I couldn't believe the change in my marriage. We did a complete 360.

I loved Marcus more than ever now. He was the most attentive and helpful husband I could've asked for. He helped me with the girls every single time they woke up. I couldn't have done this without him. He was scheduled to return to work in a couple of days. I was going to miss having him here to help me, but I knew one of us had to work.

My mom had decided to come and stay with me for a few weeks since my husband was going back to work. Me and the babies had doctors' appointments tomorrow, so I was glad that my husband would be there.

"Have I told you lately how much I love my life?" Marcus asked.

"You've told me just about every day since the twins were born, but you can tell me again," I said as I winked at him.

We were sitting on the sofa wrapped in each other's arms enjoying a rare quiet moment. The twins were asleep, and my husband had his arm around me. We were cuddled on the sofa watching *Married at First Sight*, which happened to be one of my favorite reality shows.

"Thank you for giving me our baby girls."

"Thank you too. I mean, I couldn't have gotten pregnant without your input," I said.

"HA! Ha! You're too funny," he said as he planted a kiss on my right temple.

One baby started to whine, so Marcus got up. Before he made it to the nursery, the other twin started crying. At first, it was hard to tell the twins apart, but after a couple of weeks, it became very easy. Karina was a little plumper than Marina. When I looked at Karina's chubby little face as opposed to Marina, I clearly saw the difference.

It was Karina's fault she was so greedy though. While she was sucking five ounces every five hours, Marina was only sucking four. It was crazy because they were only six weeks old.

We fed the babies, changed their diapers, then sat in matching rockers and rocked them back to sleep. After we were done getting them to sleep, we put them in their crib. I thought it was a good idea to let the twins sleep in the same crib until they were at least six months old. That way they could bond and be closer to each other. I wanted my girls to be each other's best friends. It was hard to find friends that you could count on these days. That was why I was happy when the doctor told me that I was having twins.

Not having to worry about my girls finding friends they could count on was one less problem they had to worry about. They would grow up together, play together, just do everything together.

My sister and I were close, but we weren't as close as I would've liked us to be. Growing up, we were closer. I think we just grew up and now, we didn't have time for one another. I just had twins and my sister had three children ranging from ages seven months to four years old. She definitely had her hands full.

"I'm gonna take a shower and try to get some sleep," I said.

"Okay. I'll be in to shower when you're done," he said.

I went to the bathroom and turned the water on. I scrubbed myself clean then stepped out and dried myself. Then I climbed in the bed and went right to sleep. I didn't even hear when Marcus went to take a shower.

The next morning, Marcus and I got up and got the girls ready for their appointment. I had an appointment this morning, but mine was at 11 and the twins' appointment was at nine. They had their vital signs checked before they were weighed. The doctor then checked them out and gave them a clean bill of health, which we already knew. That was a great, uneventful appointment. I wished I could say the same for my own.

We arrived at the doctor's office at 10:45. Marcus figured if we got there early, we could be seen early. However, as soon as we walked in the doctor's office, I instantly felt a draft in the room. I walked to the counter and signed in. As Marcus and I turned around, there sat the woman who accused him of being her baby's daddy with a huge smile on her face.

"Thank God! I was about to walk the hell up outta here!" she said.

"Look girl..."

She stood up while her baby laid in the carrier. "No, you look. I'm not even trying to start anything with you Marcus." Then she turned to me. "Look ma'am, my name is Kalisha Moore. I'm not trying to disrespect you at all. All I want is for Marcus to take care of my kid the way he takes care of yours."

"I'm his wife!" I said.

"Understood, and no disrespect, but when I met Marcus, he never told me he was married. So, I think this situation should stay between me and Marcus," she said.

What the hell was she talking about? Anything that had to do with my man, had to do with me!

"Well, I don't know what Marcus told you when the two of you met, but he is very married. With that being said, anything that has something to do with Marcus has a lot to do with me, especially when it has to do with a woman claiming to have a baby by him," I said.

I didn't know who this chick thought she was, but she'd better check herself. She had been coming off as mad disrespectful since day one and I wasn't going to allow it again.

"Look, all I want is for Marcus to do for my kid the way he's doing for yours. I mean, you haven't seen him before, but if you look at him, you will see the resemblance between him, your husband and your babies."

"Please don't mention my babies anymore. They have nothing to do with this conversation at all," I said. I was going to draw the line there. She knew nothing about me or my family, so she needed to leave my girls out of this shit.

I wasn't trying to be a part of none of this bullshit at all. I didn't know if Marcus was her baby's father or not, but the girl seemed adamant in her claim that he was.

"Go ahead! Look at my son and then look at your husband!"

"This has nothing to do with me," I said.

"Exactly what I was trying to say from the jump! I'm trying to be respectful of you."

"I don't mean this situation has nothing to do with me because it does. I mean, looking at your baby has nothing to do with me," I reiterated for her and the people in the back.

I was so embarrassed. I couldn't believe we were going through this shit again.

"How many times to I have to tell you that kid ain't mine!" Marcus finally spoke up.

"Marcus why the hell would I lie to you? What do I have to gain from pointing the finger at you?"

"Money! Ain't that what all chicks want when they claim a nigga is their kid father when he ain't?" Marcus asked.

"You sound real stupid right now!" Kalisha said. "I don't know nothing about your financial status or anything like that!"

"I know you don't, but that don't mean you ain't after my money!" my husband said.

"Okay, so maybe I do need your help to take care of my son financially, but this is also about your time. I want you to spend time with Cameron so he could know you," she said.

"That ain't my kid!"

"I'm not lying when I say this is your child!" she said. "If you don't believe me, we can get a DNA test done whenever you're ready. I know who my baby daddy is, and I have nothing to hide!"

"I don't need a test to tell me that this kid ain't mine!" Marcus said through clenched teeth.

"Marcus just take the test and get it over with," I said.

I was sick and tired of this shit. Of course, I wanted to believe my husband, but if taking a paternity test would get this girl off his back, then he needed to take one taken and he needed to do it with as soon as possible. It would help a whole lot if he just did it and got it over with.

"I'm not taking any damn DNA test for a kid I KNOW AIN'T MINE!!" Marcus said angrily. He walked over to the counter and looked at Rebecca. "How much longer we gotta wait before my wife is seen?"

"Uhm, the doctor will be ready for her in a couple of minutes..."

"Well, the doctor needs to hurry the fuck up! Shit, can't you call her to the back now? Check her fucking vitals and weight or something," Marcus said. "Just get us to the back!"

"Give me a minute Mr..."

"You ain't gotta call my fucking last name!" he said. "Shit, you know what it is, and I know what it is, so..."

I was pissed that Marcus was speaking to Rebecca in that manner. She was just doing her job and didn't deserve his disrespect.

"Yes sir."

Rebecca stood up and hurried to the back. I had never seen her move so quickly. Marcus' attitude definitely lit a fire under her ass. The shit would be comical if this girl wasn't still standing in my husband's face accusing him once again.

"Marcus, I really think you should just take the damn test!" I said.

What was the fucking problem with taking the test if he wasn't the father? Just because he knew he wasn't the dad, that didn't mean I knew that. He should take the test just to give me peace of mind. He felt he didn't have anything to prove, but he did. I had a ton of questions at the back of my mind, but to keep the peace, I held them inside. I didn't want me and Marcus to go back to the way things were before. However, if he didn't take that test, we would definitely have a huge problem.

"If you aren't the father like you claim, what's the problem with taking the test?" the girl asked.

"I'm not gonna let you waste my fucking time just to prove what I already know!" Marcus said.

"Then prove it to me!" I said.

"What?" he asked with a shocked expression on his face.

"You said you already know he isn't yours."

"Fuckin' right!" he said.

"Okay, then prove it to me," I repeated.

"But you said you believed me," he said.

"I do, but..."

"Then if you believe me, what's the damn problem Melina?" he asked angrily.

"The problem is this girl..."

"That girl? That girl has a name and it's Kalisha. Thank you," she said with a smirk and a smile.

"Well, KALISHA..." I paused to smirk at her ass. "Is claiming the baby is yours, so take the test and prove to her that you aren't the father."

"Yea Marcus, prove it to me. Pleeeeeeeease prove me wrong. I dare you to prove to me that my son isn't yours," Kalisha said.

"Girl please! I ain't got shit to prove to you!" he said.

"But you have a lot to prove to me... your wife!" I said as my emotions finally came to the forefront. I didn't want to show any sign of weakness in the presence of all these strangers, but I was hurt.

The only reason I could think of that would keep my husband from taking that test was if he was afraid that the truth would come out. The truth being that Kalisha's son was his. My heart was breaking in a bunch of tiny pieces and my husband didn't even seem to care. If he could put himself in my shoes for one minute, he would see that we needed this done to save our marriage.

"Melina if you don't believe me, that says a lot about our marriage," Marcus said.

"That's funny because I was actually thinking the exact same thing," I said as I wiped the tears from my eyes.

"Trust me, ain't shit funny about this!" Marcus huffed.

Since my husband wasn't going to make this easy, I decided to take my chances with Kalisha. "Can you please give me your phone number?"

"Yea, sure." I pulled out my phone as she rattled off her number.

"How do you spell your name?" I asked.

"K-a-l-i-s-h-a!"

"Thanks," I said as I locked her name and number in my phone.

"I don't know what the fuck you taking her number for. I still ain't taking that fuckin' test!" Marcus said. "Girl you better quit fucking with me and go find your real kid's father!"

I was trying to figure out why my husband was so heated. Granted, being accused of fathering a child that wasn't yours would have any man upset, but Marcus was beyond upset. He was so mad his temples were throbbing. If he would've been a bull, he would have smoke coming out of his nostrils right now. One doesn't get that mad unless there was some truth to the situation. The last thing I wanted to believe was that my husband had cheated on me and fathered a child outside of our marriage. But I couldn't be a fool and deny the shit that was staring me in the face.

Kalisha's son resembled my girls and I couldn't deny that fact. Most women would put blinders on and believe their husband just to keep their marriage on the right track. I wasn't about to do that. If my husband was this baby's daddy, then he needed to step up and be in that little boy's life. Of course, that meant I'd be filing for divorce, but that didn't have anything to do with his role as a father to our daughters.

"Melina O'Connor!" I was called to the back.

"I'll be in touch," I told Kalisha.

"Okay, thanks."

I pushed the baby stroller to the back as Marcus followed behind me. I could tell that he was angry, but I didn't care. I was tired of having this question about my husband in the back of my mind. I loved him, but the last thing I wanted was to be lied to or made a fool of. And if he was Kalisha's baby's father, he had been making a fool of me for way too long.

So, whether Marcus liked it or not, he was going to take that test... PERIODT!

Chapter eleven

Marcus

Things between me and my wife had been better than they had been in a long time... until we got to her doctor's office. I had no idea Kalisha was going to be there with her son. If I had known that shit, I would've had Melina reschedule her appointment for another date. Walking in, I just assumed it would be a normal visit. As soon as we turned around from Melina signing her name on the check in sheet, my heart dropped. There sat Kalisha with a huge smile on her face.

I couldn't believe my wife was entertaining the idea that I might be that kid's father. She had me standing there with my mouth hung open, looking every bit the gotdamn fool. Why the fuck wouldn't she support me on this matter? To stand there and tell me that she needed me to prove to her that I wasn't the father in front of strangers had me feeling some kind of way about her right now.

I didn't need a test to tell me something I already knew. I knew I wasn't that chick's baby daddy. We only slept together one fucking night! She couldn't possibly be pregnant by me after one fucking night!

When Melina took her number, that did it for me. When her name was called, I was happy as fuck. I needed her to get seen so we could get the fuck up out of here. She kept looking at me, but I didn't know what the fuck she was looking for. If she was trying to feel me out about whether I was mad or not, my facial expression should've said it all.

"Good morning Melina and Marcus!" Dr. Lambert greeted. "Let me see those beautiful babies!" She rushed up to the stroller and peeked inside at the sleeping twins. "Oh my God! They've gotten so big! They are so beautiful!"

"Thank you, Dr. Lambert," Melina said with a smile on her face.

I just sat there with a stoic look on mine. "So, tell me how you're feeling? Are you getting around okay? How's motherhood treating you?"

"I am loving every bit of being a mother. I still can't believe that I have twin daughters. I can tell you one thing though... I don't know what I would have done if Marcus hadn't been with me the past few weeks." Melina turned to look at me with a smile on her face, but I wasn't smiling at her ass.

"That's good that Marcus has been around to help you. I'm sure it was much easier with two of you than it would've been with just one," she said.

"I definitely agree with that," Melina said.

"Well, you've definitely taken off a lot of the baby weight. That's a good thing. Have you been getting much sleep?" Dr. Lambert asked Melina.

I turned their asses out for the duration of her visit. I was off in my own fucking world. I knew Melina was going to force me to take that DNA test which I really didn't feel I should have to do. Yea, we slept together, but according to what I told my wife, I hadn't slept with her. So, if I had already told her that I hadn't slept with Kalisha, why the fuck did she think I needed to take a DNA test?

The doctor questioned Melina about 15 more minutes, then we left. Melina had taken her six- week old checkup, so she didn't need to come back here. Wasn't that just our luck that her last appointment with her obstetrician would lead to a confrontation with Kalisha's ass?

After we had the kids all strapped in the car, I got behind the wheel.

"That was crazy!" Melina said. "I never expected to see that girl at the doctor's office. I had no idea she was still claiming you were the father! I say we just get the DNA test, prove her wrong and move on with our lives."

Out of my peripheral vision, I saw her looking at me, but I kept my eyes on the road. I didn't want to talk about that shit right now. Shit, I didn't wanna talk about it later either.

"Marcus are you listening to me?" I didn't respond. "Look, I know you're probably mad at me, but I really think getting that test is the best thing to do."

I still didn't respond, but I was squeezing the steering wheel so badly that my knuckles were turning white. She started talking again, but I wasn't listening at all. I couldn't believe she had the nerve to take Kalisha's number. I had already told my wife that Kalisha's baby wasn't mine. She didn't have any reason to get that girl's phone number unless she didn't believe me. And if she didn't believe me, why the hell were we still together?

I knew all of this was my fault. I knew that I shouldn't have slept with Kalisha. I knew that what I was doing was wrong, but I wasn't in my right mind at the time. I had been drinking and when she entered the living room wearing those shorts with her ass busting all out, I got weak. My dick got hard and I got weak.

Only one damn night! That was all it was... one fucking night! I never thought that I would be having this much trouble from one night of sex with a stranger. I forgot to use a damn condom that night. The worse mistake of my damn life was sleeping with that girl. I wished I could tell my wife about that mistake, but I had already told her that it never happened. How could I tell her that I had lied to her and that Kalisha's kid could be mine?

"MARCUS!! Are you gonna just ignore me all day long?" Melina asked.

"We ain't got shit to talk about!"

"What's that supposed to mean?"

"It means just what the fuck I said! You stood there and asked me to take a DNA test in front of a room full of strangers... after I had told you that I never slept with the girl! You told me you believed me..."

"I do believe you!" she interrupted.

"That's a damn lie! If you did love me, you wouldn't be asking me to take a fucking test just to please some bitch with a baby!" I said. "I mean, you don't know that girl from the man on the moon, but we've been married for seven years! Seven fuckin' years! And I gotta prove that I'm not lying by taking a test?"

"Marcus, I love you, but..."

"But what? You love me but you think that kid is mine even though I told you that it wasn't? Even though I told you I never slept with her!"

"You don't have to keep repeating yourself!"

"Obviously, I do since you still think I fucked over you!" I said.

"I'm just trying to get the girl to stop accusing you of being her baby daddy. Do you know how that makes us look as a couple to have another woman claiming that you're her son's father? And what about me? Have you thought about how I'm feeling? I just gave birth to twins and I have this woman in my face talking about a one- night stand with my husband!" she said as she started to cry.

I hadn't really thought about how she must be feeling. All I was thinking about was how I had already lied to her and I couldn't go back on that lie now. But what the hell was I going to tell her about that test. I knew my wife was not going to stop until I took it. Heaven forbid if that child was mine. I was risking my wife, my marriage and my entire life as I knew it by taking that test.

"I'm sorry that you're going through this. This was something I never expected to happen."

"I just need a test in my hand that eliminates you Marcus. I had put that woman out of my head, I swear I did. But when I saw her this morning..." She paused to catch her breath. "I just need that monkey off our backs. I want so badly to believe you babe, but when you refuse to take that test, it makes you look like you have something to hide."

"I ain't hiding shit! I just don't think it's that important for me to take that damn test when I know the kid ain't mine!"

"Just do it for me Marcus! If you care about me as much as you say you do, take the test for me! I need you to do this Marcus!" she said as she stared at me.

I could tell she wasn't going to let that shit go. I had no fucking choice but to take the test. Gotdammit!

"Fine! I'll take the damn test!" I said. "When that test comes back negative, I want an apology."

"I have no problem apologizing when I'm wrong and you know that. I'm so happy!" she said. "I feel as if a huge weight has been lifted from my shoulders."

Shit, that weight that was on her shoulders just sat on mine.

Lord please help me get out of this shit. Tell me what to do. I know I asked for something to happen before, but now I'm begging you. A heart attack, stroke, something that will keep me from having to take that test. I'm counting on you Lord.

"How soon will you get it done?" Melina asked.

"Damn bae, I just agreed to the test. Not only that, but I go back to work Monday or did you forget that?" I asked, becoming aggravated.

"No, I didn't forget. I was just asking."

"I'll let you know when I can take some more time off."

"Okay, but don't take too long," she warned.

"Yea, aight."

I was done with this conversation, but I'd realize soon enough that my wife was far from done with it.

Chapter twelve

Kalisha

I had a doctor's appointment this morning and I wasn't looking forward to it. When I came by last week for my six- week checkup on the seventh week, Dr. Lambert advised me that I had a UTI, urinary tract infection. I didn't know how the hell I had gotten that shit, but she had put me on some antibiotics to clear it up. I had a follow up appointment with her this morning, and I was hoping for some good news. Hopefully, this would be my last appointment with Dr. Lambert. She was an amazing doctor and all, but I was tired going there. I was still pissed that no one would give me any information about Marcus.

But that was beside the point. My baby was almost eight weeks old, so it was time for me to return to work. Not only that, but I had to find a daycare suitable for my son. I was able to get childcare assistance, but even with that, my portion still amounted to $50 a week. That may not seem like much to some, but to a barista at Starbucks, it was a lot.

I had to pay rent, utilities, car insurance and buy groceries. Yes, I was on Section 8 and I received food stamps, but I still didn't make enough money for all the expenses that came with having a newborn. Thankfully, I had received a ton of diapers for the baby shower, so I still had enough to last at least a couple more months.

So, I gathered my things and my baby and walked out the door, heading to the doctor's office. When I arrived, there were two other patients waiting to be seen. I blew out an exasperated breath and hoped my appointment wouldn't take all morning.

"Good morning Kalisha, how are you?" Rebecca greeted.

"Much better than the last time you saw me," I said with a fake smile.

"That's good. How is that precious little boy?" she asked as she peered inside Cameron's carrier to get a peek at him. "He is such a cutie pie!"

"Thank you. He's growing like a weed with his lil greedy butt." I smiled.

"Well, have a seat. Dr. Lambert will be with you shortly."

I turned and took a seat as one of the patient's names were called. The woman stood up and went to the back. A couple of other patients walked in and after waiting 20 more minutes, it was finally my turn. I grabbed my diaper bag and headed to the back. I had a 9:30 appointment, but it was 10:00 and I was just getting called to the exam room. My vitals were taken, I got on the scale, then peed in the clear cup.

I was taken to the exam room where I waited for Dr. Lambert another 15 minutes. Thankfully, once she got to see me, she delivered the good news and I was out of there. As I stood at the desk waiting for my paperwork from Rebecca, she decided to relay some information to me that was particularly valuable.

"Were you ever able to get in touch with your baby daddy?" she asked.

At first, I thought she was just being a nosey bitch. I wanted to go off on her ass and call her every name in the damn book, but I wasn't going to do that. I wasn't about to make myself look like some ghetto chick in this bougie ass doctor's office.

"For your information, no, I haven't be able to get in touch with him. I mean, how can I do that when no one will help me?" I asked as I glared at her sideways.

"Sorry about that, but it is against Dr. Lambert's policies to give out any patient's personal information," Rebecca stated.

"Yea, you mentioned that already. Am I done?" I asked.

I was quickly losing my patience with her ass. She wouldn't give me any fucking information, yet she was asking was I able to get in touch with Marcus. How the fuck was I supposed to do that with only his damn first name?

"Almost," she said as she typed on the keyboard. "I hate to get involved in your business..."

"Then don't! I'm not going to keep begging you for information about my baby daddy when you clearly can't help me!"

"No, I can't give you patient information, but if you stick around for a few minutes, you might get what you're looking for," she said as she winked at me.

Was this bitch making a play for me or something? Because if so, I need to knock her on her fucking ass! I'm not gay and I don't swing that way!

"What? Ain't nobody got time to be sitting up in this fucking office all day..."

"It would be worth your while. All you have to do is take a seat and wait a few minutes. If you don't want to, that's up to you. But I am trying to help you," she whispered.

"Why?"

"Why what?"

"Why are you trying to "help me"? What's in it for you?" I asked.

"Nothing is in it for me. It's just that your little boy is so cute and if his baby daddy is running from his responsibilities as a parent, shame on him," Rebecca said.

As much as I wanted to get the heck up out of there, I stuck around as Rebecca suggested. I was about to say fuck this shit and leave 15 minutes later when Marcus and his wife walked in pushing a double stroller. My heart started beating so fast that I thought it was going to bust out of my chest. I had no idea this was what I was waiting for, but I was glad I had stuck around.

After the three of us had words, and they were called to the back, I walked up out of there feeling like a proud peacock. I finally had some information on my baby daddy. I had given his wife my number, but just in case she didn't use it, I now had Marcus' last name. Once I got outside, I looked for his truck and spotted it. I walked over to it and took a picture of his license plate. You could find a lot out about a person from their last name and license plate.

I decided I'd wait to get that call from Marcus' wife before taking matters into my own hands, but if she didn't call within two weeks, I was going to have to do just that.

"Marcus O'Connor, I suggest you do the right thing because if you don't, I'm coming for you with both barrels blazing," I said to myself as I headed to my car.

Two weeks later, I was still waiting for that phone call from his wife. I decided I was tired waiting and I wasn't going to wait anymore. It was obvious that she was choosing to stand by her man and support her husband. I guess I was going to have to do a little research to see what I could find out about Marcus on my own. I logged on to the computer and typed in his name. It didn't bring up his home address, but it did give me his place of business. It said he was one of the big bosses at the company he worked for, so I knew he was getting paid. How was it that he was getting all this money, and couldn't help me take care of our son?

I wasn't trying to make any trouble for Marcus. All I wanted was a DNA test to prove that he was indeed my baby's father. I just wanted him to help me out financially and if I couldn't get him to do it voluntarily, then we'd have to do it another way... through the court system. The choice was his.

I got dress, got my son together and headed to his office building. On the drive there, I stopped by Walgreens and picked up one of those home DNA tests. I hadn't even opened the box because I didn't want him to say that I tampered with anything. I just tossed the bag on the front passenger's seat and got back on the road. I arrived at his office at almost five o'clock. I wasn't sure if he would see me or not, so I wanted to come by when he wouldn't have any appointments. It was close to the end of the business day, so I knew he would be either in his office or heading home.

I hit the up button on the elevator and waited for it to stop. Then I got in and pushed the third- floor button. When the car came to a stop, my nerves kicked into high gear. I was deathly afraid that I had come all this way for nothing. What if he didn't want to see me? What was I going to do then? Should I make a scene and demand that he see me? I didn't know what I was going to do or what I was going to tell that receptionist.

As it turned out, luck was on my side. Marcus was in the front lobby when I arrived having a conversation with a couple of people. The look on his face was one of surprise, shock, and anger.

"Please excuse me," he said.

He immediately stepped over to me in three quick strides. He grabbed me by the arm and pulled me back towards the elevators.

"What the fuck are you doing here?" he asked through clenched teeth.

"Well, since your wife didn't call as she promised, I figured I'd come over to your job and find out what's up."

"What the hell do you want girl?!" he asked as he placed his hand on top of his head. "You know, you are really starting to give me a fucking headache!"

"Well, you been gave me a headache!" I scoffed.

"What the fuck do you want from me?"

"You already know what I want," I said. "I want a DNA test to prove that you're my son's father so you can help me take care of him."

"So, you want money?" he asked.

"No. I mean, yes. I mean..."

"Fuck it! You need to get the hell out of here!" he said as he pushed the down button on the elevator.

"I'm not going anywhere until we hash this out!"

"Hash what out? I already told you I ain't that kid's daddy!"

"I know what you said, but I know what I know. I haven't slept with anyone in that time frame except you. You're the only one who can be my son's daddy and I'm not leaving here until you take this test!" I said as I held up the Walgreens bag.

The elevator dinged and he waited for me to get on it. When I didn't get on the elevator, he grabbed my arm.

"Let go of me!" I fussed as he tried to get me in the elevator.

"Get the fuck out of here Kalisha!"

"If you don't let go of my arm, I swear I'm gonna scream bloody murder up in this bitch!" I said.

He quickly released my arm and raised his hands in the air. At that moment, a white man walked by and looked at the two of us. "Is everything alright here Marcus?" he asked.

"Everything is fine Mr. Perkins, sir. Are you leaving for the day?" Marcus asked.

"As a matter of fact, I am. Can I speak to you in private for a moment?" Mr. Perkins asked.

"Yes, sir."

He walked to the side and Marcus followed him. "I'm not sure what is going on with you and that woman Marcus, but may I suggest you take your personal business to your office?" Mr. Perkins asked.

"You're absolutely right, sir and I apologize. I was just about to do that when you walked by," Marcus responded.

"Good because this is a really bad look for you right now. Your personal and private business should not be anyone else's. Got it?"

"Yes sir." The elevator dinged and the man hopped in, giving Marcus a stern look.

"See what the fuck you did?" he asked angrily.

Marcus turned and stomped to his office and you better believe I followed his ass. He opened the door and locked it once I was inside.

"Why the hell are you even here?"

"I told you why..."

"How did you find me?"

"It wasn't hard once I had your last name, Mr. O'Connor. You'd be surprised what information you could find on Google and Bing," I said with a smile.

"I don't give a fuck how you found me. You can't be coming around my office making scenes and shit!" he fussed.

"I wouldn't have had to come here if you would've called to get that test done," I countered. "And I never made a scene, that was your doing. Everything that's going on right now is because of you. I tried to keep this shit quiet, but you keep running away from your responsibilities as a father, and that ain't gonna cut it!"

"What do you want Kalisha? Money?" he asked as he walked over to his desk. He sat down in the chair and pulled out his checkbook. He wrote on the first blank check, tore it out and stood up. He walked over to me and handed the check to me. "Here!"

I took the check and saw that he had written me a check for ten racks. I had never seen so many zeros on a check before. I had never been given this much money before. That was a lot of money.

"Well, this is definitely a start baby daddy," I said with a smile as I shoved the check in my diaper bag before he could change his mind.

"A start my ass! That muthafucka is the starter and finisher!" he said. "And I'm not your baby daddy!"

"So, you're giving me hush money?" I asked.

"I'm giving you money to get the hell out of my life Kalisha..."

"Marcus, we have a son! Doesn't that matter to you at all!" I asked feeling hurt. I looked at my little boy every day and thanked God for bringing him into my life.

I hadn't planned on having kids right now. I was only 24 years old and had a job that paid peanuts. I didn't even get to go to college or nothing, so I didn't want to have the responsibility of a child so soon. But once I found out that I was pregnant, I made the decision to be a mother. I decided it was time for me to grow up and accept my responsibility as a mom. I owed it to Cameron because he didn't ask to be here.

I unstrapped my baby boy from his carrier and held him in my arms. "Don't you want to hold your son?" I asked as tears threatened to fall. "He's your firstborn."

"I ain't trying to hear all that shit! Take the money and get the hell out of my office!" Marcus fumed.

"Look at him Marcus! He looks just like your daughters."

I brought the baby closer to him so he could see that the only difference between my son and his daughters was the gender. My baby looked just like him and his other kids, which meant his genes were strong as hell.

He looked at my son and for just a smidge of a moment, it looked like he saw what I knew he would see. That my son was his. Then just as fast, he said, "You have the check, now get out of my office and don't fucking come back!"

"If this check was all you thought I wanted, you're wrong! I want you to be a part of Cameron's life. I can't do this alone Marcus and I shouldn't have to since I didn't get pregnant by myself!"

"IT WAS ONLY ONE DAMN NIGHT!! ONE FUCKIN' NIGHT!!" he yelled, which caused Cameron to jolt out of his sleep and start crying.

"Now look what you did! Stop yelling like that around our son!" I fussed as I comforted my baby by rocking him and rubbing his little back. I was trying my best to calm him down.

"None of this would be happening if you would just leave!"

"I'm not leaving until we take this test, and if I have to leave without you taking it, I'll just come back every damn day until you do!" I said with a smile. He thought it was a game, but it was far from that. "Look Marcus, I realize that you're a married man. Had you told me that before we slept together..."

"I did..."

"No, you did NOT! Because had you told me, I never would've slept with you. Getting pregnant by a married man was never on my bucket list, but it happened. Now, we have to be adults about this and handle it the best way we can. My son shouldn't have to suffer because you decided to cheat on your wife. Please don't make me get these white folks in our business," I said.

He looked at me sideways before asking, "What white folks?"

"The people from the child support office," I said smugly.

"What the fuck?! So, money is what you're after!" he said as he walked back to his desk. He sat down, opened his checkbook and started writing again. He continued to fuss calling me all kinds of gold diggers and shit like that as he wrote. “If I would’ve known you were a gold digger, I never would’ve fucked you!”

“Well, according to you, we didn’t have sex that night! But clearly,” I said as I pointed to our son. “Clearly, that was a lie! You gave me a ride home and then came inside and gave me another ride.”

He rolled his eyes at me as he tore the check from the checkbook and walked around the desk again. He thrust the check in my face and my eyes dropped to the floor. It was a check for another ten thousand bucks.

“Are you kidding me right now?” I asked.

“Does it look like I’m kidding? You got 20 G’s out of me. Now, if you’re finished milking me like a fuckin’ cow, I need you to leave my fuckin’ office!”

“Marcus it isn’t about the money! Please listen to me…”

“I don’t wanna hear shit!” he said.

“I’m serious about coming up here every day until you take this test,” I said.

“WHAT?! YOU GOT 20 G’S AND YOU STILL TALKING ABOUT THAT STUPID TEST!!” he fumed.

“I want the test because I wanna prove to you that I’m not lying about you being my son’s father. So, if that means I have to give this money back, I’m prepared to do that,” I said, even though I didn’t really want to give him the money back.

"I don't know what you think a test will do for you. I still ain't gonna be in that kid's life!"

"So, even if he's your son, you will continue to deny him?" I asked. "Your firstborn. Your only son." Now that shit was hurting me to my core. How could he be so heartless to not want to be in this precious little boy's life?

"Give me the fucking test! I'll take it, just to prove to you that I ain't his daddy! Once I have that piece of paper telling you what I already know, I never wanna hear from you again!" he said as he scowled at me. He signed as he held his hand out. "Deal?"

I reached my hand out and shook his. "Deal. I mean, if you aren't Cameron's dad, there won't be a reason for me to reach out to you again."

"You probably wanted this dick again anyway," he said as he opened the box and sat on the edge of his desk.

"Boy bye! Ain't nobody even thinking about your dick. I just want you to be a father to my son," I said. "Your son!"

The thought of riding his big dick had crossed my mind a few times. Hell, I hadn't been with anybody since I slept with Marcus. My pussy was so tight, there was no way anybody was getting in there without the help of a crowbar and some KY Jelly. I watched as

Marcus swabbed the inside of his cheek before putting the Q-tip thingy in the little clear bag and sealing it.

I took one of the swabs, bent over and did the same thing with Cameron. He fussed a little, but eventually, I got it done. When I stood up, I caught Marcus looking at my ass.

"See something you like?" I asked.

"Nah. Not a damn thang. Ain't nobody tryna get caught up in yo shit again!" he said.

"Whatever!"

I placed the swab in another clear bag and sealed it. I grabbed a pen off of Marcus' desk and wrote his name and my son's name on each bag. Then I put the bags containing the swabs in the yellow envelope provided by the company. I filled out the paperwork and closed it.

"I'm gonna drop this off to the post office first thing in the morning."

"How long before we get the results in?" he asked.

"I think seven to ten days," I remarked.

"SEVEN TO TEN DAYS?! THEY DIDN'T HAVE A RUSH ORDER?!" he bellowed.

"I don't know. I don't have the extra money to pay for a rush order fee, so it is what it is. In seven to ten days, I'll be contacting you with the results."

"And if your son ain't mine..."

"But he is..."

"But if he ain't..."

"But he is..."

"Girl shut the fuck up and quit playing with me! If he ain't mine, I never wanna see you again Kalisha! I'm not bullshittin' with you!" Marcus said.

"You ain't got shit to worry about if my son isn't yours, because he is. When that test comes back positive, you will have a lot of explaining to do to your wife."

"Don't you worry about me and my wife! Worry about finding your real baby daddy!" he said smartly.

"I already know who my baby daddy is," I said.

"Then you better inform him that he has a kid," he said.

"Already done." I picked up my baby carrier and diaper bag. "You know, I thought after that night we had a vibe. I actually thought you were special. When I found out you were married, I was devastated. Not so much for me, but for our son because I knew you were going to deny him. I thought you would take one look at him and fall in love with him the way I did. I never expected you to just deny him like that."

"What did you expect Kalisha? I have a wife..."

"And we have a son! Isn't your flesh and blood more important?"

"I don't know that he's my flesh and blood yet."

"Yea, you do. For some reason, you won't admit it, but you know that Cameron is your son."

"I don't know that Kalisha," he said.

"You do know that. It's cool. You can keep denying it all you want, but by this time next week, you'll be singing a different tune. Thanks for the child support," I said as I walked towards his office door, twisting my ass from side to side.

I could feel his eyes on my ass which was why I put an extra twist on it. Marcus could deny until the sun came up tomorrow, but at the end of the day, I knew the truth and soon, he would know too.

As soon as I got in my car, I called Donya. "Hey are you home?" I asked.

"I'm almost there. Why... what's up?"

"I'm on my way. Please tell me you have something to drink," I said.

"You know I do, but is it okay for you to be drinking? You know you just had a baby," she said.

"My doctor gave me the all clear, so I can do whatever I want to. I can drink, have sex, do whatever I wanna do. I just need something to drink and when I tell you about my day, you'll understand why."

"Oh Lord! Well, come on over. You have my baby with you?"

"Yea, he's sleeping, I think. He's gonna need a bottle and diaper change when I get there."

"Well, I'll feed and change him while you get your little drinky drink on," she said with a chuckle.

"I'm on my way!"

"Okay."

I was only 20 minutes from Donya's place. By the time I got there, Donya's car was parked in front of her place. I was glad because I really needed that drink.

Chapter thirteen

Donya

I didn't know what was going on with my girl Kalisha, but if she needed a drink it must be something deep. I walked in the house and went straight to the kitchen. I pulled a bottle of strawberry flavored Ciroc out of the wine rack and put it in the freezer. Then I headed to the bedroom. After slipping my heels off and putting my hair in a ponytail, I stripped and hopped in the shower. When I was done, I dried off and threw on a pair of shorts, socks and a t-shirt. By the time I was done, Kalisha was knocking on my door.

I opened the door, hugged her quickly and took the baby. "Can you change his diaper while I fix his bottle please?" she asked.

Cameron was fussing and sucking his tiny little fist. "Damn girl, you got my baby starving!"

"I know. I didn't think that I was going to be at Marcus' office as long as I was..."

"Wait, wait, wait! Did you say you were at Marcus' office?"

"Yes, girl. Remember I told you that his wife was supposed to call me about the DNA test?" she explained while shaking Cameron's freshly made bottle.

She walked over to where I had just finished changing Cameron's diaper. She handed me the bottle and took the wet diaper. While I fed the baby, Kalisha placed Cameron's diaper in a scented bag and tossed it in the trash. I watched as she went to the freezer and pulled out the Ciroc bottle. She got a glass from the cabinet and came to sit on the sofa.

She poured herself a glass and took a sip. "So, what happened with Marcus? How did you end up at his office?" I asked.

She had told me all about running into Marcus and his wife at the doctor's office two weeks ago. I told her that Marcus' wife wasn't going to call her, but she swore the woman was on her side. Or rather the side who would tell her the truth. I guess she decided to stick by her cheating man.

"Well, I decided to take matters into my own hands. I went online and looked up Marcus O'Connor. What came up was that he was an executive at that chemical plant on Fulshear?"

"What? An executive?"

"Yes girl. Marcus is making big money and refusing to acknowledge his child! I couldn't believe it when I walked into his office!" she said.

"Wow! So, what happened when he saw you?"

"Girl he literally tried to push me in the elevator to send me back home!"

"You're kidding!" I said with my mouth open.

"Yes, if it wasn't for the white man, that nigga was about to throw my ass in that elevator!"

"What white man, girl?!"

"Some white man. He looked like a big boss or something! He told Marcus to take his business to his office and that's exactly what he did. He went to his office and I followed him in," she continued. "But you will never guess what happened when we got to his office."

"Please don't tell me that y'all had sex again..."

"Hell no!" She reached in her diaper bag and pulled out a check and handed it to me.

"He gave you a check?" I asked as I took it.

"Look at for how much!" she said as her eyes widened, and she took another drink.

I opened the check and my mouth fell in Cameron's lap. I looked at Kalisha and said, "This is a check for 10 grands!"

"Shit, I know!"

"Why did he give you a check for 10 grands? Are you sure you didn't sleep with him?" I asked. Shit, men didn't go around writing checks for ten thousand dollars for nothing. I was wondering if he had convinced him to let him sign over his rights and this was some kind of payment for that.

"Didn't I tell you no?!" she asked with a smirk on her face.

"I'm sorry girl, but that's a lot of money!" I said as I gave the check back to her.

"Girl, I asked him if that was hush money... like for me to keep quiet so his wife doesn't find out Cameron is actually his."

"And?" I asked as I put Cameron over my shoulder to burp him.

"He said it was money for me and Cameron to disappear out of his life..."

"And you still took it? What were you thinking? I sure hope you didn't sign any kind of paperwork to that effect!" I said.

"No, I definitely did not! I told him that it wasn't just about the financial support. I told him that I wanted him to spend time with Cameron the same way he did with his other kids..."

"What did he say to that?" I asked.

"He said that he wasn't going to be in Cameron's life because Cam wasn't his. I forced him to look at my child and for a split- second D, I know he saw the resemblance. I could've seen it in his eyes."

"Wow! And I bet he still didn't admit it huh?"

"Girl no! But it's cool because by the time I left his office, I had the DNA I needed for the test..." she said as she produced the yellow envelope.

"Whaaaaaat?! How the hell did you manage that?" I asked.

I couldn't believe she had managed to secure Marcus' DNA. From what Kalisha told me a couple of weeks ago, Marcus was adamant about not taking that test.

"He did it to prove a point that Cameron wasn't his. He said when the DNA test comes back negative, he wants me to stay out of his life. I told him if, and that's a very strong if, that test comes back negative, I won't have a reason to be in his life. Girl, he really believes he isn't Cameron's daddy," she said as her voice cracked.

"Aw, don't cry Kalisha. You got what you wanted. You got his DNA and when the test comes back that he is the father, he will have to suck it up and be there for Cameron."

"What if he still doesn't want to be in my baby's life?"

“He will. I mean, Cameron is his firstborn son. What man doesn’t want anything to do with his son?” I asked.

“I guess.”

“Look at this baby. Who wouldn’t wanna be in his life?” I asked, already knowing the answer.

“His daddy,” she responded quietly. She poured herself another drink and sipped almost half the glass.

“Look, I know you’re upset, but don’t go letting that man and his actions turn you into an alcoholic,” I warned.

“Girl bye! Ain’t nobody gonna turn into an alcoholic from a couple of glasses of vodka!” she said.

“Okay. Well, the way you are sucking down that vodka, you and Cameron may have to spend the night. I can’t let you drive with all that alcohol in your system,” she said as she placed my sleeping baby between us on the sofa.

“I only had two glasses,” she argued.

“Two big glasses!” I countered. “I’d never forgive myself if something happened to you and my godchild.”

“Well, thanks for letting us stay the night.”

“No thanks needed. That’s what friends are for and we’re practically sisters.”

"That's true." It looked like she had something else on her mind. She didn't look upset or anything, just in a daze or something.

"What are you thinking about?" I asked.

"Marcus..." she said with a smile.

"What about Marcus?"

"You should've seen the way he was looking at my ass when I bent over to swab Cameron for his DNA." She giggled. "When I stood up, his eyes were dead on my ass." More giggling. "He still wants me D," she said in a slurred tone.

"You better leave that man alone sis. He's married and doesn't even wanna claim his own son! He ain't no good for you," I said.

Why the hell were we even having this conversation? Marcus had been ducking and dodging her for months! Since before Cameron was born. Now she was sitting here drunk and thinking about him!

"I don't want him either. Well, that's not totally true." She giggled. "I just want his dick!" She busted out laughing that time.

"Sssshhhh! You'll wake him up!" I said as I patted Cameron's back.

"Ssshhhh! Sorry, but Marcus has some good dick! It's fat and round and damn, he was hitting my spot..."

"Ugh!" I shuddered. "TMI!"

"Sorry sis. I guess seeing him today and this alcohol is making me wanna fuck!" she said as she touched my thigh.

"Okay!" I said as I stood up and grabbed the bottle of alcohol and the glass from her hand. "You have officially reached your limit!"

I walked to the kitchen and put the glass in the dishwasher and the liquor in the fridge. Kalisha had definitely had enough to drink.

By the time I went back in the living room, she had fallen asleep on the sofa. I went and put Cameron in my bed because in the state my bestie was in, he definitely couldn't sleep with her. Then I went back in the living room and took off Kalisha's shoes and stretched her out on the sofa. I covered her with a throw blanket that I kept on the back of the sofa and went to the bedroom.

I went back to the living room to get the diaper bag. I brought it to my room. I couldn't believe that Marcus had given Kalisha $10,000 to stay out of his life. That man knew he was wrong for that shit. I had to see that check again, just to make sure Kalisha would be able to cash or deposit it... whatever she chose to do with it.

"What the hell is this?" I asked myself as what looked like a second check fell on the floor. I opened it and I could hear my mouth bang against my hardwood flooring as it fell. “That nigga gave her two checks! 20 grands! What the hell was going on?”

Why would Kalisha tell me about one check but not the other? What was she hiding that she didn’t want me to know about? I put the checks back in her diaper bag, got down on my knees beside my bed and prayed. I prayed that Marcus wasn’t taking advantage of my best friend. I prayed that Kalisha wasn’t allowing him to take advantage of her.

As I stared at the sleeping baby in my bed, I prayed that Kalisha and Marcus would be able to come to some kind of reasonable arrangement to coparent Cameron. He deserved to have both his parents in his life.

“Please God, let my friend make the right choices for this baby’s sake,” I prayed.

Chapter fourteen

Porsha

Two days later…

"Oh shit! Yea, that's it! Right there!" I cried as Chandler pushed his dick up against my G-spot. "Yaaasss! Go deeper!"

He was behind me banging me out from behind. He had my pussy wide open as he drove his dick in and out of me with fervor. That man had my nose wide open just like my kitty. I loved Chandler so much and I truly believed that he was my soulmate. I hoped that he felt the same way about me, but since I didn't get a ring yet, it made me wonder.

As I arched my back with my belly on the pillow, Chandler squeezed my ass cheeks as he plowed deeper. We had been making love for what seemed like two hours.

We were all sweaty, but he had just got his second wind. I had came so many times that I lost count. I was so tired, and my kitty was sore, but I wanted Chandler to bust his second nut. When I finally felt him squeezing my buns and his body go rigid, I knew he was at that point. Of course, I didn't mind pleasing my man. It's just that at 30 weeks pregnant, I couldn't do it as long as he liked.

But I never complained about it. Why would I? I loved sex just as much as he did and if I didn't satisfy my man, he'd look for it somewhere else. I wasn't about to risk that shit happening again. So, no matter how tired I was or how much my jaws hurt, I was going to do what I had to do to please Chandler. After all, he was mine, so it was my responsibility.

"Oh fuck!" he howled as he finally busted his nut inside me.

I collapsed on my side since he had been hitting it from behind. He turned towards me and kissed me on the mouth. "Damn bae, I didn't think you'd ever bust," I said as I inhaled and exhaled deeply.

"Shit, that's what you get for getting yourself pregnant." He laughed.

"Uh, excuse you, but I didn't get myself pregnant!" I said.

"You know what I mean."

"Uh huh."

Chandler's phone started ringing. I immediately looked at the clock on my nightstand. "Who could that be?" I asked, already getting suspicious.

"I don't know bae." He slid out of bed and pulled his phone from his pants pocket. By that time, it had stopped ringing. Before he could unlock it to see who called, it was ringing again. Okay, now I was on tens. Who the hell was calling my man at 11 o'clock in the evening?

"Who is it?"

"Shawn," he said as he answered the phone. "Wassup man?"

I couldn't hear what was being said, but from what I could tell from Chandler's demeanor it wasn't good. "What the fuck?!" he asked as he jumped out of the bed.

He grabbed his boxers, pants and shirt and went into the bathroom while still on the phone. He sounded super upset. About two minutes later, he rushed out the bathroom like his underwear was on fire. He put his shoes on and was heading out the room.

I jumped out of bed and waddled after him butt ass naked.

"Babe where are you going? What happened?" I asked.

"Somebody fucked up the shop!" he said as he grabbed his keys.

"What?"

"Somebody fucked up the shop! I gotta get down there!"

"Be careful babe," I said.

"I will. I'll be back as soon as I'm done down there."

With that being said, he rushed out of the house. I locked the door and headed back to the bedroom. I wondered who the hell had fucked up his shop. Chandler got along with everybody. I went to the bathroom and turned the shower on. After I peed all the excess fluid from my vagina, I slid the glass door to the shower open and stepped in.

As I lathered my body up, I thought about how Chandler must be feeling. That carwash meant a lot to him. It was his first time being a business owner and he loved working there. I was proud of him too. Proud of the way he had made it happen. He wanted something, saw a way to get it and did it.

His place was very successful too. I guess that Maya chick knew what she was doing after all. I had my doubts about her when I first met her because she was in my man's arms. Chandler had gotten upset with me because of the way I acted, but I didn't know one woman who would've been happy to see her man in that situation.

Shit, any woman in this city would be lucky to have Chandler for her man. But he chose me to be his woman… well, sort of. I had to get rid of that Maya chick first. Now that she was out of the picture, well, not completely, but personally. I didn't know why she didn't tell Chandler that we had spoken on the phone that night. Shit, I was prepared to tell him that I didn't know what he was talking about. I was going to deny, deny, deny!

When I was done with my shower, I stepped out, dried off and got dressed. I was always hot at night, so I just put on some boy shorts and a tank top. Then I climbed in bed and turned on the television. As I channel surfed, I remembered my conversation with Donya earlier. She had mentioned to me that Kalisha had gone to Marcus' job to confront him and get him to take the DNA test. I was shocked and proud of how Kalisha was handling things.

She truly believed that Marcus was her child's father and she was going to make noise until she was heard. I would've given up a long time ago. I was lying. I would've done the same thing Kalisha was doing. What shocked the hell out of me was when Donya said that Marcus wrote Kalisha a check for ten racks. I was stunned.

That was a lot of fucking money to be giving to a woman he claimed he didn't believe was his baby mama. Hell, me and Chandler had been together for four years, off and on. Not once had he ever given me that kind of money, and I knew he had it.

Kalisha had definitely gotten her a big money baller! Donya said she didn't really want the money though. She wanted the man to be a father to her son. I didn't blame her though. Shit, we were mothers, not fathers. And as mothers of little boys, we couldn't teach them the important things like their father could do. We couldn't teach them to stand and pee. If a woman did that, she would have pee all over the toilet seat and her leg and shit. That was a nasty thought.

Little boys needed their fathers to mold them into men. I didn't know what Kalisha was going to do about Marcus, but I was sure she had a plan. Shit, she was 10 G's richer today than she was last week.

I watched *Keeping up with the Kardashians* until they were watching me. I wasn't sure what time it was when I fell asleep. All I knew was that I was sleeping, and Chandler walked in slamming doors and shit. I jumped up in bed thinking someone was breaking in or something. I wiped the sleep from my eyes and turned the bedside lamp on. Chandler was sitting in the chair in the corner of the bedroom weeping.

Damn, it must be really bad.

I walked over to him and sat on the ottoman across from him. “You wanna talk about it?” I asked in a soft tone.

“My shop is ruined bae!” he said as he looked up with tears in his eyes. “They trashed my shit!”

I sat on his lap and held his head against my chest. “I’m so sorry babe. Did you call the police?”

“Yea, that’s what took me so long to get here. They were asking all kinds of questions about if I had enemies or shit like that. I don’t have no damn enemies!”

“Did you look at the video surveillance?” I asked.

“Yea, but those fools wore masks!”

“How many were there?”

“Three!” He pulled his phone out of his pocket and unlocked it. He scrolled through then gave me the phone. “Look! Look at what the fuck they did to my shop!”

I scrolled through the pictures and saw that the perpetrators had busted out the windows, spray painted the outside, tore up the inside. It was awful.

“It’s gonna be okay babe.”

“Okay? How the hell is it gonna be okay Porsha? They fucked my shit up! Did you not see the damn pictures?!”

"Okay, I know you're upset, but I'm gonna need you to calm down and quit talking to me like that!"

"I'm sorry bae. I'm not mad at you. I'm pissed at this situation. Who the fuck would do me like that?" he asked.

"I don't know, but I'm sure the police will find them. In the meantime, just file a claim with the insurance company and they will cut you a check to fix it. You will see. It'll be okay and you can build a bigger and better carwash!" I said in an effort to get him out of his funk.

"I guess," he said.

"Don't guess babe. You have to know that things will work out. The cops will find those responsible and you will open your shop again. You'll see," I said as I held him close.

"Thanks babe."

"Anytime babe. I'm here for you."

"It just sucks that someone would do that shit, ya know?"

"Yea, I know. But don't worry. The police will catch them and if they don't, someone will come through for you. The streets are always talking," I said.

"You're right. Once people on the streets find out what happened, someone will talk," he said.

"Yep, that's exactly what I'm saying!"

He kissed me on the lips. “Mmmm,” he moaned as he rubbed my ass.

I felt his manhood growing underneath my ass and all I could do was roll my eyes. My man was ready for sex again and I still hadn’t recovered from the sex we had engaged in earlier. “You smell so fucking good,” he said as he nuzzled my neck.

He lifted me up and stood from the chair and carried me to the bed. I watched as he undressed and then climbed in bed with me. I knew by the time he’d be done with me, my pussy would be raw, but if he needed me and my pussy to make him feel good, so be it.

Thankfully, our lovemaking session didn’t last that long. After I came twice and he came once, we laid in each other’s arms. I was too exhausted to go to the bathroom to pee.

Chapter fifteen

Chandler

When Shawn called after 11 o'clock, I knew something was wrong. No one ever called that late unless it was an emergency. When he told me there was a problem at the carwash, I was thinking something minor that he couldn't resolve on his own. Never had I imagined it was something like the shit that went down. How the hell could that shit have happened? People around here knew me, and they knew how I got down.

I think because I bought a legit business, they must've forgotten how I used to be. And I said used to be because I tried my best not to get down like that anymore. I tried to run a legit business and handle myself accordingly. Now, I was going to have to figure out who fucked up my spot like that. Those niggas really went off with the damage too. It was like they wanted to make a statement and lucky for them, I read that shit loud and clear, but we'd see who had the last laugh.

I didn't know if it was the fact that she was pregnant that was maturing Porsha or what, but my baby was coming through these days. She was really surprising me. It made me start to think that she might be ready for marriage. But was I ready?

I knew I was ready to be a dad and I'd do anything for Porsha and CJ. I'd just have to think about that marriage thing a little longer. I couldn't let my mom and girl pressure me into marriage. But to be honest, Porsha hadn't been bothering me to marry her lately. She seemed happy with the way things were going between us, and I surely was.

When she comforted me about my shop and gave me all that encouragement, she made my heart swell. I had to give her some more of this dick. Afterward, we fell asleep exhausted from all that good loving.

The next morning, I woke up later than I wanted to. I had some phone calls to make concerning the repairs on my shop. First, I contacted Allstate so they could come down and do an inspection on the shop. Then I hit up Vaughn to let him know what happened, but I wasn't surprised when he told me that he had already heard.

"Man don't worry. I put my men on the streets to find out who did that shit! We gon' find them muthafuckas so don't worry!" Vaughn assured me.

"Thanks bro. I knew if anyone had my back, it was you," I said.

"Shit, you got that right! We been bros for way too long, so just know that I gotchu. Anyway, how's my sister in law? She getting big or what?"

"Man, if she getting big. Her ass waddling like a duck and shit. Watch, I'ma take a picture and send it to you. I can't wait for her to have my lil man though," I said.

"I know you can't. Being a father is one of the most important jobs any man can have. It's up to us to teach our sons how to be men," he said.

"You right. But look, I got a couple of more calls to make, but hit me up if you hear anything about them muthafuckas, you dig?"

"Yea, I gotchu."

We ended the call and I made a few more calls. My mom called me while I was on the other line, so I had to call her back.

"Hey ma."

"Baby what's this I hear about your carwash getting trashed?"

"Damn! News travels fast huh?"

"Yea, so tell me what happened."

"I don't know ma. Three lil niggas busted in my place and fucked it all up..."

"Do the police know who did it? You had cameras in there, right?"

"Yea, I have cameras, but those punks wore masks. I couldn't see who they were, but no worries. I got my boys out looking for them," I said.

"Did you call the police?" my mom asked.

"Of course, I did ma. You ain't raised no dummy. If I wouldn't have called the police, I wouldn't be able to get the police report to file the claim with the insurance company. I called the insurance company too and they said the adjuster is supposed to contact me within 24 hours to come inspect the damage."

"Well, that wasn't the point I was trying to make."

"What is your point ma?"

"Well, if you contacted the police, you need to let them do their jobs instead of getting your boys to do your street justice.

"Nobody said that ma. I just wanna know who did it, that's all."

"Baby, you can fool some of the people some of the time and yourself all of the time. But one thing you can't do is fool your mama. I know you better than anyone else on this planet, so just remember what I said. Now, how's my daughter in law doing?"

"She's still asleep," I said.

"Still asleep? It's almost noon," my mom said.

"I know ma, but she stayed up late waiting for me last night. So, she's a little worn out."

"Well, tell her to call me when she gets a chance and give her a hug for me."

"I will ma. Love you."

"Love you too baby," she said as we hung up.

I didn't know who the fuck thought it was a good idea to fuck with me, but they would soon find out that was the wrong thing to do. While I heard what my mom said about street justice, she already knew how we handled things in the hood.

Them niggas are in for a rude awakening...

Chapter sixteen

Kalisha

Five days later...

I had been waiting on pins and needles for the results of the DNA test to come in the mail. If I would've paid the rush fee, I would've gotten the results in my email days ago. But I didn't mind waiting. It wasn't as if I didn't know what the results were going to be anyway. Marcus was my son's father and there wasn't a shadow of a doubt in my mind. So, if he thought that $20,000 was going to get me out of his life, he had better think again. I had no plans to go anywhere.

Cameron was his son and that test would prove it. I had to think of what I wanted to do with my life. I was tired working at Starbucks. That money Marcus gave me helped me to make some decisions in my life that was better for my son. I quit my job at Starbucks and started school. I thought about going online but didn't want to be cooped up in the house all day. So, I decided to go on campus.

I decided to go to school for something in the medical field. I was too jittery when it came to blood, so being a nurse was definitely not something I wanted to do. However, medical billing and coding was right up my alley. So, I dropped Cameron to the daycare and went to enroll at the university. By the time I was done, I had registered for all my classes, which started in two weeks.

I was so excited and couldn't wait to share the news with Donya.

"Hey, you. What are you up to?" she asked.

"Guess where I'm coming from."

"Oh God! Please don't tell me you went by Marcus' office and you had sex with him!" she said.

"Damn! All you think about is me and Marcus having sex huh?" I asked as I busted out laughing.

"Girl bye! Ain't nobody thinking about you and Marcus having sex. I was saying that's where you're coming from since you were lusting over him a few nights ago."

"I think that was the alcohol talking."

"Okay. So, where are you coming from?" Donya asked.

"You were supposed to guess, but since you aren't guessing, I may as well just tell you. I just enrolled at TSU," I said excitedly.

"Oh my God! Are you serious?"

"Dead ass!"

"Aw, Kalisha. I'm so proud of you! You're taking steps for a better future for you and Cameron," she gushed.

"Yea, I sure am. Not that our future was looking bleak. I mean, I did add four zeros to my account recently," I said with a chuckle.

"That you did. Did the check clear yet?"

"Yep. All the money is mine!"

Marcus had given me that money to disappear, but that wasn't going to happen. As long as my son's veins were filled with his blood, I would keep coming for him. He should've told me that he was married when we met. If he had told me that, he wouldn't have gotten any of my cookie and we wouldn't be in this situation.

"That's good Kalisha. Where are you on your way to now?" she asked.

"I'm about to go by the daycare and scoop up my baby. I had to drop him off so I could go down to the school and handle my business."

"I'm really glad you did that, and you'll be glad you did it too."

"I am glad," I said.

"Good. Where else do you have to go?"

"Nowhere. To be honest, I'm anxious to get home to check the mail. I've been waiting on it for the past few days. I'm about to call the lab and ask them where's my fucking test results!"

"Just be patient. It'll come soon."

"It better," I said.

"Well, I gotta run. I have a meeting in a few minutes," she said.

"Okay. I just pulled into the daycare anyway. I'll call you later."

"Okay."

We ended the call and I got out of the car and went inside to get my son. My baby was now three months old and the spitting image of his dad. After kissing his little cheek, I placed him in the car and strapped him in. Then I got behind the wheel and drove home.

I couldn't wait to check the mail because something told me today was the day. I parked my car in front of the mailboxes and got out, locking the doors behind me. I turned the key and pulled the mail out. As bad as I wanted to check it now, I needed to feed my baby and get him settled before I checked it.

So, I got back in the car and went around the corner to my place. I climbed out of the car after shutting the engine off and grabbed my son from the backseat. I picked up his diaper bag and my purse and unlocked the door to my apartment while locking the doors to my car.

After giving my baby a bottle, I changed his diaper and placed him in his swing. As the swing rocked him while playing lullabies, I grabbed the stack of mail I had shoved in the diaper bag. As I fumbled through the mountain of bills, I finally came across a white envelope labeled 'Genovate DNA'. I immediately opened the letter and went straight to the bottom for the results, 99.99999% positive for paternity.

"YES! YES! YES!" I screamed happily as I stared at the results. I immediately called Marcus' job.

"Rawlins Chemicals, how may I help you?"

"I need to speak with Marcus O'Connor please."

"May I ask whose calling?"

"Kalisha Moore," I responded.

"Please hold." She clicked the line and a couple minutes later, she came back on the line. "I'm sorry, but Mr. O'Connor is in a meeting. Would you like to leave a message?"

"Yes, please have him call me at 3469922872."

"I'll pass the message along. Have a nice day."

Two days later, Marcus was still giving me the run around, just like before. I thought about going to his office but decided against it. I didn't want to embarrass myself or get him fired. Now that I had the proof I needed, I refused to be ignored.

I had another idea. One that would surely get his attention…

Chapter seventeen

Marcus

Kalisha didn't give up. For the past two days she had been calling my job like she was my side chick. The shit was embarrassing to be getting all these pink messages from Lynette's nosey ass. I couldn't understand what was so important that she had to keep calling me. I was sure by now she had the test results and the kid wasn't mine. I told her when those results came back, I was done with her. But she was seriously tripping on me right now.

I had Lynette lie and tell her that I was in a meeting every single time she called. I prayed she would get the message and stop calling me. Like damn, didn't she get the picture that I didn't want to be bothered? What kind of question was that? Of course, she didn't.

I gave her 20 G's and she was still bothering the fuck out of me. If someone had given me that much money, I would forget why the fuck I was trying to get in touch with them. I would just let the shit be, but I could tell Kalisha wasn't about to do that.

However, had I just answered her call, none of the events that followed would've ever happened. I was sitting at my desk busting my ass when my wife came busting into my office. The look on her face had me thinking some crazy shit. What was wrong with her? Where were the girls? Did someone die?

"Babe what are you doing here? Where are the twins?" I asked nervously.

She was breathing hot and heavy like she was having a heart attack or something. "What's wrong with you? Did something happen to my mom? Did something happen to Ms. Belinda?" I continued questioning her. I was now standing in her face trying to figure out what was wrong with my wife, but she wasn't telling me shit.

"Why did you come here baby? What is the problem?"

She dug in her purse and pulled out an envelope. She handed it to me. Shit, it looked like the average letter addressed to me in a woman's handwriting.

Oh Lord, she thinks I'm cheating.

That was the first thought that popped into my head.

"What the fuck is this?" I asked.

"Open it," she said. She stood there with her arms over her chest.

I opened the envelope and pulled out the letter. I started reading it and my mouth fell to the floor. I looked up at my wife who had tears in her eyes. But as hurt as she was, she still managed to punch the shit out of me.

POW!

To be continued...